POP CULTURE
GOES TO WAR

f. J. Jane film (p. 107)

POP CULTURE GOES TO WAR

Enlisting and Resisting Militarism in the War on Terror

Geoff Martin
and
Erin Steuter

LEXINGTON BOOKS
A division of
ROWMAN & LITTLEFIELD PUBLISHERS, INC.
Lanham · Boulder · New York · Toronto · Plymouth, UK

Published by Lexington Books
A division of Rowman & Littlefield Publishers, Inc.
A wholly owned subsidiary of The Rowman & Littlefield Publishing Group, Inc.
4501 Forbes Boulevard, Suite 200, Lanham, Maryland 20706
http://www.lexingtonbooks.com

Estover Road, Plymouth PL6 7PY, United Kingdom

British Library Cataloguing in Publication Information Available

Library of Congress Cataloging-in-Publication Data

Martin, Geoff, 1963–
   Pop culture goes to war : enlisting and resisting militarism in the war on terror / Geoff Martin and Erin Steuter.
      p. cm.
   Includes bibliographical references and index.
   ISBN 978-0-7391-4680-4 (cloth : alk. paper)—ISBN 978-0-7391-4681-1 (pbk. : alk. paper)—ISBN 978-0-7391-4682-8 (electronic)
   1. Militarism—Social aspects—United States—History—21st century. 2. Popular culture—United States—History—21st century. 3. War on Terrorism, 2001–2009—Social aspects—United States. 4. Military-industrial complex—United States—History—21st century. 5. United States—Military policy—21st century. 6. War and society—United States. 7. War in mass media. I. Steuter, Erin, 1963– II. Title.
   U21.2.M363 2010
   306.2'70973—dc22

                                                                                          2010010543

Printed in the United States of America

Contents

Acknowledgments

IT IS OFTEN SAID THAT THE CONCEPT OF "CRISIS" IS ASSOCIATED with the ideas both of "danger" and "opportunity." That there is danger is clear. We are reminded every day that there is the danger of permanent war, of economic collapse, of sovereign bankruptcy, and environmental catastrophe. What we hope becomes clear in this book, however, is that opportunity is also all around us. We believe that the above conditions are intimately connected to the rise and persistence of militarism in the United States and the Western world, but when we look just below the surface we see opportunities to work for change. Artists, comedians, street performers, writers, musicians, and activists of all kinds have joined forces with traditional political actors to persist in exposing militarism in U.S. life. So our thanks first go to all the performers, writers, activists, and legions of creative people whose efforts to undermine militarism have provided us with so much raw material to analyze and to highlight.

Erin Steuter values the opportunity to work closely with engaging undergraduate students at Mount Allison University whose inspiration and research assistance has been very helpful over the last number of years. Thanks go to Amy Bright, Laurel Carleton, Emily Cornford, Sarah Dogherty, Dorian Dorn, David Morse, and Halley Roback for sharing their intelligence and energy in helping make a formidable task a little less daunting. We also thank brick artist Andrew Becraft, who kindly provided us with the clever cover art.

Geoff Martin would like to thank a number of his professors over the years who have taught him a great deal about U.S. politics, foreign policy, and American studies more generally. At Purdue University in West Lafayette, Indiana, he benefited from the teaching and guidance of Julie Erfani, Myron Hale, Michael Stohl, Rolf Theen, and Michael Weinstein. He also owes a debt of gratitude to Robert W. Cox and James N. Rosenau, both of whom recognized the importance of culture in the study of global relations and foreign policy before it was fashionable to do so. Finally, being a young academic in the last twenty years has not been easy. He is grateful to his late father, J. Robert Martin, and his mother, Lois F. (Morell) Martin, for their unstinting support over the years. The Martins and Morells, the Joneses and the Cassidys, and our other cousins in the human family, built a society in the twentieth century out of the ruins of war that was progressive and worth saving. It is that vision as much as anything that is now under threat and which we must defend.

Introduction

Without war, ancient civilization could not have existed. . . . We shall see that modern society, on the other hand, would be destroyed by war.

—Gugliemo Ferrero, 1899[1]

THE YEAR 2009 OPENED ON AN OPTIMISTIC NOTE. The American public elected a "change" candidate, Barack Hussein Obama, to the White House. The world witnessed greater jubilation in the United States than it had seen in decades. Candidate Obama promised to change the usual way of doing things in Washington, D.C., by ending the war and pulling out of Iraq, by repairing U.S. relationships with its North Atlantic (NATO) allies, and by bringing fiscal sanity back to the U.S. federal government. With a Democratic Congress and president, surely it was only a matter of time before the United States would free itself from the grip of the madness of militarism that had defined its domestic and foreign policy since 9/11.

For eight years, the United States and the world lived with a U.S. president who seemed to have little regard for U.S. or global public opinion, international law, alliance relations, democracy and liberalism, or the good sense of people of good will. That president was sworn into office in January 2001 under the cloud of a disputed election. Eight months later, he was eager to declare himself a "wartime president" after a small group of predominantly Saudi terrorists crashed U.S. domestic airliners into the two main towers of New York's World Trade Center, the Pentagon, and a farmer's field in Pennsylvania. In the seven years that followed, under that president's leadership, the U.S. Congress voted to restrict civil liberties, expand police and military powers, cut income taxes twice, borrow from future generations, narrow the separation between church and state, start wars in Afghanistan and Iraq, continue with financial deregulation, and establish secret prisons both outside and inside the United States, among many other measures. That new Conservative age (and Republican majority), which some, like White House advisor Karl Rove, thought would last for a generation or more, appears to have come to an end.

Yet, as each month of the Obama era unfolds, increasing numbers of concerned citizens and global observers see hope for a peace agenda and the promise of a change in foreign policy dissipating. Since taking office, continuity has outweighed change in the president's decisions as well as those of the Democratic Congress. An early disappointment came in Obama's February 27, 2009, speech at Camp Lejeune, South Carolina, where the president backed away from his campaign commitments to end U.S. overseas wars,[2] shortly followed by the decision to restart military tribunals to charge and try captured prisoners from the "War on Terror." The new administration ruled out investigations of Bush administration officials who justified and authorized "aggressive interrogation techniques," like "water-boarding," which the Obama administration has equated with torture. The fact that senior Bush officials could be charged for "waging an aggressive war," among the highest of crimes against humanity, is not even mentioned. There is no sign that the Foreign Intelligence Surveillance Act (FISA) will be amended to give Americans back the rights of privacy that were taken away in the Bush era. President Obama's decision to appoint General Stanley A. McChrystal, former commander of the secretive Joint Special Operations Command (JSOC), as supreme U.S. commander for Afghanistan raised eyebrows because of allegations of JSOC involvement in torture and assassinations.[3] The Obama administration proposes to continue to increase military spending, to escalate the war in Afghanistan, and very possibly to continue to station a large number of U.S. forces in Iraq on permanent bases over the long term.

To the surprise of many, President Obama won the 2009 Nobel Peace Prize, a controversial decision, as he himself admitted, "because I am at the beginning, and not the end, of my labors on the world stage." Whether the prize was awarded because of the relief that he was not George W. Bush, or to encourage the better angels of his character, or to reward him for his first six months in office, is the subject of considerable debate.[4] The president's acceptance speech, delivered on December 10, 2009, in Oslo, Norway, is important because it provided a clear indication that Candidate Obama was long gone, replaced by a leader who accepts the bipartisan, establishment view common to virtually every administration from FDR through Clinton. Even as he quoted from both Martin Luther King Jr. and Gandhi, Obama reaffirmed virtually every article of faith of the United States as a militaristic global power. He said that war of some type is inevitable, based on a pessimistic view of the "facts" of human nature, and that as president he reserves the right to use the military to protect the United States and its interests. He presents the United States as always the victim, and never the aggressor. Even as the Western countries *were* contemplating negotiations in Afghanistan, Obama was saying that there is evil in the world and "negotiations cannot convince al-Qaeda's leaders to lay down their arms." In the Middle East "the conflict between Arabs and Jews seems to harden," and apparently the superpower has played no role in enabling this over many decades. In the last sixty years, the United States was a force for peace and freedom in the world, and prevented World War Three. He says that "the instruments of war do have a role to play in preserving the peace," though "war promises human tragedy." Further, at the heart of war there are "two seemingly irreconcilable truths—that war is sometimes necessary, and war at some level is an expression of human folly."[5] This speech may turn out to contain the kernel of an "Obama Doctrine," which is that apart from certain aspects of the George W. Bush era, he embraces the mainstream, bipartisan mythology and common cause of the twentieth-century presidents.

The concerns are not only about the presidency, but about Congress as well, along with many other social institutions. In late May 2009, the U.S. Senate voted 90–6 to strip funding for closing Guantánamo's Camp X-ray, the United States' controversial prison camp for War-on-Terror detainees located in Cuba. (Only three senators voted against the larger $91 billion funding bill for the wars in Iraq and Afghanistan, despite the continuing unpopularity of those wars.) This act of defiance by the president's own party was based largely on fear, on the fear that somehow these captives, whom it is assumed are a threat to the United States, will be released onto U.S. streets or back to their home countries, only to rejoin terrorist organizations. Senate Republicans spent weeks whipping up this fear and in the end a large majority of Senate Democrats sided with them. A campaign promise to rethink how the United States treats detainees was realized by the announcement of the trial of Khalid Sheikh Mohammed in the U.S. District Court in New York, though Attorney General Eric Holder then reversed himself and said he will be tried elsewhere. Others will be tried in front of military commissions. While Obama has announced at least a one-year delay in closing Guantánamo's Camp X-ray, with Congress's support the bulk of the remaining Guantánamo detainees will be relocated to an empty prison in Thompson, Illinois.[6] Closure does not mean release.

The fact that we are witnessing policy continuity instead of the much-desired and promised transformational change in the United States' relations with the global community reflects the persistence of militarism. Militarism is an approach to the world in which global problems are defined primarily as military problems, where the first response of political leadership, and a segment of the population, is the resort to force, and where pride of place in American life is given to the military and to a culture of violence. Chalmers Johnson, who has provided such a cogent critique of the "blowback" of aggressive American foreign policy, has noted that for militarism to be present, there must be "the emergence of a professional military class and the subsequent glorification of its ideals"; the "preponderance of military officers or representatives of the arms industry as officials of state policy"; and the "devotion to policies in which military preparedness becomes the highest priority for the state."[7] In this book, we will demonstrate that these conditions exist in contemporary American society, and that they are reinforced by our popular culture; a military-industrial-entertainment culture that sells war through our games and leisure activities. But that which can be created and reinforced through popular culture can also be undermined by it and artists, performers, and activists are using creative tools to mobilize resistance to militarism.

Despite the partisan change in the United States in 2008, militarism does not seem to have been weakened. If anything, it may be pursued in a more "competent" manner, compared to the specific tactics of the Bush era. This is reminiscent of the transition from President Eisenhower to Kennedy, in which, by pointing to a false Soviet advantage in missile technology (the so-called missile gap), John F. Kennedy promised to prosecute the Cold War more competently, thereby escalating the intensity of conflict between the two global superpowers.

In July 2009 a poll conducted in twenty countries representing more than 60 percent of the world's population found that in fifteen of nineteen countries—excluding the United States—the majority saw Washington as bullying other countries with the threat of its powerful military. In seventeen of nineteen countries, according to the poll, the United States was seen as not obeying international law.[8] Even domestically, a July 2009 poll showed that a majority of Americans opposed both the war in Afghanistan and the war in Iraq with 63 percent opposed to the war in Iraq and 53 percent opposed to the war in Afghanistan.[9] On December 1, 2009, President Obama announced his own troop surge in Afghanistan, which will put thirty thousand more troops in that country over eighteen months.[10] Not including private mercenaries, this will put U.S. and allied forces up to 137,000, which exceeds the Soviet commitment in the 1980s. President Obama got a short-term boost from the announcement, according to the Quinnipiac University National Poll of December 8, 2009. That poll indicates that by a margin of 58 to 37 percent, Americans approve of Obama's decision to send thirty thousand more combat troops to Afghanistan, and by 60 to 32 percent they approve the president's plan to begin withdrawing combat troops from Afghanistan in July 2011. Interestingly, by a 45 to 40 percent margin respondents do not believe that this last promise will be kept.[11]

So how do we explain the continued militarist policies of the new administration and Congress in light of the opposition expressed by American and world opinion? For some observers, this continuity can be explained by the role of money in U.S. politics. Barack Obama raised $750 million for his primary- and general-election campaigns and he accumulated some major political debts, as did members of Congress. Given the context of a political establishment where accumulating money and power are the highest values, continuity in U.S. behavior can be seen as the result of conceding to pressure from a multitude of interests who want overseas trading and investment opportunities, and access to and control over natural resources, such as oil and natural gas, in their pursuit of an expansion-oriented capitalist economy. Military power is a means of achieving or guaranteeing these goals. Other observers would emphasize that as a superpower—the world's lone military superpower—the United States will always be concerned with its position, and will always fear being knocked off the "top of the hill" by an upstart, whether it is China, the European Union, or a revived Russia. Third, some observers point to pro-Israel political forces in the United States, whether Jewish, Christian, or otherwise, as an explanation for many aspects of U.S. foreign policy, particularly in the Middle East.

While there is merit in each of these arguments, and while a single explanation is unlikely to explain fully a complex phenomena like the continuity of militarism, the central argument of this book is that the continuity of militarism in U.S. life and foreign and defense policy is related to many decades in which U.S. domestic popular culture has tended to reinforce rather than undermine militarism. Andrew Martin notes that there are important links between popular culture and militarism:

> Popular culture in the United States is where war comes from and where it is made possible—even desirable—and it is where it ends up, as the lived experience of war is fed back to us in displaced forms and narratives. It is one of the key sites where social norms and identities are constructed and valorized; it is where culture in all its complex tangles of residual, dominant and emergent forms overlaps and is enfolded back into structures of authority and control. It is through this process that the lived experience of insecurity, of uncertainty about the motives and aims of outsiders (the possible evil ones), are best viewed both as constructs and as constructed.[12]

This culture of militarism means that in so many instances, the political leadership's first response to any challenge is to consider the use of military force, and they do this counting on significant support from the American public. The government uses popular culture symbols as they call for support for war and the culture industries and consumers respond through the production and consumption of cultural products that support the war. Criticism of the war is also expressed through popular culture, as resistors signal their opposition through creative cultural expression. An example of this can be currently seen in the debate over Afghanistan as the "good war."

Afghanistan as the "Good War": "Our Cause Is Just"

Shortly after his election, President Obama announced that he would send almost 20,000 more troops to Afghanistan, increasing by nearly 50 percent the 36,000 American troops already there, and as we have seen he announced a further increase in December 2009.[13] Afghanistan is now being portrayed as the "good war," especially compared to Iraq, by the president and other supporters of a militarist American foreign policy. The notion of the "good war" comes from the noble cause of World War II, a war that garnered tremendous popular support because the United States and the world faced a clear threat from the aggression of Germany and Japan, and in victory the United States was rich, powerful, and magnanimous. The opposite of a "good war" is one in which the reasons for U.S. involvement are not clear and victory was not achieved. In Korea, the United States achieved only a stalemate, and in Vietnam, a quagmire with tremendous loss of life on all sides. Public opinion turned against the war in Iraq as it became clear that the premise for the war was based on false claims and that a liberation of the Iraqi people would not be swiftly achieved. Thus the Iraq War, or Bush's war, is being characterized as the bad war, while rhetoric mounts to justify the continuation of the war in Afghanistan.

Obama's announcement of the first troop escalation in Afghanistan was accompanied by leading political pundits and think tank commentators expressing their support for the "good war" in Afghanistan and echoing a series of talking points that make the case for the development of a renewed Afghan mission. Peter Bergen supports "winning the good war" by arguing that the United States must stay the course in Afghanistan and that the United States has the capacity to be successful there, and can improve the welfare of the country, where the British and Soviets did not.[14] The normally liberal Center for American Progress (CAP) issued a report that could have come from the Bush administration, advocating short-, medium-, and long-term goals for the United States in Afghanistan, which involve a significant troop and aid increase in that country over the next five to ten years.[15] In addition, U.S.

allies who are participating in the Afghanistan mission, including the United Kingdom, Canada, and Australia, also are using "good war" imagery to justify the war in the face of their own skeptical, domestic publics.[16]

But many progressive commentators, who provided accurate and insightful cautions about the original rush to war in Iraq, are skeptical about seeing Afghanistan as the "good war"—one that has to be fought and won at all costs. John Pilger, a reliable war correspondent of long standing, challenges the idea that the Afghanistan War is a "noble effort," certainly a core requirement of the "good war" school. He refutes this by discussing his efforts to meet with "Marina," an activist of the Revolutionary Association of Afghanistan Women (RAWA), in Kabul; this is difficult because in post-Taliban Afghanistan she and her sisters risk arrest for their activities, and must keep a low profile. She understands, Pilger tells us, that Western motives in the Afghanistan War are not noble, but as we see all too often, motivated by the goals of acquiring more power and treasure. As Pilger says, "The truth about the 'good war' is to be found in compelling evidence that the 2001 invasion, widely supported in the west as a justifiable response to the 11 September attacks, was actually planned two months prior to 9/11." He points out that the Clinton administration had signed a secret memorandum with the Taliban for the construction of a natural gas pipeline, but the Taliban appeared to be losing ground to the Northern Alliance and therefore were not a stable and reliable partner. In early 2001 the Taliban proposed to oust Osama bin Laden, by exiling him to Peshawar, Pakistan. Pilger continues: "A tribunal of clerics would then hear evidence against him and decide whether to try him or hand him over to the Americans. Whether or not this would have happened, Pakistan's Pervez Musharraf vetoed the plan."

In July 2001, fed up with the Taliban, the United States decided that in the coming months it would bomb the country and oust the Taliban government.[17] The "unexpected" attacks of 9/11 made it easy for the Bush administration to get domestic support. We say "unexpected" because on August 6, 2001, President Bush received a president's daily brief entitled "Bin Ladin Determined to Strike in the U.S."[18] At its root this is hardly a noble war, forged as it is in the desire for geopolitical control and access to energy. Osama bin Laden was wanted in the United States before 9/11, because of his past attacks on U.S. assets, but apprehending him was not the highest priority for either the Clinton or Bush administrations.

Tariq Ali also convincingly demonstrates the Afghanistan is not a "good war," but he does this by showing that this war was never a "struggle of good versus evil," another typical core value. Rather, the U.S.-led effort there is a bundle of contradictions. The United States and its allies invaded Afghanistan after 9/11 with little understanding of the country and the situation has not improved since. As Ali points out, the Western state-building project in Afghanistan was flawed from the beginning, for it aimed "to construct an army able to suppress its own population but incapable of defending the nation from outside powers; a civil administration with no control over planning or social infrastructure, which are in the hands of Western NGOs; and a government whose foreign policy marches in step with Washington's. It bore no relation to the realities on the ground."[19] Those realities included an ethnically diverse country, dominated by various regional strongmen who are more than prepared to take over from where the ousted Taliban left off. The initial U.S. choice for president, Hamid Karzai, runs a government characterized by massive corruption which is barely able to control its own capital city, let alone the country. It was the preference of the British and U.S. governments that someone other than Karzai win the 2009 election, but because he successfully rigged that election, and because his main challenger refused to contest a runoff election against him, Hamid Karzai will rule for the next five years, or less, if he is removed by force.[20]

This view is not just held by the contrarian left. While most of the media coverage parrots the line that Afghanistan always was and still is a war worth continuing to fight, there have always been military officers and intelligence operatives, usually retired, who have challenged the common view of the Afghanistan War. In 2009, a documentary entitled "Security" was released by the "Rethinking Afghanistan Project" and provides new revelations of diplomats and intelligence officials who dissent from the Bush and Obama view of the Afghanistan War. Robert Baer, former CIA field operative in the Middle East and the author of *See No Evil*, says: "The notion that we are in Afghanistan to make our country safer is complete bullshit." Further, Graham Fuller, a former CIA station chief in Kabul, says that: "Both wars have made the world much more dangerous for Americans and for any American presence overseas."[21]

In December 2009 President Obama pushed the "good war" claim a little further, making the claim that "our cause is just." While he did not quite go so far as to invoke "just war doctrine" on behalf of the Afghanistan War, in his speech to cadets at the U.S. Military Academy, he did go to great lengths to argue for the justice of the Afghani war, compared to Iraq and especially in comparison to the U.S. war in Vietnam.[22]

The fact that governments, military leaders, and political pundits are using the term the "good war" (or even "just war"), in justifying the war in Afghanistan is not an accident. The term is consciously chosen because it resonates with cultural associations that will help to sell the war to the public as a legitimate and worthy cause. Carl Boggs and Tom Pollard explain in their book *The Hollywood War Machine* that the Office of War Information began a propaganda campaign in 1941 to "forge a deep cultural orientation toward warfare as a method for protecting U.S. national interests—in other words, to instill in the vast majority of Americans an ethos of the good war."[23] The film industry embarked on the production of patriotic pro-war films that built support for World War II but that also romanticized and enabled U.S. militarism for decades afterwards. Boggs and Pollard examined scores of Hollywood films and they characterize the "good war" formula as containing the following elements: (1) that the military campaign is a wholly noble one, which makes combat possible to bear; (2) that the war is a struggle between good and evil and the opponent is therefore devoid of human qualities; (3) that the conflict revolves around predominantly white, male heroism; (4) that military units are diverse in ethnic and class terms, and that the military goals are widely accepted among the groups they represent; (5) the soldiers possess professional and stoic heroism in the face of battle; and (6) the armed unit is cohesive and has its own set of rules, which an outsider must adopt to be accepted.[24] When the government, military, and think tank fellows advocate in favor of continuing the U.S. war in Afghanistan they are calling on our conscious and unconscious familiarity with these Hollywood themes in order to convince us to stay the course, and support the war. As Boggs says, the focus of the Good War theme in the movies is on "noble American military triumphs over evil monsters" in which the "the larger motifs of patriotism, male heroism, and essential goodness of U.S. military action were taken for granted."[25]

With the campaign in Afghanistan being characterized as a "good war," we see fresh examples of the ways in which cultural products can both support and oppose policy. There has been an explosion of new merchandise to help people show their support for the war, and persuade others of its value, including buttons, coffee mugs, barbeque aprons, T-shirts, and other items. There are racist bumper stickers for your car that have slogans, such as "Al Qaeda Hunting Club" and "I do not brake for turbans," which threaten violence and portray Arabs as subhuman prey. Then there are the blood-thirsty messages that you can emblazon on your coffee cup, such as "Understanding Terrorism One Bullet at a Time," "Pro-torture—It's Fun to Make Terrorists Cry," and "If We Weren't Supposed to Kill People, God Wouldn't Let Us Be So Good at It." Third, there is the glorification of the military and the sentiment of "supporting the troops," but with a negative edge, such as on T-shirts for soldiers and their fellow travelers, with phrases such as "Me at Work, Doing the Job That Cowards Won't Do," "Land of the Free Because of the Brave," and "Get Behind Our Troops or Get in Front of Them." Finally, the militarist sentiment that blames those who oppose the United States' willingness to engage in permanent war can be found on barbecue aprons that bear

slogans such as "PEACE Kills," "Give War a Chance, That's All We Are Saying," and "It's About Liberty, Stupid."[26]

Nor is it the case that satire and irony are dead now that Obama is in
power, as though all the satirists and bloggers were simply puppets of the
mainstream of the Democratic Party. David McGinn floated this idea in
Toronto's *National Post* around inauguration day, quoting Nicholas Kristof
and Joan Didion among others, arguing that there would be a rise of intel-
lectualism and hope and a decline in pessimism, irony, and satire.[27] But even
a year into the Obama era we can see that this is not the case, and it becomes
clearer with each passing month. If a president pursues the same policies, he
can expect both the same support and send-ups in the popular culture. On the
side of support, some cultural support for militarism is partisan, in the sense
that a Republican president might get stronger support for the same policies
than a Democrat. In the case of Obama, some militarists have breathed a sigh
of relief or have actively supported the continuity. Country performer Toby
Keith, known for his patriotic tune "Courtesy of the Red, White and Blue
(The Angry American)," written after the 9/11 attacks, was invited, ironically,
to play at the Nobel Peace Prize Concert in Denmark in December 2009,
despite his strong pro-war views. "If President Obama has to send (more)
troops into Afghanistan to fight evil, I'll pull for our guys to win, and I won't
apologize for it," Keith told the Associated Press. "I'm an American, and I do
pull for our team to fight evil." Many Norwegians and peace advocates have
expressed dismay that the Nobel Committee would include pro-war performers at a peace concert.[28]

As for criticism, even before his inauguration, and in anticipation of tough
times ahead, Urbandictionary.com sold merchandise for its entry "Obomba,"
which says "I used to like Obomba, but now I think he is crazy," to be used
"to insult Barack Obama if he decides to bomb people when he becomes
President of the United States."[29] In a related sentiment, there are also bumper stickers and magnets that say "I voted for Obama, not Obomba."[30] The
political cartoonists haven't stopped either, exemplified by a cartoon labeled
"Obama's Vietnam," which shows two young people looking at a movie
poster with a pitch that says "If you think we won the first time, think again
. . . ," for a movie entitled "Afghanistan II." The teenaged young woman tells
the young man "I am so not ready for this sequel."[31] Some products cater to
both sides, an expression of the way that Obama himself is now an ambiguous
figure. Samuelpnewton has created a black T-shirt which says "Obama a Real
American Hero," in the style of the G.I. Joe T-shirts. This T-shirt could appeal
to antiwar activists disappointed in Obama's embracing of militarist policy, or
it could be worn by Obama supporters who see it as a boost to the president
and his defense credentials.[32]

The satirical newspaper the *Onion* ran one of their trademark mock news stories with a headline on March 20, 2009, that read, "U.S. Troops in Iraq Excited to Finally Return to Afghanistan." According to the *Onion* satirical story, "Members of the U.S. Armed Forces were reportedly overcome with feelings of joy, nostalgia, and optimism this week after learning they would soon be withdrawn from Iraq and allowed to finally return home to Afghanistan." Further, the writers quote a certain "Cpl. Douglas Robinson, who hasn't seen the barren hills and smoking craters of his beloved Kabul in nearly six years." Apparently, some soldiers are saying this would be the first chance to be reunited with their children in Afghanistan, some of whom they have never seen. A "Lt. David Shapiro" says "I can't wait to meet my little princess, Badria . . . I just hope her mother isn't still angry at me." The reader is also told, at the end of the story, that "Amid all the fanfare, there was some unpleasant news. Troops in the 11th Marine Regiment were ordered early Tuesday morning to ship off to the United States, a distant foreign land, filled with bizarre customs, strange beliefs, and millions of people they do not know or understand."[33]

While we will see more of Jon Stewart in chapter 7, suffice it to say here that he has taken up every opportunity to attack the Obama administration, particularly as they show weakness or look too much like the Old Regime. On his December 2, 2009, program, Stewart had some fun with Obama's speech announcing his Afghanistan (or "Eff'dghanistan," as Stewart would say) troop surge. He starts the segment by asking the question, "Is thirty thousand troops the military equivalent of taking two Advil? No matter what the problem, that's what they do . . . ," noting the similarity between the Bush Iraq and Obama Afghanistan surges. He then structures the segment in a call-and-response fashion, with Stewart saying what Obama will *not* say, only then to show a clip in each case in which Obama does just what Stewart said he wouldn't do. With a gas mask as a prop, Stewart says that Obama is different from Bush, and that he "won't mention 9/11 . . . he won't dip into the well-worn bucket of fear . . . he won't engage in absolutist rhetoric . . . he won't reference unnamed, domestic vague critics. . . ." In each case he shows a clip in which Obama does just that, to the laughs of his audience. He then says "to fill out your Bush card, you just need a Freudian gaffe," and then shows a clip in which Obama says "bring the war to an *irresponsible* end," by mistake. After noting that Obama says he has ordered a surge but will not stay indefinitely, Stewart then puts on a John F. Kennedy accent (or is it *The Simpsons'* Mayor Quimby character?) and says "Our resolve is unwavering, but it turns out that our Discover card is over the limit."[34]

In this book we will discuss how popular culture feeds into a militaristic society, but as the above vignette shows, popular culture has also been a space for opponents of militarism. As the reader will see, popular culture sometimes advocates militarism because major business interests promote it in their economic and/or ideological interests. The transnational corporations that own major media outlets may also be weapons producers, or vendors of products the sale of which will increase from militaristic endeavors. Corporate leaders may be ideological conservatives who believe that by serving militarism they serve God, or from a secular perspective, that by serving militarism they serve the "national interest." Militaristic culture and policy, once it gets on a roll, can create an audience that wants more militaristic culture and policy.

This book is inspired in part by the ideas of the Reverend Dr. Martin Luther King Jr., both those trumpeted by the media and those neglected. In the last year of his life, Dr. King realized that as a Christian pastor his struggle was not just for civil rights for African Americans, but also to uplift the poor and create justice in the world. In a brilliant but underappreciated speech at the Riverside Church in New York City, delivered on April 4, 1967, Dr. King said that the U.S. war in Vietnam was a sign of U.S. domination and aggression, it consumed people and valuable resources on both sides, and even threatened the American soul:

> If America's soul becomes totally poisoned, part of the autopsy must read: Vietnam. It can never be saved so long as it destroys the deepest hopes of men the world over. So it is that those of us who are yet determined that America will be are led down the path of protest and dissent, working for the health of our land. . . . We can no longer afford to worship the god of hate or bow before the altar of retaliation. The oceans of history are made turbulent by the ever-rising tides of hate. And history is cluttered with the wreckage of nations and individuals that pursued this self-defeating path of hate.[35]

While most of Dr. King's words in his last year were harshly criticized in his day, and are largely ignored today, each new generation must be reminded of his message. As the quote at the beginning of this chapter suggests, and as Dr. King said over forty years ago, it is far from clear that a society with a militaristic culture like the United States today can survive in the long term unless it can find a way to change. When Gugliemo Ferrerro wrote at the beginning of the twentieth century, he was part of a now largely forgotten global movement of people who understood, reflecting on the U.S. Civil War and other military conflicts, that the "war system" that the nineteenth century bequeathed to the twentieth century was becoming ever more destructive and ever more difficult to control.[36] The horrors of war in the twentieth century have been well documented and presented visually, including in the neglected work of Ernst Friedrich, founder of the Anti-War Museum in Berlin.[37] We are now in a period where increasing numbers of people are coming to the same conclusion as we close out the first decade of this new century and millennium, regardless of the partisanship of our leaders. The war system may have seemed tolerable in the forty years of the Cold War, because while it took a tremendous toll in the global south, it prevented yet another total, general war in the north. Our fear is that our current course means a forty-year period of real war all over the world.

We believe there are people of goodwill in U.S. society and politics who want to reduce militarism, cut military spending, and create a more peaceful and just world at home and abroad. We believe that a militaristic culture is a wall that they run into, even if economic, resource, and political pressures in favor of militarism wane, and this book is intended to shed light on the role culture plays in promoting, and ultimately undermining, militarism.

The Plan of the Book

In the first chapters we will discuss the costs and benefits of war, historically and today, and show the extent to which continual war is not a sustainable course of action for the United States or the world. In chapters 2 through 6 we discuss the ways in which popular culture has been and is used to prepare the population to be receptive to war, to accept the need for war on the eve of its outbreak, and to stay the course with all its sacrifices as the wars drag on. We will also provide the reader with some analytical tools to make sense of the seemingly confusing reality that we live in. In chapter 3 we will focus on children's toys, in which war and soldiering of various types are common. Video games and popular music often glorify war and encourage patriotism. For many decades, Hollywood and the Department of Defense have had a hand-in-glove relationship in which script changes have been traded in exchange for access to military equipment, bases, and personnel. The news media were "stenographers to power" in the run-ups to the U.S. invasions of both Afghanistan and Iraq, offering no challenge to claims we now know to be false or mistaken, and which many dissenters confidently denied at the time. In a militaristic society the charge of being "unpatriotic" is one of the most serious, and some journalists and media outlets will seemingly do almost anything to avoid it. In the space of only months, torture in popular culture made the transition from being a sordid technique used in sixteenth-century Tudor England and 1960s-era Vietnam (by the North Vietnamese!), to one proudly on display on a weekly basis on television programs like *24*, and in U.S.-run prisons in Iraq and elsewhere.

As we will show in chapters 7 and 8, in both the past and present culture has been a means for people to oppose militarism, not just support it.

Through music and song, film, television, theater, and the visual arts, people have objected to militarism and have built movements through these means to end wars, like in Vietnam, and to end conscription as part of that struggle. Whether culture changes slowly or quickly, it is a means for both supporting and challenging militarism. We believe that this opposition to militarism through culture played a significant role in undermining the George W. Bush administration as well as Republican Party, and the same effort can continue to have a significant impact in national politics.

Notes

1. Gugliemo Ferrero, *Militarism: A Contribution to the Peace Crusade*, trans. Anon. (Boston: L. C. Page and Company, 1908).

2. "Text: Obama's Speech at Camp Lejeune, N.C.," February 27, 2009, *New York Times*, www.nytimes.com/2009/02/27/us/politics/27obama-text.html (accessed July 13, 2009).

3. See, for example, James Petras, "Obama's Animal Farm: Bigger, Bloodier Wars Equal Peace and Justice," Global Research, www.globalresearch.ca/index. php?context=va&aid=13644 (accessed July 13, 2009).

4. By a 66 to 26 percent margin, Americans said that he did not deserve the Nobel Peace Prize. Quinnipiac University, "Obama Gets Surge in Afghan War Approval, Quinnipiac University National Poll Finds; but Only 26% of U.S. Voters Say He Deserves Nobel Prize," Quinnipac University Polling Institute, December 8, 2009, www .quinnipiac.edu/x1295.xml?ReleaseID=1402 (accessed January 10, 2009).

5. All references to the Obama speech come from Barack Obama, "Remarks by the President at the Acceptance of the Nobel Peace Prize," Oslo City Hall, Oslo, Norway, December 10, 2009, White House Press Office www.whitehouse.gov/the-press-office/ remarks-president-acceptance-nobel-peace-prize (accessed January 9, 2010).

6. C. Parsons and J. Oliphant, "Illinois Prison for Guantanamo Detainees Faces Tough Vote in Congress," *Chicago Tribune*, December 16, 2009, www.chicagotribune .com/news/nationworld/sns-dc-congress-prison,0,4703026.story (accessed January 10, 2010).

7. Chalmers Johnson, "American Militarism and Blowback," in *Masters of War: Militarism and Blowback in the Era of American Empire*, ed. Carl Boggs (New York and London: Routledge, 2003), 19–22.

8. Howard LaFranchi, "Views of the U.S. and Its Role in the World Remain about as Negative as before Obama's Election, according to New Poll That Represents Nearly Two-thirds of the World's Population," *Christian Science Monitor*, July 7, 2009, www.csmonitor.com/2009/0707/p02s05-usfp.html (accessed July 24, 2009).

9. Associated Press, "Poll Details: Majority in U.S. Oppose Both Wars," July 23, 2009, www.google.com/hostednews/ap/article/ALeqM5ilEurPdCgm_t5kD1mnU3r YmSwQsAD99K7VL01 (accessed July 24, 2009).

10. "Obama's War: The American President's New Plan for Afghanistan Is Roughly What the Generals Ordered," *Economist*, December 2, 2009, www.economist.com/world/unitedstates/displayStory.cfm?story_id=15004081 (accessed January 10, 2010).

11. Quinnipiac University, "Obama Gets Surge in Afghan War Approval."

12. Andrew Martin, "Popular Culture and Narratives of Insecurity," in *Rethinking Global Security: Media, Popular Culture and the "War on Terror,"* ed. Andrew Martin and Patrice Petro (New Brunswick, NJ, and London: Rutgers University Press, 2006), 108.

13. Helene Cooper, "Putting Stamp on Afghan War, Obama Will Send 17,000 Troops," *New York Times*, February 17, 2009.

14. Peter Bergen, "Winning the Good War: Why Afghanistan Is Not Obama's Vietnam," *Washington Monthly*, July/August 2009, www.washingtonmonthly.com/features/2009/0907.bergen.html (accessed July 21, 2009).

15. Lawrence J. Korb, Caroline Wadhams, Colin Cookman, and Sean Duggan, "Sustainable Security in Afghanistan: Crafting an Effective and Responsible Strategy for the Forgotten Front," Center for American Progress, March 24, 2009, www.american progress.org/issues/2009/03/sustainable_afghanistan.html/ (accessed July 21, 2009).

16. For sources along these lines, see "Afghan Strategy 'to Make UK Safer,'" *Daily Mirror*, July 13, 2009, www.mirror.co.uk/news/latest/2009/07/13/afghan-strategy -to-make-uk-safer-115875-21516302/ (accessed July 22, 2009); Murray Dobbin, "Afghan-istan Transforms Canada," *Act for the Earth*, August 13, 2008, http://activistmagazine .com/index.php?option=content&task=view&id=919&Itemid=144 (accessed July 22, 2009); and "Afghanistan—Rudd's Good War a Catastrophe," *Solidarity Magazine* 1, June 2008, www.solidarity.net.au/1/afghanistan-rudds-good-war-a-catastrophe/ (ac-cessed July 22, 2009).

17. John Pilger, "The 'Good War' Is a Bad War," *Zspace*, January 10, 2008, www .zcommunications.org/zspace/commentaries/3313 (accessed July 21, 2009).

18. Thomas S. Blanton, "The President's Daily Brief," *The National Security Ar-chive*, www.gwu.edu/~nsarchiv/NSAEBB/NSAEBB116/index.htm (accessed January 16, 2010).

19. Tariq Ali, "Afghanistan: Mirage of the Good War," *New Left Review* 50 (March–April 2008), www.newleftreview.org/?view=2713 (accessed July 21, 2009).

20. Associated Press, "With Few Options, U.S. Accepts Karzai: Analysis," November 2, 2009, www.msnbc.msn.com/id/33574404/ns/world_news-south_and_central_asia/ (accessed January 10, 2010).

21. "Three Former Top CIA Agents Say War in Afghanistan Making World More Dangerous," *Huffington Post*, August 23, 2009, www.huffingtonpost.com/2009/08/23/ three-former-top-cia-agen_n_266721.html (accessed February 15, 2010).

22. Barack Obama, "Remarks by the President in Address to the Nation on the Way Forward in Afghanistan and Pakistan," White House Press Office, December 1, 2009, www.whitehouse.gov/the-press-office/remarks-president-address-nation-way-forward-afghanistan-and-pakistan (accessed January 10, 2010).

23. Carl Boggs and Tom Pollard, *The Hollywood War Machine: U.S. Militarism and Popular Culture* (Boulder, CO, and London: Paradigm Publishers, 2007), 69–70.

24. Boggs and Pollard, *The Hollywood War Machine*, 126.

25. Carl Boggs, "Pentagon Strategy, Hollywood, and Technowar," *New Politics* 11, no. 1 (2006), www.wpunj.edu/newpol/issue41/Boggs41.htm#r7 (accessed July 21, 2009).

26. "Afghanistan Souvenirs & Items," Cafe Press, http://buttons.cafepress.com/afghanistan_flair (accessed July 22, 2009).

27. Dave McGinn, "The Art of Obama," *Weekend Post* (Toronto), January 16, 2009, www.nationalpost.com/arts/story.html?id=1185377 (accessed July 22, 2009).

28. Associated Press, "Peace Prize Ceremony Performance by Pro-war Country Singer Toby Keith Dismays Norwegians," *New York Daily News*, December 11, 2009, www.nydailynews.com/news/world/2009/12/11/2009-12-11_country_singer_toby_keith_.html (accessed January 23, 2010).

29. "Obomba," Urban Dictionary, www.urbandictionary.com/define.php?term=Obomba (accessed July 22, 2009).

30. "I Voted for Obama Not Obomba," Carry a Big Sticker, www.carryabigsticker.com/obama_not_obomba.htm (accessed July 22, 2009).

31. Abu Cihan, "Obama's Vietnam," PhotoBucket, July 2009, http://media.photobucket.com/image/obama%20afghanistan%20political%20cartoon%20july%202009/AbuCihan/cartoon20080722.gif (accessed July 22, 2009).

32. See "Obama GI Joe Retro Logo Shirt Designs," Zazzle, www.zazzle.ca/obama_gi_joe_retro_logo_shirt-235711972476296911 (accessed February 18, 2010).

33. "U.S. Troops in Iraq Excited to Finally Return to Afghanistan," *Onion* 45, no. 12 (March 20, 2009), www.theonion.com/content/news/u_s_troops_in_iraq_excited_to (accessed July 22, 2009).

34. *The Daily Show*, episode #14153, December 2, 2009, www.thedailyshow.com/videos (accessed January 16, 2010).

35. Martin Luther King Jr., "Beyond Vietnam—a Time to Break Silence," April 4, 1967, Meeting of Clergy and Laity Concerned at Riverside Church in New York City, www.americanrhetoric.com/speeches/mlkatimetobreaksilence.htm (accessed June 4, 2009).

36. This useful term comes from the work of Samuel Kim and Richard Falk, both distinguished academics, and the latter of whom was in 2008 appointed Special Rapporteur for the Palestinian Territories by the United Nations Human Rights Council.

37. Ernst Friedrich, *War Against War!* (Seattle: The Real Comet Press, 1987).

1

The Price of War

The Costs of the Military Industrial Complex

IN A MILITARISTIC SOCIETY, the dominant impression that citizens get about war from their culture is one of war as a noble and glorious endeavor. In the case of the United States, it is said that the War of Independence was fought for freedom from the British Empire; the Civil War was fought to end slavery; World War I was fought to "make the world safe for democracy"; and World War II and the Korean Conflict were fought, by the "greatest generation," to defend the world against totalitarian aggression. The United States became a continental power by the 1890s, a great power by the 1920s, and one of two superpowers by the late 1940s, all as the result of war. Depending on citizens' perspectives, they can believe that the United States has used militarism to promote the cause of peace and freedom, or they can believe that the members of the American elite use war to increase and preserve their power and treasure at the expense of people at home and in other lands.

Some wars are harder to spin as noble or glorious, such as the Mexican-American War of 1848, the genocidal wars against the American Indian in the 1880s, or the Spanish-American War of 1898, because they were so clearly based upon a desire for territorial expansion. Other conflicts are still highly contested, like the Vietnam War, which militarists regard as a "noble effort" which the U.S. military was "not allowed to win," while critics view it as a colonial war of aggression against Vietnam and its neighbors, in which the United States was defeated by an under-armed and determined nationalist population in both the North and the South. Militarism wraps itself in a mantle of glory but it conceals the ugly reality that war brings death, destruction, and losses that are physical, financial, and moral.

Where Have All the Soldiers Gone?

There are many ways in which militarism is valued and glorified, but behind the parades and patriotic bunting, war always carries a high cost. The price of war in a militaristic society has been and continues to be a costly one, in humanitarian, economic, political-legal, and moral terms, certainly for the world but also at home. In the U.S. War of Independence, the Continental Army lost 4,435 soldiers; in the U.S. Civil War it was 550,000, while it was 116,708 in World War I, 407,316 in World War II, 54,246 in the Korean Conflict, and 58,168 in Vietnam, and as of this writing, over 4,700 in Afghanistan and Iraq.[1] Add to these totals millions more in combat wounded, many of whom spend a lifetime coping with the wounds of war. Often ignored, denied, and undercounted are the civilian casualties numbering as many as one million in the current War on Terror alone.[2] There are always new weapons for both soldiers and civilians to contend with; smart bombs and land mines, daisy cutters, and bunker busters or more recently, the increased use of deadly white phosphorus.

In the last hundred years the United States has consistently fielded the superior technological force (with the exception of the early period in World War II), with an advanced air force, navy, and army, so it has always exacted a far greater toll on its enemies, such as millions of killed and wounded through aerial bombardment in WWII, two million in Vietnam, and one million in Iraq alone most recently. For every killed and wounded civilian and soldier on both sides, there is a mother, father, brothers and sisters, aunts and uncles, to grieve and to potentially take up arms in retaliation, thereby continuing the cycle of violence.

One of the more articulate of grieving parents is "Peace Mom" Cindy Sheehan, whose son, U.S. Army Specialist Casey Sheehan, was killed in Iraq on April 4, 2004. She is a cofounder and current president of Gold Star Families for Peace and is now a passionate and vocal opponent of U.S. militarism. As she said in her 2009 Memorial Day address, five years after her son's death, "Casey will always be my hero, but he was a victim of U.S. imperialism and his death should bring shame, not pride, as it did not bring freedom to anyone." For her, the rows of headstones in the military cemeteries, so prominently featured on television on the last weekend in May, inspire "horror, regret, pain and a longing for justice."[3]

In a militaristic society like the United States there is a veneer of valuation of military service, but below this surface the current reality is that service people are underpaid, underarmed, underarmored, and underled. Potential soldiers are often deceived in an effort to get them to join the all-volunteer military, and the frequent desire to obtain "money for college" often leaves them with less resources than they expected. Military recruiters have been under so much pressure to meet targets that they have lied to and strong-armed potential recruits.[4] A provision in the No Child Left Behind law allows recruiters to go into public schools that receive federal funding, gain access to students' personal data, and cultivate potential recruits. According to an army manual, savvy recruiters should eat in the school cafeteria, befriend administrators, bring coffee and donuts for teachers, and buddy up to team captains and student body presidents to win the hearts and minds of other students.[5] Recruiters are upfront about their plans to use school lists to aggressively pursue students through mailings, phone calls, and personal visits—even if parents object. "The only thing that will get us to stop contacting the family is if they call their congressman," says Major Johannes Paraan, head U.S. Army recruiter for Vermont and northeastern New York. "Or maybe if the kid died, we'll take them off our list."[6]

Feminist activist Martha Burk points out that the marines are trying to recruit more women for the War on Terror by advertising in magazines read disproportionately by women, yet they do not reveal the limitations that female recruits face in the jobs they could be assigned, the unlikeliness of promotion for women in this patriarchal institution, or the risk to them of sexual assault by their colleagues, commanders, and even recruiters.[7] Predictably, military recruiting became easier in 2009 because of the economic downturn, which aggravates what is already called the "poverty draft."[8] According to a 2007 Associated Press analysis, nearly three-fourths of U.S. troops killed in Iraq came from communities where the per capita income was below the national average. More than half came from communities where the percentage of people living in poverty topped the national average.[9]

The Pentagon unilaterally extends tours of duty beyond the commitments that service members agree to. Members of the U.S. National Guard, who signed up to protect their home states, found themselves called up and sent to Iraq or Afghanistan. For those who have done their service and seek to come home, many find that their active duty service contract has been extended through the "stop-loss" provisions or they are reactivated from "individual ready reserve" and sent back over to Iraq or Afghanistan, a lesser-publicized form of involuntary service that has been fueling the troop supply for the wars in Iraq and Afghanistan.[10] As the United States faced an increasingly difficult fiscal crisis because of Bush-era tax cuts and increased military spending, the troops payed the price. Based on a doctrine of war supported by Defense Secretary Donald Rumsfeld, too few troops were sent to Iraq, they were sent with too little armor on their vehicles, and they were sent without a sound occupation plan or exit strategy. Critics of the Bush invasion plan have argued there was no exit strategy because there was no intention to leave. Because of the shortage of soldiers to guard ammunition and explosive warehouses in Al Qa Qaa, and other sites,these installations were sacked, so the raw materials for what would become improvised explosive devices (IEDs) became available to the insurgency.[11] Because of the privatization mania of the administration, soldiers are often fed and supplied by private corporations, who skim profits off the top, and soldiers work side-by-side with mercenaries, so-called private contractors, who made many times as much money for safer assignments.[12] U.S. soldiers who believe that the Iraq War is a war of aggression and a violation of international law are given no recourse but to continue to follow orders, desert, or go absent without leave (AWOL). This just scratches the surface of the "mistakes" to which the political establishment now obliquely refers.

For the veterans who are not killed, but who return with wounds visible and invisible, increasingly the militarized society does not keep its promises to them either for the sacrifices they make. Since the Vietnam era the Veterans Administration (VA) has been underfunded and it has been overwhelmed by the numbers of military personnel who have survived serious wounds and loss of limbs, only to be transferred to state-side military and VA hospitals like Bethesda Naval Hospital and Walter Reed Army Hospital. There is a growing consensus that Walter Reed Army Hospital is underfunded, understaffed, and semi-privatized, and provides substandard care to many wounded personnel.[13] Psychological treatment for veterans, including those with post-traumatic stress disorder (PTSD), is inadequate, and suicide rates among active-duty and returned soldiers are alarming.[14] Returning warriors are also responsible for increasing numbers of domestic assaults; just under 1.2 million vets were arrested in 2007.[15]

When Women Pay the Cost of War

Humanitarian costs of the militarized state go well beyond the sacrifices of soldiers, touching those least likely to be combatants. Feminist scholar Cynthia Enloe notes that both at home and abroad, women in particular pay a steep price for militarism. In Iraq, Afghanistan, and other objects of military action, rape and prostitution follow in the army's wake, and it is women who become personally insecure when the army leaves its barracks.[16] Military training frequently encourages the hatred and belittling of women. The use of gender slurs motivates men to act aggressively, both toward women within their own culture and women of the "other" culture.[17] War and militarism are the masculine activities of a patriarchal society, and while they hurt everyone, they reduce the power of women and reinforce women's subordination at home and abroad.[18] Susan Faludi argues convincingly that conservatives used the 9/11 attacks to try to put women back into traditional gender roles in the United States, which was rather ironic considering that the United States was attacked by a movement devoted to the same traditionalist role for women. She states that European nations that experienced terrorist attacks, such as Spain in March 2004 and Britain in July 2005, responded to their terrorist attacks by treating them as criminal matters to be methodically investigated and prosecuted. "They did not react by calling for the return of manly men and submissive women. There was something peculiar in our response, peculiar to us as a nation."[19] She points to American conservatives' regressive fixation on Doris Day womanhood and John Wayne masculinity, featuring trembling-lipped "security moms" and swaggering presidential gunslingers. Compared to FDR's initiatives to bring women into the workforce and public funding for daycare during WWII, the Bush-era response has been to undermine women's economic and reproductive independence.[20]

The Profits and Losses of War

As of February 2010 the wars in Afghanistan and Iraq have cost the U.S. taxpayer over $964 billion, though this is a running total, and like the national debt clock, it is immediately an underestimate once the number is committed to paper.[21] As their best projection, Joseph Stiglitz and Linda Bilmes's book title says it all: *The $3 Trillion War.*[22] To put this in context, the combined annual total of the military budget of every other country in the world is $670 billion.[23] In response to ludicrously low Bush administration claims of the Iraq War's likely costs, economist James K. Galbraith stated that the real economic costs are impossible to be certain of because assumptions about the longevity and "success" and ultimate impact of the effort are unknown.[24]

While militarists claim that this kind of expenditure can be good for the economy, the predominant view of economists is that military spending on war is on balance bad for the economy because it shifts resources away from expenditures and benefits that do far more good for the society. For example, while the military does employ people, it employees fewer people per billion dollars spent than would be employed through the hiring of teachers, nurses, or construction workers. Teachers improve the skills, productivity, and earning capacity (and taxpaying ability) of students, which is good for both the economy and a democratic polity. A better educated population makes for better citizens. To put it in the language of the economists' "human capital approach," school teachers create high school and college graduates who will produce wealth in future economic production. Nurses and other health care professionals create a healthier population, which is a more productive population. And construction workers employed to build infrastructure create transportation systems that improve society's quality of life and make it possible for goods and services to get to and from markets. Government spending on the military is harmful because it doesn't produce any positive results unlike spending on health or agriculture, which return an improved economy.[25] While militarists argue that military spending and research lead to spin-offs in the form of technological products, scientists argue that direct research, rather than indirect research, in the development of these products would lead to quicker development with less overall expenditure.

A 2006 poll offered respondents the chance to reallocate the federal foreign policy budget. When offered a list of alternative security measures, the majority of respondents stated that they are most interested in having their legislators increase funding for: reducing U.S. dependence on oil; increasing port security; international police and intelligence cooperation to go after terrorist networks, working through the UN to strengthen international laws against terrorism and to ensure the cooperation of UN members in enforcing them; fighting the global spread of HIV/AIDS; preventing the spread of nuclear weapons by securing nuclear materials in the former Soviet Union; and increased spending on programs to promote dialogue and intercultural understanding between the United States and the Muslim world.[26]

At the end of WWII, the United States had the world's leading economy, held 80 percent of the global gold supply, and the continental United States was undamagd by the war. In WWII the United States produced real products on a scale unprecedented in human history. The United States was a power house in this "real economy," whether it was agriculture or manufacturing, in the production of all the tangible products that people needed and wanted. As the real economy of the militaristic state declines, the country is becoming more militaristic, seeking to win and control by force of arms that which—like markets and territory—it can no longer win commercially. Thus the United States invaded Afghanistan and Iraq in part for reasons of commercial gain and energy security, taking these markets away from other powers, including the Europeans and those in east Asia, particularly China and Japan, who were prepared to deal purely on a commercial, contractual basis. The United States wants *control* of oil and natural gas, not just the ability to purchase it at the global market price. Control gives U.S. voters potential employment, U.S.-based corporations a flow of profits, and the U.S. government a potential veto over the foreign policies of oil-importing rivals. The U.S. attacks on Afghanistan and Iraq are not like the "police actions" or "covert ops" of old, in which the marines or CIA were sent in on small-scale, limited term assignments in Iran, Lebanon, the Dominican Republic, Haiti, and so many others.

Even in the case of Vietnam, there was a nominal government that the United States said it was *supporting.*

It is no coincidence that the global economic crisis struck, beginning in the United States, in 2008–2009. Faced with slow growth in the 1990s and early in this decade, U.S. policy makers, both Democrat and Republican, resorted to a series of financial tricks to generate demand in the domestic economy. In the 1990s, people were encouraged to borrow against the rising values of their homes and stock portfolios, in order to make up for the fact that average wages and salaries after inflation have not increased since the mid 1970s.[27] In the 2000s more and more people were encouraged to buy houses, in part by deregulating the home mortgage business and by a low-interest-rate policy pursued by the Federal Reserve. The "dot.com" bust in the 2000–2002 period and the later collapse of corporate darlings like Enron and WorldCom was only the dress rehearsal for the sub-prime mortgage crisis and the global financial and economic meltdown that persists well into 2010. The real economy of the United States, such as automotive production, has largely been hollowed out, and nobody is quite sure which economic sector will be the engine of a hoped-for recovery.[28] Despite the potential for this decline in traditional technologies and industries to open the door to a new green and prosperous postindustrial economy, in the militaristic state, the military-industrial complex is promoted as the leading candidate for the engine of economic recovery.

One hundred years ago, historians and students of politics were interested in the economics of imperialism and their work has lessons to teach us today. They were faced with questions such as, does a country benefit from being an imperial power, when the tally of expenses and revenues is calculated? If not, why do countries pursue this policy? Writing from an economic perspective in the beginning of the twentieth century, liberal British political economist John Hobson noted that the United Kingdom paid a steep price for the British Empire, and that the economic costs of empire, including funding the Royal Navy and administering colonies and dependencies, outweighed the benefits accruing to the United Kingdom.[29] He explains this anomaly, in terms that few mainstream U.S. commentators seem to have come to terms with. The United Kingdom pursued this policy in part because the benefits of empire were narrowly distributed to the ownership class in Britain, while the costs, including the eventual costs of the empire, were widely shared by the population in the form of higher taxes, fewer services, industrial decline, and blood. By 1945, at the end of World War II, the British people were fed up with the costs of empire and elected a Labour government that redirected public resources to public education, health care, transportation, and state enterprises instead of to the military.

Besides control of and revenues from oil, U.S. investors have much to gain in getting access to new markets. In April 2008 it was announced that a major project will be undertaken in Iraq to create a Disney-style theme park in Baghdad.[30] To be constructed on fifty acres adjacent to the Western-constructed and secure "Green Zone," this facility will have an amphitheater, shops, cafes, a museum, amusement-park rides, a water park, and other attractions. The investors also plan to give away two hundred thousand skateboards to young people to use a series of elaborate skateboard parks. This theme park is very symbolic of why the Western powers are in Iraq. It provides an investment opportunity—involving hundreds of millions of dollars if it comes to pass—for *C3*, a Los Angeles–based holding company established by Llewellyn Werner, who stated in his pitch for the project "I'm a businessman. I'm not here because I think you're nice people. I think there's money to be made."[31] The Baghdad Zoo and Entertainment Experience (BZEE) was given a green light from the Pentagon and an endorsement from General David Petraeus, and a fifty-year lease for the land from the City of Baghdad for an undisclosed price.[32] It amounts to the privatization of public space, including the Al Zawra Park and the Baghdad Zoo. Having allowed the Iraqi museums to be looted in 2003, the new forms of culture being developed by the United States in Iraq seek to win hearts and minds through the introduction of Western entertainment and culture, while collecting a tidy profit.

The United States is fighting two intractable wars which appear to involve long-term commitments, it is living through the worst economic crisis since the Great Depression of the 1930s, its federal public debt has reached and exceeded $12 *trillion*, and economic inequality, a legacy of the last thirty years of federal public policy, is the worst it's been since the 1920s. The lesson of John Hobson's analysis is that the net costs of empire, which are certainly being felt, will not be distributed evenly among American families. In the unlikely event that they are, these costs will be more than affordable for the richest fifth of the U.S. population, the part of the population that has seen its net worth grow staggeringly over the last twenty-five years.

I Wasn't Using My Civil Liberties Anyway

The United States republic was founded on the idea that people's civil liberties must be protected from abuse of government power, but over the last two hundred years it has often been a struggle to guard these liberties. The outbreak and conduct of war has been the opportunity for those in government who want to increase state power at the expense of the people. In the late eighteenth century the country lived under Alien and Sedition Acts, the right of habeas corpus was suspended during the Civil War, war critics were persecuted during World War I and the Red Scare that followed it, and Japanese Americans were interned in camps during World War II. The anticommunist McCarthyite witch hunts during the Cold War and the government's surveillance of civil rights and antiwar groups in the 1960s and early 1970s provide more recent examples. The attack on civil liberties in the 2000s has a long pedigree, and conflict with an external enemy was and still is the mechanism that makes this attack possible and successful, at least for a time.

Political leaders have historically used war as a pretext to gain and exercise greater control. The War on Terror has seen an unprecedented rollback of constitutional civil liberties and increased surveillance of U.S. citizens. The Patriot Act, put together in just forty-five days from 9/11 to the day that Bush signed it into law, has been characterized as a veritable "wish list" of powers that the law enforcers had been after for years but that would never have withstood the opposition from civil liberties groups or the public had 9/11 not provided the perfect opportunity to pass it.[33]

Political leaders have used the 9/11 attacks to justify the unconstitutional arrest of innocent immigrants based on Arab stereotyping; the illegal detention of Arab and Muslim Americans and their improper treatment during extended confinement; prisoner abuse of alleged terrorism suspects in Guantánamo Bay military prison; the allowance of improper search and seizure of American citizens without due cause; prohibited travel based on racial profiling; bully tactics employed with impunity by local police in efforts to undermine free speech; and other clear indications of the Patriot Act's unconstitutional enforcement. A war government has broadened the definition of "terrorism" to include acts of civil disobedience such as trespassing on military bases, anticapitalist protests, and strikes; increased the powers of state surveillance on its own citizens; and curtailed free speech and political dissent. In July 2008, the American Civil Liberties Union reported that the nation's terrorist watch list had reached one million names. The actions of former U.S. attorney general John Ashcroft—and by extension, the George W. Bush administration—have used the Patriot Act to justify what is essentially a dictatorial police state. In an article entitled, "Fascist America, in 10 Easy Steps," Naomi Wolf documents the way in which the war president and administration is following the same script any "would-be dictator must take to destroy constitutional freedoms": ranging from "invoking a terrifying internal and external enemy" to "creat[ing] a gulag" to spying on everyone to harassing opposition to controlling the media to calling dissent treason to "suspend[ing] the rule of law."[34]

War, particularly the unending war of the militaristic society, has exacted a political-legal-moral cost for the United States felt both externally and internally.

Externally the United States has lost a good deal of its political influence with its allies as well as its standing in international legal circles. While there have always been both external and internal skeptics of U.S. good faith during the Cold War period, from the 1940s through the early 1990s, in the last ten years this skepticism has become much more widely shared in the world's capitals and at home. The Bush administration was so full of bravado, swagger, and testosterone that traditional U.S. allies such as France, Germany, and even Canada were defiant or at least kept their distance. Even those governments that supported U.S. plans in Afghanistan and Iraq, like the British, Dutch, and Australians, generally did so despite the opinions of their publics and in many cases they paid the price electorally in the years after. George W. Bush presented former prime ministers Tony Blair (United Kingdom) and John Howard (Australia) with the Presidential Medal of Freedom in the dying days of his administration, as thanks for their cooperation in the "War on Terror," but by then they had both left office facing tremendous public opposition to their participation in the Iraq War.[35]

At home, the U.S. electorate seems to have little ability to change the direction of the country. Despite the fact that the Democrats took control of Congress in the 2006 elections, and despite the strong case urging the House of Representatives to hold impeachment hearings on George W. Bush, these hearings, let alone an impeachment vote and Senate trial, never happened.[36] The Democrats under Speaker Nancy Pelosi declared early in 2006 that impeachment was "off the table." Despite their majority, and despite President Bush's low approval ratings, the Democrats in the 110th Congress ratified much of Bush's policy, including the wars in Iraq and Afghanistan, specifically legitimizing his military commissions and "warrantless wiretapping" policies through legislation known as the Military Commissions Act and the amendments to the Foreign Intelligence Surveillance Act (FISA). Concerns continue to be expressed about whether individual rights will be protected under the new administration: "President Obama may mouth very different rhetoric," said Anthony D. Romero, executive director of the American Civil Liberties Union. "He may have a more complicated process with members of Congress. But in the end, there is no substantive break from the policies of the Bush administration."[37]

Domestic Sacrifices

For years the public has opposed the U.S. wars in Afghanistan and Iraq, and yet despite the results of the 2008 elections, there are no signs these wars will end anytime soon. Henry Giroux notes, "The radical shift in the size, scope, and influence of the military can also be seen in the redistribution of domestic resources and government funding away from social programs into military-oriented security measures at home and abroad."[38] As Frances Fox Piven argues, a major goal of pursuing the wars of the last ten years has been to implement the conservative program, including reducing the domestic welfare state, including governmental contributions to education, pensions, public Medicare, and to social assistance.[39] On domestic issues, particularly in health care, public support for a single-payer public health care system cannot break through into public discourse except in the most marginal fashion, in the personages of Representative Dennis Kucinich (D-OH) and Senator Bernie Sanders (I-VT) and a few others. At a Town Hall meeting on health care in August 2009, President Obama said to a questioner, "you are absolutely right that I can't cover another 46 million people for free . . . we're going to have to find money from somewhere."[40] The elephant in the room is that because of militarism, the U.S. government does not have the resources to provide its people with public health care comparable to that enjoyed by the other advanced, industrial countries.

According to journalist George Monbiot, the U.S. federal government "is now spending as much on war as it is on education, public health, housing, employment, pensions, food aid and welfare put together."[41] That critic of an earlier Empire, John Hobson, also pointed one hundred years ago to the incompatibility between imperialism abroad and genuine democracy and social reform at home.[42] As Chris Hedges has said more recently, "The embrace by any society of permanent war is a parasite that devours the heart and soul of a nation. Permanent war extinguishes liberal, democratic movements. It turns culture into nationalist cant. It degrades and corrupts education and the media, and wrecks the economy. The liberal, democratic forces, tasked with maintaining an open society, become impotent."[43] While the United States continues to present itself as the world's greatest country, as a model, as a beacon, and a moral force for good, the number of skeptics both outside and inside has never been greater. As he admits, President Obama has a lot of fence mending to do, though it is not clear how successful he will be if he wholeheartedly adopts the militaristic policies, both foreign and domestic, of the past.

Often ignored but very real in its consequences are the environmental costs of militarism. As Barry Sanders notes in *The Green Zone*, the U.S. Department of Defense (DoD) is the largest single consumer of energy in the world, using about the same amount of energy as the African country of Nigeria, which has 140 million people.[44] There are 1.4 million employees in the DoD, stationed at hundreds of bases worldwide. The United States has a six-hundred ship navy, over 85 percent of which is fueled by oil products. The air force and other branches have thousands of combat, transport, and other planes, and the army has tens of thousands of vehicles of all types. Since this is the military, fuel efficiency isn't a priority, and the DoD guzzles gas. All of these bases and equipment take energy to produce building materials and construct them. But the environmental impact goes well beyond just the consumption of fossil fuels. Many weapons in the U.S. arsenal are composed in part of depleted uranium (DU), which acts as a penetrator, increasing the effectiveness of the weapon, particularly against armor. Composed mainly of uranium-238 (u-235 is used in nuclear fission), DU remains where it has exploded and emits low-level radiation, relatively speaking, but has an extremely long half-life of 4.5 billion years, which is the period over which half the remaining radioactive material will decay. Arguably, there is no truly safe level of exposure to radiation and the United States is dropping thousands of tons of DU per year in war zones like Iraq and Afghanistan. White phosphorus, which is only supposed to be used for nighttime illumination, produces a gas that is also an environmental contaminant. The U.S. wars in Afghanistan and Iraq have increased fuel consumption, but also combustion in the war zones, including oil well fires in Iraq. Since militarism begets militarism and war begets war, we must consider not only U.S. military expenditures but also those of other countries. Even though the United States is by far the largest military force, the rest of the world's militaries are undoubtedly a significant addition when it comes to the environmental footprint of the military.

Finally, as we would expect in a militaristic society, the military establishment becomes more powerful over time and intrudes as well into previously domestic jurisdiction. Domestic policing has become militarized and the military is taking an interest in domestic policing. Activities like "counterterrorism" and "controlling immigration" are attracting Pentagon involvement, and the Department of Defense now places military units on alert for events like national political conventions in case of "civilian disorder."[45] The Bush administration tried and succeeded for a year (2007–2008) in reducing limits on the ability of the U.S. military to do domestic law enforcement (by repealing sections of the *Posse Comitatus* Act of 1878), though those restrictions were restored in a bipartisan fashion by senators Patrick Leahy (D-VT) and Kit Bond (R-MO). Also worrying has been the training of military units to do domestic operations as part of the military's Northern Command.[46] As Peter Kraska argues, "distinctions between military, police, and criminal justice are blurring," in that domestic police are becoming more militarized, with heavy weapons and military-style training, and the military is working more closely with police on domestic issues such as drug interdiction.[47] U.S. prisons are becoming more militarized, and the military now runs prisons all over the world, not just for convicted personnel but for "detainees," those who in the past were identified as "prisoners of war." It should be clear that as the United States becomes a more militaristic state, on a gradual basis it is also being transformed in many other ways.

Can We Justify the Costs of War?

Given the high costs of war in lives, dollars, liberties, reputation, and the health of the planet, is military action ever justified, and if so, under what circumstances? President Obama called for Europeans to participate in the war in Afghanistan by referring to the war as "just," a term usually reserved for theological debates about whether state-sanctioned bloodshed can be morally justified.[48] The just war tradition, which goes back thousands of years and was founded by major Roman Catholic thinkers such as St. Augustine and St. Thomas Aquinas, emphasizes prudence in the deliberation on whether to go to war, as well as placing restraints on the ways in which war is conducted. According to the just war tradition, the strongest case to go to war is in genuine self-defense; when your country has been attacked by another state. Based on the United Nations Charter, which binds the United States since it is a ratified treaty, a state-oriented military defense is acceptable only when the global community cannot or will not respond to the aggression.[49]

The United States has been attacked twice in the last hundred years, in World War II and 9/11, but the United States has initiated warfare, and has interfered in other countries, many dozens of times in the same period. The United States distorts the just war principle of defense by artificially extending it to any country that it considers in its "vital interests." The U.S. government has defined its "vital interests" to be global, and with allies or clients all over the world the United States reserves for itself alone the right to sail the seven seas and intervene anywhere anytime. As a militaristic state the United States has been engaging in "wars of choice" rather than necessity, while the just war tradition is based in the assumption that there will be genuine necessity as a precondition to go to war. The just war tradition does not fully account for the struggle against terrorist groups, and it does not anticipate that citizens may believe that they are merely retaliating against the enemies who have attacked them, when in fact the targets of war often have more to do with preserving and enhancing a superpower's treasure and power than a proven complicity in an attack on the United States.

Even though the United States was attacked on 9/11, in a militarized society where people are told to defer to political and military leaders, it is easy for these same leaders to "massage" the facts and misrepresent the situation to get the necessary consent to go to war against the enemies that suit their political and economic agenda. As seen in the sentiment "When Timothy McVeigh attacked Oklahoma City, did we bomb his home state of Michigan?" many people questioned why the United States would attack Afghanistan because of the presumed presence of Saudi citizen Osama bin Laden. The construction of the threat of weapons of mass destruction and the falsification of a link between Saddam Hussein and al-Qaeda were the pretext for the Iraq War. Given the options of prosecuting the 9/11 masterminds through the U.S. domestic justice system or the International Criminal Court, was it really justified or necessary to attack two countries that were not responsible for the attack on the United States? The Peabody award–winning antiwar documentary *Why We Fight* features a grieving father who lost his son on 9/11. The father recounts the sad and compelling story of how he eagerly supported the Iraq War out of a desire for revenge, but that now he feels betrayed and exploited by his government. The documentary reveals that this one father's story parallels the story of the nation who were all grieving after the 9/11 attacks and whose leaders took advantage of that anger and grief to mislead the American public into war.[50]

So Who Wants War Anyway?

If war has great costs in humanitarian, economic, and political-legal-moral terms, and it is rarely justified, why is the United States in a condition of seemingly permanent war? A central answer must be found in the concept of the military-industrial complex (MIC). The MIC concept has an honorable pedigree. It was first raised within the mainstream by none other than retiring president Dwight D. Eisenhower, the supreme military commander of the victorious Allies in World War II, who also served as U.S. president from 1953 to 1961. His comment, though well known, is worth reproducing in detail:

> This conjunction of an immense military establishment and a large arms industry is new in the American experience. The total influence—economic, political, even spiritual—is felt in every city, every State house, every office of the Federal government. We recognize the imperative need for this development. Yet we must not fail to comprehend its grave implications. Our toil, resources and livelihood are all involved; so is the very structure of our society.
>
> In the councils of government, we must guard against the acquisition of unwarranted influence, whether sought or unsought, by the military industrial complex. The potential for the disastrous rise of misplaced power exists and will persist.
>
> We must never let the weight of this combination endanger our liberties or democratic processes. We should take nothing for granted. Only an alert and

knowledgeable citizenry can compel the proper meshing of the huge industrial and military machinery of defense with our peaceful methods and goals, so that security and liberty may prosper together.[51]

The idea that arises from this is that the wars in the first half of the twentieth centuries created their own "war lobby." Where there has also been a recognition of the category of the "war profiteer," World War II created massive pro-war interests to advocate for war and they perfected the use of culture to convince average people that war was necessary and even desirable. Before World War II, the United States was at war for certain periods, and then not at war, as though the switch had been and could be turned on and off. The United States had a small but capable permanent military (army, navy, and Marine Corps), able to engage in whatever "police actions" were ordered, but this military was certainly not in a position to threaten the Republic. After World War II, people expected the same kind of demobilization as was seen in 1919, but it did not materialize. The Czech coup of 1948, in which the pro-Soviet Czech Communist Party took over the country, the Chinese revolution in 1949, and the outbreak of the Korean War in June 1950, were *interpreted* as signs of the Soviet threat of worldwide aggression, despite the recent wartime alliance between, chiefly, the United States, the United Kingdom, and the Soviet Union. Just as the attacks of 9/11 could have been interpreted as a massive civilian crime requiring a massive law-enforcement-based response, those events in the late 1940s and early 1950s also could have been interpreted differently. But they were not.

After the Korean War the United States was fully engrossed in what came to be called the Cold War, a not-quite-war in which the United States and its NATO allies would prepare for war but would not fight directly with the main adversary, the Soviet Union and its allies in the Warsaw Pact. The 1950s saw increased military expenditures, including U.S. funding of the French colonial war in Indochina, and then Americanization of the war in Vietnam in the early to mid-1960s. The United States was "at war with Asia" for over twenty-five years, half of which saw direct U.S. military involvement. This was also the McCarthy period, in which U.S. citizens who were allegedly procommunist and prosocialist were branded as "un-American" and hauled in front of congressional committees, fired from their jobs, and blacklisted from the education sector and the entertainment industry. The precedent for this was the "Palmer raids" during and after World War I, in which the political left, including anarchists and communists, were attacked and in some cases deported from the United States. Even with the end of the Cold War in 1990, the United States in the Clinton era saw only a very tiny "peace dividend." It is no exaggeration to say that the United States was in a state of war readiness for fifty years before 9/11, and this can certainly be attributed in part to the MIC.

As Chalmers Johnson has pointed out, since U.S. withdrawal from Vietnam in 1975, militarism has become more dangerous because it has increasingly taken on a civilian form. During the early Kennedy and Johnson administrations, it was the uniformed generals who were hawkish. After Vietnam, particularly in the Republican administrations of Reagan and the two Bushes, the civilians have been more hawkish than those with combat experience. The central lesson taken from the Vietnam experience by these civilian actors was that military planners must be more secretive and must centralize power in the hands of hawkish proponents of military action. This resulted, in the 2000s, in the extraordinary sight of President Bush challenging militants planning strikes on U.S. forces in Iraq to "Bring it on!" and civilian managers, like Dick Cheney, Condoleezza Rice, Donald Rumsfeld, Paul Wolfowitz, and others, calling the shots on how to fight in Iraq and Afghanistan, despite their "chicken hawk" lack of combat experience, and having benefited from college deferments or soft assignments in the Vietnam era.[52]

Of course over the years there have been various efforts to elaborate on the MIC. Nick Turse's book *The Complex: How the Military Invades Our Everyday Lives* shows how almost every American "is, at least passively, supporting the Complex every time he or she shops for groceries, sends a package, drives a car, or watches TV—let alone eats barbeque in Memphis or buys Christian books in Hattiesburg. And what choice do you have? What other brand of computer would you buy? Or cereal? Or boots?"[53] For some, the word "congressional" should be added to the combined forces of military and industrial, in order to note the widespread influence of the complex on Capitol Hill. For others, the community of "intelligence" should be included since they play an increasing role.[54] In the last ten years, but going back to the Reagan era, one could also add "contractor/mercenary" because this is a new source of political support for overseas intervention and a permanent war footing.[55] That the MIC is still relevant there should be no doubt. As Peter Phillips wrote recently, with reference to the Obama administration:

> Lockheed Martin gave $2,612,219 in total political campaign donations, with 49% to Democrats ($1,285,493) and 51% to Republicans ($1,325,159). Boeing gave $2,225,947 in 2008 with 58% going to Democrats, and General Dynamics provided $1,682,595 to both parties. Northrop Grumman spent over $20 million in 2008, hiring lobbyists to influence Congress, and Raytheon spent $6 million on lobbyists in the same period. In a revolving door appointment, Obama nominated Raytheon's senior vice president for government operations and strategy, William Lynn, for the number two position in the Pentagon. Lynn was formally the Defense Department's comptroller during the Clinton administration.[56]

Ralph Lopez noted in a September 2009 article that as much as 80 percent of Congress members' war chests come from outside their states or districts, and that the amount of money received from an industry with an interest in legislation is a good predictor of how the member will vote. His solution is to ban contributions from outside the state or district, to try to return the country's politics to the vision where elected people are accountable to their electors, not distant donors.[57]

As another dimension of the MIC, some observers ultimately explain, and support militarism, by referring to political rather than military or economic motives. This view is captured by those who defend the presidency of George W. Bush by saying that "he kept us safe." Referred to as "realism" by academic political scientists, this is a "power politics" analysis that says that great powers and the twentieth- and twenty-first-century phenomenon, superpowers, must behave in certain ways because other states in the world will behave this way. The dominant view in this tradition is the "balance of power" view, claiming that there will always be between two (1945–1990) and five (1820–1919) dominant powers that will all try to preserve and enhance their wealth and power, and must do so lest they be taken advantage of by others. It is worth noting that this way of thinking is not for public consumption, but consistently seems to dominate when policy makers are in private.

Since 1990 we have seen the revived relevance of another Realist tradition, the "hegemony" view. In A. F. K. Organski's pioneering work, the typical global structure of the states' system was not so much a balance of power but a pyramid. There was a dominant state on top, like the United States after 1945 (and especially after 1990), and others who were trying to knock the United States off its pedestal and take over.[58] It was taken for granted by both schools of thought that these great/superpowers tended to act in an "imperial" fashion. It also explains why a superpower continues to behave in an imperial fashion even when it has seemingly no enemies, and certainly no enemies of even remotely comparable power.

The United States as a War State

Since the collapse of the Soviet Union, and the emergence of the United States as the world's lone military superpower, there has been an increasing acceptance by American political leaders that the United States is an empire. Imperialism is "the process whereby the dominant politico-economic interests of one nation expropriate for their own enrichment the land, labor, raw materials, and markets of another people."[59] In 1941 Henry Luce, multimillionaire owner of *Time*, *Life*, and *Fortune* magazines, stated that the time had arrived for the United States "to exert upon the world the full impact of our influence, for such purposes as we see fit, and by such means as we see fit."[60] This sentiment has a contemporary advocate in the Project for a New American Century (PNAC), a group of U.S. Neoconservatives who argued for a more assertive U.S. policy during the late Clinton era, many of whom had a chance to implement this vision as senior officials in the Bush administration. In their signature document, "Rebuilding America's Defenses: Strategy, Forces and Resources for a New Century," published in September 2000, PNAC argues, rather starkly, and early in the document, that the United States should ensure that it maintains its global military superiority, so that it can "defend the American homeland," "fight and decisively win multiple, simultaneous theater wars," and "perform the 'constabulary' duties associated with shaping the security environment in critical regions."[61] This view accepts the legitimacy of policies that would, undertaken by any other state, be labeled by the United States as imperial and aggressive.

In the late 1980s, Yale historian Paul Kennedy argued that the United States was risking "imperial overstretch."[62] As we have seen, PNAC has been much more open and direct, but they are not alone. Niall Ferguson, for example, offers a sanguine and benign view of the U.S. Empire in his book *Colossus: The Price of America's Empire.*[63] This should be no surprise, since a "realist" will say that the obligations and benefits are inevitably thrust upon a superpower—the only question is how well the situation will be managed. This was a book of the moment, which was optimistic about U.S. militarist behavior and denied the concerns of the more prudent, albeit minority, of scholars. One of these prudent thinkers was and is John Ikenberry, Albert G. Milbank Professor of Politics and International Affairs at Princeton University. Though also a student of "power politics," Ikenberry expressed skepticism in a series of articles about the course of action being advocated by PNAC, Bush, and the imperial planners who believed they could dominate the United States and the world for a generation.[64] In *A People's History of American Empire*, Howard Zinn evocatively asks, "Have not the justifications for empire, embedded in our culture, assaulting our good sense—that war is necessary for security, that expansion is fundamental to civilization—begun to lose their hold on our minds?"[65]

Blowback

It is sobering to consider that one of the challenges of ending militarism is that in a way it is self-perpetuating, literally. This is because, apart from everything else, conflict begets conflict, and one of the mechanisms is "blowback."

As Chalmers Johnson writes, "[t]he term 'blowback', which officials of the Central Intelligence Agency first invented for their own internal use . . . refers to the unintended consequences of policies that were kept secret from the American people."[66] In the recent past the media have presented world events in the framework of forced naiveté, in which news anchors report on events and throw up their hands unknowingly, instead of looking into the historical background and precedents or interviewing someone who can shed light on the situation. The concept of blowback helps us see that much of the conflict in the world can be traced to past actions by many states and other actors, including the leading superpower of the last sixty-five years. So the poor relations between the United States and the new progressive governments of Latin America is blowback from U.S. domination in the 1970s and 1980s; distrust of the United States in the Middle East is blowback from increasing U.S. support of Israel over particularly the last thirty years, along with U.S. support for authoritarian regimes in the past (e.g., Iran, Iraq) and the present (e.g., Saudi Arabia). Much has been done in secret, and the U.S. people are encouraged to forget so much anyway that the distinction between "secret" and "public" may be meaningless. The fact that things were done in secret or have been forgotten makes it that much harder to raise those past actions as believable explanations for current developments. Having cried "wolf" and been wrong regarding weapons of mass destruction (WMDs) in Iraq in the early 2000s, there are many in the world who are skeptical of U.S. concerns expressed over Iran and North Korea. This is just scratching the surface. This is blowback, and this makes ending militarism more difficult.

The Role of American Exceptionalism in Militarism

One of the reasons that the United States persists in its militarist foreign policy, despite the facts that the costs of war are high, the domestic and global reaction is unfavorable, and the results of blowback may well be making U.S. citizens less safe, is found in the notion of "American exceptionalism." As historian Howard Zinn says, the core of American exceptionalism is the idea "that the United States alone has the right, whether by divine sanction or moral obligation, to bring civilization, or democracy, or liberty to the rest of the world, by violence if necessary."[67] He and many others note that this idea goes back to the European founding of colonies in New England in the seventeenth century, when Governor John Winthrop referred to his Massachusetts Bay Colony in 1630 as a "city on the hill." Since then it has been a common belief that the United States of America is special, that it represents a departure from its European roots, that it is specially blessed by God, and ordained to extend "peace and freedom" in the Americas and around the world. As Zinn notes in the same essay and throughout his large body of work, this self-confidence has often come at a terrible price to other peoples, whether it was the American Indian who was slaughtered, starting shortly after Winthrop uttered his famous words, or many peoples in the world, in Mexico, the Philippines and elsewhere, who have been killed directly or indirectly by U.S. forces, and saw their opportunity for genuine self-government taken away. The "historic mission" of the United States has often been a good cover for the search for power and treasure, whether in the nineteenth and twentieth centuries, or in the early 2000s.

Over the last couple of centuries, presidents and leading thinkers have been inspired by American exceptionalism in their view of the world. The Monroe Doctrine, proclaimed by President James Monroe in 1823, declared that no further European colonialism would be permitted in the Americas, leaving the United States to dominate the hemisphere. The idea of "Manifest Destiny" was coined by John O'Sullivan in the 1840s; he regarded the U.S. war with Mexico as "the fulfillment of our manifest destiny to overspread the continent allotted by Providence for the free development of our yearly multiplying millions."[68] President Theodore Roosevelt coined what has come to be known as the "Roosevelt Corollary" to the Monroe Doctrine, that the United States reserves the right to intervene in Caribbean and Latin American countries in cases where these countries cannot pay their debts, and in order to maintain "stability." All told, in the twentieth century the United States intervened militarily all over the Americas, and after World War II, U.S. concerns became increasingly global. U.S. presidents from across the narrow spectrum behaved in ways consistent with these ideas, but during the eight years of the Bush era these ideas, such as divine ordination of the United States' exclusive moral certitude, were pushed much farther than they have been in some time, particularly compared to the previous thirty years.

The legacy of this is that the United States is to some degree an isolated state, as illustrated by its cultural relations with other parts of the world. The country's historic mission provides the more overconfident among U.S. citizens with a grand idea of the country's popular cultural achievements. Norman J. Pattiz, a U.S. media executive, founder of Radio Sawa, and tapped to establish more pro-Western outlets in the Middle East, is quoted as saying that exposure to television programs like *Friends* "are what's needed to improve the Iraqis' understanding of what we're all about."[69] The superiority of Western, and more specifically U.S., civilization is assumed, as is the legitimacy of ramming it down people's throats at the end of a bayonet. To the extent that Iraqis are influenced by these sorts of programs and understand the United States better, it will undoubtedly be at the expense of their own civilization.

American exceptionalism is a deep-seated cultural value shared by many in the United States that leads them to overblown self-confidence and sense of the special virtue of the United States. It is part of why, culturally, so many in the United States (and particularly among the governing elite) are so suspicious of international law, the United Nations, the International Criminal Court, and even the concerns of U.S. allies. Even if global institutions are largely the creation of the United States, the U.S. people, led by the elite, will be open to the idea that they have fallen under the control of those in the "Old World" of Europe, or dubious people in the global south. The United States was born through war, and achievement through war and violence is a persistent theme in U.S. life. It allows people in the United States to say they live in "the greatest country in the world," though many outside the United States don't agree. It allows presidents, and other conservative militarists (the take-no-responsibility crowd), to dismiss any criticism of the United States as coming from what they call the "blame-America-first crowd." It allowed officials of the Bush administration to dismiss concerns of its opponents on the Iraq invasion as part of "Old Europe." It allows the United States to declare its professional baseball championship "the World Series," even though any U.S. national baseball team can face stiff competition from other national teams. It allows U.S. citizens to refer to themselves as "Americans," a phrase that chafes especially for those in Central and South America, who see themselves as Americans too.

American exceptionalism feeds into (the Realist) power-politics theory, where the world is a "self-help" system in which every state must look out for its own interests and cannot trust anyone else.[70] As Stanley Hoffmann once said, the contemporary study of international relations is a U.S. social science.[71] One could say that this science embraces the doctrine of American exceptionalism writ large, designed to govern the thinking of the whole world. The problem is that as an underlying part of U.S. culture it predisposes the country to militarism. The most educated part of the U.S. population, those who have heard of the Monroe Doctrine, the Roosevelt Corollary, and the "greatest generation" that won World War II, is most likely to believe the myth of American exceptionalism.[72] The children of the more affluent are less likely to serve on the front lines, and still more likely to be officers if they do serve at all. The average person, part of the majority and less well educated, and less indoctrinated with mythology, has reason to resist militarism because their kids are more likely to serve in the military for economic reasons, and to end up directly in harm's way. They also have less to gain personally than the affluent, who are invested in the stock market and will potentially benefit from the profits of the military-industrial complex. They have the most to lose when (and not "if") the welfare state, including Social Security and Medicare benefits, are cut to pay war debts.

Conclusion

We have seen that the death tolls from U.S. wars have been high and that the country now faces challenges in recruiting personnel for its contemporary wars. Despite the effort to recruit more women the military remains a firmly patriarchical institution. The economic and financial costs of war to the country as a whole are steep, but may suit the economic motivations of the elite who have the most to gain. Militarism means that the country pays a price in lost civil liberties, which are hard to recover even when the war ends. Domestic government spending priorities are hamstrung by militarism, ignore environmental impacts, and the military establishment intrudes on more and more "domestic" areas of jurisdiction. We explored whether the just war tradition provides any cover for the U.S. propensity to go to war, and argue that these were wars of choice in which the United States did not come close to exhausting alternatives to war. Given the unpopularity of current U.S. wars, we addressed the question of why these wars happen, noting the economic and political forces behind them. As the United States has become increasingly militaristic it is acceptable to admit that it is imperial, and we also see that conflict perpetuates itself because of "blowback" from past secret U.S. initiatives. "American exceptionalism" is a long-standing cultural value that promotes the separation or alienation of the United States from other states, as well as feelings of U.S. superiority, thereby making it easier to lay the ground work for overseas wars.

Over the history of the U.S. republic, occasional voices have been raised with warnings for their fellow citizens. In his farewell address, George Washington warned against "foreign entanglements" in the form of alliances, because of the harm they could do to the young republic. Thomas Jefferson was a known opponent of the institution of a standing army. President Eisenhower warned of the influence, "sought or unsought," of the military-industrial complex. Dr. Martin Luther King warned that the soul of America was at risk because of its domestic and foreign policies in the 1960s. No longer voices in the wilderness, these concerns over the future of the United States have been picked up by the mainstream, and the small number of dissenters has grown and is having an increasing impact on the public.

The concerns of internal dissenters are well founded. While most people were not paying attention, the United States has become an increasingly militaristic state and some observers openly admit that the country has become a new form of Empire. This has exacted a great humanitarian toll in both civilian and military casualties, it has sapped the U.S. economy, aggravated its environmental problems, and undermined the potential for U.S. liberal democracy and republican ideals. Catherine Lutz effectively identifies the far reaching costs of militarism:

Militarization is simultaneously a discursive process, involving a shift in general societal beliefs and values in ways necessary to legitimate the use of force, the organization of large standing armies and their leaders, and the higher taxes or tribute used to pay for them. Militarization is intimately connected not only to the obvious increase in the size of armies and resurgence of militant nationalisms and militant fundamentalisms but also to the less visible deformation of human potentials into the hierarchies of race, class, gender, and sexuality, and to the shaping of national histories in ways that glorify and legitimate military action.[73]

As we will show in the rest of this book, popular culture has been one of the means through which militarism has been created, but it can also be a means of undermining it.

Notes

1. "America's Wars," Department of Veterans Affairs, 2008, www1.va.gov/opa/fact/docs/amwars.pdf (accessed February 23, 2010).

2. David Goodner, "American Genocide in the Middle East: Three Million and Counting," *Global Research*, August 8, 2007, www.globalresearch.ca/index.php?context=va&aid=6531 (accessed August 15, 2009).

3. Cindy Sheehan, "The Day of the Dead," *Truthout*, May 25, 2009, www.truthout.org/052509A (accessed May 25, 2009).

4. Katrina vanden Heuvel, "Recruiters Sink to New Lows," *Nation*, June 21, 2005, www.thenation.com/blogs/edcut/3705/recruiters_sink_to_new_lows (accessed May 28, 2009). These issues are well summed up in "Tomgram: Nick Turse on 12-Pentagon Steps to a Misfit Military," *TomDispatch*, September 14, 2006, www.tomdispatch.com/post/121072/nick_turse_on_12_pentagon_steps_to_a_misfit_military (accessed May 28, 2009).

5. Vanden Heuvel, "Recruiters Sink to New Lows."

6. David Goodman, "No Child Unrecruited," *Mother Jones*, November 2002, www.motherjones.com/politics/2002/11/no-child-unrecruited (accessed July 27, 2009).

7. Martha Burk, "Advertising for Trouble," *Huffington Post*, May 23, 2008, www.huffingtonpost.com/martha-burk/advertising-for-trouble_b_103298.html (accessed July 12, 2009).

8. "U.S. Military Meets, Exceeds Recruiting Goals for April 2009," The Tension Blog, May 12, 2009, thetension.blogspot.com/2009/05/us-military-meets-exceeds-recruiting.html (accessed June 10, 2009).

9. Jorge Mariscal, "The Making of an American Soldier: Why Young People Join the Military," *Sojourners*, June 26, 2007, www.alternet.org/story/52233/ (accessed July 27, 2009).

10. Sarah Lazare, "Involuntary Military Service Under the Radar," *Truthout*, May 1, 2009, www.truthout.org/052109R (accessed May 28, 2009).

11. Ann Scott Tyson, "GAO Faults U.S. Military over Munitions in Iraq," *Washington Post*, March 23, 2007, www.truthout.org/article/gao-faults-us-military-over -munitions-iraq (accessed May 28, 2009).

12. Jeremy Scahill, *Blackwater: The Rise of the World's Most Powerful Mercenary Army*, rev. ed. (New York: Nation Books, 2008).

13. Judith Coburn, "Tomgram: Judith Coburn, Caring for Veterans on the Cheap," *TomDispatch*, April 27, 2006, www.tomdispatch.com/post/80291/judith_coburn_ caring_for_veterans_on_the_cheap (accessed May 28, 2009).

14. Suzanne Goldenberg, "Pentagon Counts the Psychological Cost of Iraq War as Survey Reveals Suicide Levels," *Guardian*, March 29, 2004, www.guardian.co.uk/ world/2004/mar/29/iraq.usa (accessed May 27, 2009).

15. Penny Coleman, "The Tragedy of Our 'Disappeared' Veterans," *AlterNet*, August 12, 2009, www.alternet.org/world/140828/the_tragedy_of_our_%27disappeared %27_veterans/ (accessed August 13, 2009).

16. Cynthia H. Enloe, *Does Khaki Become You? The Militarisation of Women's Lives* (Boston: South End Press, 1983).

17. Lucinda Marshall, "The Connection between Militarism and Violence against Women," *Znet*, February 21, 2004, www.zmag.org/znet/viewArticle/9041 (accessed July 10, 2009).

18. This paragraph draws on Cynthia Cockburn, "Why Feminist Anti-militarism?" Women in Black UK, March 1, 2003, www.womeninblack.org.uk/Feminist%20Anti militarism.htm (accessed July 10, 2009).

19. Susan Faludi interviewed by Rashi Kesarwani, "Susan Faludi: America's Terror Dream," *Nation*, November 12, 2007, www.thenation.com/doc/20071126/kesarwani (accessed August 15, 2009).

20. Susan Faludi, *The Terror Dream: Fear and Fantasy in Post-9/11 America* (New York: Metropolitan Books / Henry Holt and Company, 2007).

21. National Priorities Project, http://costofwar.com (accessed February 23, 2010). See the site for a more recent figure.

22. Joseph E. Stiglitz and Linda J. Bilmes, *The Three Trillion Dollar War: The True Cost of the Iraq Conflict* (New York: W. W. Norton, 2008).

23. Stockholm International Peace Research Institute, *2008 Year Book on Armaments, Disarmament and International Security for 2007*, www.sipri.org/year book/2008/05 (accessed August 10, 2009).

24. James K. Galbraith, "What Economic Price This War?" *Common Dreams*, March 24, 2003, www.commondreams.org/views03/0324-02.htm (accessed May 27, 2009).

25. The classic work on this is by Seymour Melman, *Pentagon Capitalism: The Political Economy of War* (New York: McGraw-Hill, 1970).

26. Miriam Pemberton, "Poll: Fewer Guns, More Talk," *Foreign Policy In Focus*, October 27, 2006, www.fpif.org/fpiftxt/3649 (accessed August 10, 2009).

27. The key work that inspires this analysis is by Robert Brenner, *The Economics of Global Turbulence: The Advanced Capitalist Economies from Long Boom to Long Downturn, 1945–2005* (London and New York: Verso, 2006). Particularly important is his concept of "asset price Keynesianism."

28. Louis Uchitelle, "Once a Key to Recovery, Detroit Adds to the Pain," *New York Times*, June 1, 2009, p. B1.

29. John A. Hobson, *Imperialism: A Study* (Ann Arbor: University of Michigan Press, 1905/1965), especially part I, chap. 4, "Economic Parasites of Imperialism."

30. Michel Chossudovsky, "War Propaganda: Disneyland Goes to War-Torn Iraq," *Global Research*, April 28, 2008, www.globalresearch.ca/index.php?context=va&aid =8837 (accessed July 13, 2009).

31. Scott Thill, "Introducing Disney-Iraq: The Unhappiest Place on Earth," *Alter-Net*, August 1, 2008, www.alternet.org/world/93251/introducing_disneyiraq%3A_the_unhappiest_place_on_earth/ (accessed July 26, 2009).

32. Jared Jacang Maher, "Drop Boards Not Bombs: Llewellyn Werner Thinks Skateparks Could Get Iraq's Economy Rolling," *Denver Westword News*, October 1, 2008, www.westword.com/2008-10-02/news/drop-boards-not-bombs/ (accessed July 20, 2009).

33. Jim Cornehls, "The War on Civil Liberties Continues," *Z Magazine Online*, July 2006, www.zmag.org/zmag/viewArticle/13711 (accessed July 27, 2009).

34. Naomi Wolf, "Fascist America, in 10 Easy Steps," *Guardian*, April 24, 2007.

35. Nico Hines, "President Bush Awards Tony Blair Presidential Medal of Freedom," *Times of London*, January 13, 2009, www.timesonline.co.uk/tol/news/world/us_and_americas/article5511389.ece (accessed June 2, 2009).

36. See, for example, D. Loo and P. Philips, eds., *Impeach the President: The Case against Bush and Cheney* (New York: Seven Stories Press, 2006); See also N. Wolf, *The End of America: Letter of Warning to a Young Patriot* (White River Junction, VT: Chelsea Green, 2007).

37. Charlie Savage, "To Critics, New Policy on Terror Looks Old," *New York Times*, July 1, 2009.

38. Henry A. Giroux, "The Emerging Authoritarianism in the United States: Political Culture under the Bush/Cheney Administration," *symploke* 14, nos. 1–2 (2006): 98–151.

39. Frances Fox Piven, *The War at Home: The Domestic Costs of Bush's Militarism* (New York: The New Press, 2004).

40. "Transcript: President Obama Holds Town Hall in Belgrade, Mont.," *Washington Post*, August 14, 2009, www.washingtonpost.com/wp-dyn/content/article/2009/08/14/AR2009081402355.html?sid=ST2009081402514 (accessed August 15, 2009).

41. George Monbiot, "States of War," *Guardian*, October 14, 2003, www.common dreams.org/views03/1014-09.htm (accessed July 15, 2009).

42. Hobson, *Imperialism: A Study, 1905/1965*, part II, chap. 1, "The Political Significance of Imperialism."

43. Chris Hedges, "The Disease of Permanent War," *Truthdig*, May 19, 2009, www .alternet.org/politics/140106/the_disease_of_permanent_war/?page=1 (accessed July 21, 2009).

44. From *The Energy Bulletin*, cited in Barry Sanders, *The Green Zone: The Environmental Costs of Militarism* (Oakland, CA, and Edinburgh: AK Press, 2009), 9.

45. Chalmers Johnson, *Sorrows of Empire: Militarism, Secrecy, and the End of the Republic* (New York: Henry Holt, 2004), 119.

46. "Is Posse Comitatus Dead? U.S. Troops on U.S. Streets," *Democracy Now!* October 7, 2008, www.democracynow.org/2008/10/7/us_army_denies_unit_will_be (accessed August 15, 2009).

47. Peter B. Kraska, "The Military-Criminal Justice Blur: An Introduction," *Militarizing the American Criminal Justice System,* ed. Peter B. Kraska (Boston: Northeastern University Press, 2001).

48. Caren Bohan and Noah Barkin, "Obama Seeks More European Help in Afghanistan," Reuters, April 3, 2009.

49. This discussion is inspired in part by Michael Walzer's classic work, *Just and Unjust Wars: A Moral Argument with Historical Illustrations,* 4th ed. (New York: Basic Books, 2006).

50. Eugene Jarecki, *Why We Fight,* DVD, 2005.

51. Dwight D. Eisenhower, *Public Papers of the Presidents,* Dwight D. Eisenhower, 1960, 1035–40, farewell speech, http://coursesa.matrix.msu.edu/~hst306/documents/indust .html (accessed June 2, 2009).

52. Chalmers Johnson, *The Sorrows of Empire: Militarism, Secrecy and the End of the Republic* (New York: Metropolitan Books / Henry Holt and Company, 2004), 60–61.

53. Nick Turse, *The Complex* (New York: Metropolitan Books, 2008).

54. Chalmers Johnson and Tom Engelhardt, "The Military-Industrial Complex," July 28, 2008, *TomDispatch,* www.antiwar.com/engelhardt/?articleid=13214 (accessed June 2, 2009).

55. Frida Berrigan, "Military Industrial Complex 2.0," *TomDispatch,* September 15, 2008, www.commondreams.org/view/2008/09/15-3 (accessed June 2, 2009).

56. Peter Phillips, "Obama Administration Continues U.S. Military Global Dominance," *Dissident Voice: A Radical Newsletter in the Struggle for Peace and Social Justice,* February 19, 2009, http://dissidentvoice.org/2009/02/obama-administration-continues -us-military-global-dominance/ (accessed July 13, 2009).

57. Ralph Lopez, "Why the Wars Roll On: Ban Campaign Money from Outside the District," *Truthout,* September 9, 2009, www.truthout.org/090409A (accessed February 16, 2010).

58. A. F. K. Organski, *World Politics,* 2nd ed. (New York: Alfred A. Knopf, 1968).

59. Michael Parenti, *Against Empire* (San Francisco: City Light Books, 1995), chap. 1, www.michaelparenti.org/AgainstEmpire.html (accessed June 3, 2009).

60. George McKenna, *The Puritan Origins of American Patriotism* (New Haven, CT: Yale University Press, 2007), 246.

61. Project for a New American Century, *Rebuilding America's Defenses: Strategy, Forces and Resources for a New Century* (Washington, DC: PNAC, September 2000), iv, www.newamericancentury.org/RebuildingAmericasDefenses.pdf (accessed June 3, 2009).

62. Paul M. Kennedy, *The Rise and Fall of the Great Powers: Economic Change and Military Conflict from 1500 to 2000* (New York: Random House, 1987).

63. Niall Ferguson, *Colossus: The Price of America's Empire* (New York: Penguin, 2004).

64. See G. John Ikenberry, "America's Imperial Ambition," *Foreign Affairs*, September/October 2002, www.foreignaffairs.com/articles/58245/g-john-ikenberry/americas-imperial-ambition (accessed June 3, 2009).

65. Howard Zinn, Mike Konopacki, and Paul Buhle, *A People's History of American Empire* (New York: Metropolitan Books, 2008).

66. Chalmers Johnson, *Blowback: The Costs and Consequences of American Empire* (New York: Henry Holt and Company, 2000), 8.

67. Howard Zinn, "The Power and the Glory: Myths of American Exceptionalism," *Boston Review*, November 24, 2006, http://bostonreview.net/BR30.3/zinn.html (accessed June 11, 2009).

68. Cited in Zinn, "The Power and the Glory."

69. Pattiz quoted in James Castonguay, "Intermedia and the War on Terror," in *Rethinking Global Security: Media, Popular Culture and the "War on Terror,"* ed. Andrew Martin and Patrice Petro (New Brunswick, NJ, and London: Rutgers University Press, 2006), 169.

70. A major thinker in this "Neorealist" tradition is Kenneth Waltz, whose groundbreaking work was *International Politics* (New York, 1979).

71. Stanley Hoffmann, "An American Social Science: International Relations," *Daedalus* 106, no. 3 (1977): 41–60.

72. See Roger Cohen's mixed review of Godfrey Hodgson's book *The Myth of American Exceptionalism*, in the *New York Times*, April 24, 2009. Cohen writes from the perspective of a believer in American exceptionalism, in which the United States is the "universalist embodiment of liberty, democracy, the rule of law and free enterprise." See www.nytimes.com/2009/04/26/books/review/Cohen-t.html?pagewanted=1&_r=2 (accessed June 12, 2009).

73. Catherine Lutz, "Making War at Home in the United States: Militarization and the Current Crisis," *American Anthropologist* 104 (September 2002): 723.

2

The Call to Arms

Popaganda Persuades the Public to Go to War

ESPITE THE FACT THAT THE UNITED STATES MAY BE A WAR STATE with a tradition of pride in its role as a global superpower, it is nevertheless true that the U.S. population is quite resistant to the idea of participating in or starting wars. Sixty-five percent of Americans say the United States has been "too quick to get American military forces involved" in international conflicts, and an even higher percentage wants the United States to put more emphasis on diplomatic and economic methods in combating terrorism.[1] Many global victims of the militarist policies of the war state recognize the distinction between the actions of the state and the wishes of the American people when they say, "my dispute is with the U.S. government, not the U.S. people."[2] Historians have demonstrated that U.S. citizens were lukewarm about fighting the British in the War of 1812 and Mexico in the 1840s. The Spanish-American War of 1898 was famously the war that made William Randolph Hearst's active promotion of war in his newspapers the subject of critique and mockery from a generation of "muck-raking" journalists. The United States entered World War I only in 1917, almost three years after it began, and entered World War II in December 1941, twenty-eight months after the British declaration of war and only after the United States was attacked at Pearl Harbor. Many Americans generally held to President George Washington's views that it was unwise to get caught up in the affairs of others.

The resistance of the U.S. public to support going to war continued in more recent times and to this day. Lyndon Johnson won landslide reelection as president in 1964 based on portraying his opponent, Barry Goldwater, as a reckless extremist who would involve the United States in overseas wars, including a nuclear war with the Soviet Union, and then Johnson proceeded to escalate U.S. forces in Vietnam from fifteen thousand to over five hundred thousand. (This parallels the Obama campaign's highlighting of Senator McCain's admission that U.S. forces could be in Iraq for one hundred years, a scenario which may actually come to pass even under Democratic presidents.) The Johnson administration was able to rally public opinion in favor of U.S. escalation in 1965 only because of public outrage over an "attack" on U.S. naval ships in the Gulf of Tonkin, an attack which, it was revealed years later, never happened. With the U.S. military defeat in Vietnam in 1975, the American public's justified skepticism regarding overseas intervention was characterized by the militarists as "Vietnam Syndrome," as though opposition to invading other nations was a form of ailment that required treatment. This was also the era of a resurgent Congress, which felt betrayed by the executive branch which pursued war with Vietnam. Investigative committees, such as those chaired by Senator Frank Church, developed the War Powers Act and the Foreign Intelligence Surveillance Act (FISA), which were aimed at curbing the president's power to rush to war. In the 1980s, the so-called syndrome continued as a majority of people opposed U.S. direct military intervention in Central America. As a result, the Reagan administration turned to covert means in order to support authoritarian, anti-Communist regimes and anti-governmental militias, including in the Iran-Contra scandal.[3] The U.S. invasion of Grenada in 1982, code named "Operation Urgent Fury," was sold to the people as necessary to protect U.S. medical students in the wake of a coup that brought a hard-line socialist leader to power on the small Caribbean island, though it was later revealed they were never under threat.[4]

When the U.S. government elites decide that there is a "security issue" that needs to be addressed, they lay the ground work in the public mind for military action, and they strike when an "incident" provides the necessary rationale for action. This is not a new phenomenon, in that even the casual student of U.S. history will have heard of the "Chesapeake Incident" (War of 1812), the "sinking of the USS *Maine*" (Spanish-American War), the "sneak attack on Pearl Harbor," the "North Korean Invasion of the South," "Soviet Missiles in Cuba," the "Gulf of Tonkin Incident," the "Soviet Invasion of Afghanistan," "Cuban and Nicaraguan support for the El Salvador insurgency," the "Iraqi Invasion of Kuwait," and "Iraqi connections to al-Qaeda and WMDs," all of which were official reasons for the threat of, or resort, to war. Just as these rationales go back to the birth of the republic, so too governmental techniques are not new. As John M. Barry has written:

> Then, during the World War, President Woodrow Wilson turned the desire for community into something foul by encouraging, manipulating, and exploiting

the nation's fears. His administration warned of hidden enemies undermining the nation, enemies to be found and cast out. George Creel ran Wilson's propaganda machine and demanded "100% Americanism." At his peak 150,000 people worked under his umbrella. . . . One newspaper editor complained, "Government conscripted public opinion as they conscripted men and women and materials. . . . They mobilized it. They put it in charge of drill sergeants. They goose-stepped it."[5]

It is important to note that even as the self-appointed global police officer, not every international invasion or crisis is defined as a security threat for the United States. During the Cold War between the United States and the Soviet Union, each superpower seemed to recognize that the other had a "sphere of influence" in which each had, with some limits, a free hand. More recently, the world's refusal to intervene in the Rwanda genocide of 1994, in which a million people were killed, and its ongoing unwillingness to intervene in Sudan, despite humanitarian reason to do so, is an indication of both elite and popular disinterest in those parts of the world.

Manufacturing Consent for War

The story of the U.S. republic is that over time and through social struggle, slavery was ended, women won the vote, African Americans emerged from the "Jim Crow" system of discrimination, gays and lesbians make gradual progress in struggling for equal rights, and the development of campaigns for educational reform, peace, the environment, and many other causes is on the rise. This greater sophistication on the part of the people of U.S. society has necessitated more capable state and elite efforts to promote their policies, which are otherwise quite unpopular. As historian Gabriel Kolko has written recently:

> There are indeed problems with the public but it invariably senses realities and its constraints well before the politicians—who use the public and then ignore it. The party out of office will cater to mass opinion but usually forgets it once it comes to power.[6]

States which want to go to war against the wishes of their citizens turn to propaganda as a tool of persuasion. "Propaganda is a set of methods employed by an organized group that wants to bring about the active or passive participation in its actions of a mass of individuals, psychologically unified through psychological manipulation and incorporated in an organization."[7] As a term it is associated with authoritarian and totalitarian states like Nazi Germany and the Soviet Union, which had ministers in the government devoted to persuading the public of the rightness of government policy and courses of action. Large-scale social control has been one of the biggest challenges of the twentieth century and it has not diminished in the new one we have now entered. As Nazi propaganda chief Joseph Goebbels said:

> If you tell a lie big enough and keep repeating it, people will eventually come to believe it. The lie can be maintained only for such time as the State can shield the people from the political, economic and/or military consequences of the lie. It thus becomes vitally important for the State to use all of its powers to repress dissent, for the truth is the mortal enemy of the lie, and thus by extension, the truth is the greatest enemy of the State.[8]

As a matter of policy, one of the biggest challenges in the contemporary society is to convince citizens to go to war, particularly when their country has not been attacked. This was articulated openly by Hermann Göring, field marshal of the Nazi German air force (*Luftwaffe*), at the Nuremberg Trials, as follows:

> Of course the people don't want war. But after all, it's the leaders of the country who determine the policy, and it's always a simple matter to drag the people along whether it's a democracy, a fascist dictatorship, or a parliament, or a communist dictatorship. Voice or no voice, the people can always be brought to the bidding of the leaders. That is easy. All you have to do is tell them they are being attacked, and denounce the pacifists for lack of patriotism, and exposing the country to greater danger.[9]

As the U.S. population becomes increasingly sophisticated and democratic-minded, governments have had to increase their efforts at "manufacturing consent" for military actions. The idea of the "manufacturing of consent," pioneered by Noam Chomsky and Edward Herman, reflects the fact that when the U.S. state pursues unpopular policies, instead of changing the policy the state actors try and often succeed in "manufacturing consent" for the policy in U.S. society.[10] If the U.S. democratic process really resulted in a state that is responsive to the people, then propaganda or the manufacturing of consent would be unnecessary. This is why people across the political spectrum are concerned about governmental interference in, and manipulation of, society, because they have a vision of government responsive to, rather than lording it over, the people.

When the 1980s-era U.S. ally Saddam Hussein invaded and took over Iraq's former province, Kuwait, in 1990, it wasn't clear what the reaction of the George H. W. Bush administration would be, let alone that of the American people. George H. W. Bush decided to make the Iraqi invasion of Kuwait a test of U.S. resolve and commitment to "freedom and democracy." Certainly, and importantly, this would provide reassurance to the U.S. arms industry that the front-page news of the collapse of the Soviet Union and the end of the Cold War would not negatively impact their bottom lines. It would also assure U.S. allies in the Middle East, such as the Saudis, that the United States could be counted on to quell any threats to the authoritarian kingdoms in a number of Middle Eastern states.

But the American people took some convincing that the United States should ship troops to Saudi Arabia and Qatar and then oust Iraq from Kuwait. George H. W. Bush made the usual claims, that this was a fight for democracy, even though Kuwait was an emirate with *no elections*. (Kuwait is less "democratic" than Iran, however flawed Iranian elections were and are.) For its part the Kuwaiti royal family, through a front known as the Citizens for a Free Kuwait, hired one of the United States' leading public relations firms, Hill and Knowlton, and spent millions of dollars in promoting the importance of American participation in the war. Its boldest act was to send a young Kuwaiti woman, identified only as "Nayirah," to appear in public before the U.S. Congressional Human Rights Caucus on October 10, 2000, three months before the launch of the first Gulf War. She related the story of Iraqi forces entering a Kuwaiti hospital, taking babies out of incubators, leaving them on the floor to die, and then taking the equipment back to Iraq. The "incubator babies" story was a major talking point for those who advocated that a coalition of civilized states was virtually under a humanitarian obligation to expel Iraq from Kuwait.

This would have been a significant war crime had it happened, but it did not. Amnesty International and other human rights organizations revealed that the incident was a hoax and that "Nayirah" was a member of the Kuwaiti royal family and the daughter of Saud Nasir al-Sabah, Kuwait's ambassador to the United States, who had much to gain by the American protection of Kuwait. American government complicity and the lack of journalist investigation meant that the public reacted with horror to the incubator baby story and soon gave their support for the "Desert Storm" invasion of Iraq in 1991.[11] John Stauber and Sheldon Rampton, founders of PR Watch, note that if Nayirah's outrageous lie had been exposed at the time it was told, it might have at least "caused some in Congress and the news media to soberly reevaluate the extent to which they were being skillfully manipulated to support military action."[12]

It should be clear that over the last twenty years state propaganda, with the collusion of the mainstream media, has been of vital importance in persuading the U.S. people to support wars. As Stuart Cross argues, the discourse that develops after the "threat" or the "attack" is the product not just of government but also forces in civil society, such as the media, business interests, unions, religious organizations, and voluntary associations.[13] The difficulty of this persuasion has increased because without the Soviet Union it has been harder to claim that there are believable threats to which the United States must respond. Perhaps for this reason direct attack, either of Kuwait in 1991 or the United States on 9/11, has been an important precondition for intervention.

Boiling the Blood and Narrowing the Mind

While a high percentage of U.S. citizens supported the U.S. invasion of Afghanistan in October 2001, as much out of pure rage and revenge for 9/11 as anything else, the fact that the Bush administration needed to spend many months beating the drums of war, using misleading and even false information, to convince Americans to support invading Iraq in 2003 is fresh in people's memories. These events are so recent and public disquiet over the lies are so fresh that it almost seems unnecessary to rehearse them. But memories fade quickly enough. It is well established that U.S. neoconservatives used the 9/11 attacks as a sort of "shock" to enable them to impose their agenda, developed over the thirty-year period, on an unwilling country.[14] At home this included more tax cuts, deregulation, imposing conservative Christian moral standards, discouraging trade unions, and a crackdown on the civil liberties and civil rights traditions of the country. People would be more subject to surveillance and government oversight, and the disadvantaged could not expect government help in improving their condition. Internationally, this meant flexing of U.S. military muscle in Afghanistan, where the 9/11 attackers trained, and Iraq, which had no connection to the 9/11 attacks.[15]

In 2002 and early 2003, in speech after speech, officials of the Bush administration gave the clear impression that Iraq was connected to 9/11, and that the ousting of Saddam Hussein by force would be a valid move in the War on Terror. They did this directly by claiming that there were high level meetings in Vienna between the Saddam Hussein regime and a senior al-Qaeda official, a charge that has since been refuted. They then claimed with certainty that Hussein had weapons of mass destruction (WMDs), and that he was a threat both to his neighbors and the United States as well. To make it easy medicine to swallow, Defense Secretary Donald Rumsfeld said that the invasion would be successful with a relatively small force, that it would cost the U.S. Treasury only a few billion dollars, that the U.S. military would be greeted as liberators, that the occupation would prove to be temporary and uncomplicated, and that the reconstruction of Iraq would be paid for from Iraqi oil revenues.

Iraq was represented as a robust, military monster, *not* a country that had been defeated in war in 1991 and that was still suffering under crushing UN sanctions.

The Bush administration used the Rendon Group, a PR firm, to help create the "Iraqi National Congress," headed by Iraqi opposition figure Ahmed Chalabi, as the U.S. favorite to take over the country. Chalabi was one of the sources of information about Iraqi WMDs that the administration knew or should have known was false.[16] In his now famous State of the Union speech in early 2003, Bush made what turned out to be a false claim that Iraq was trying to acquire "yellowcake" (a low-grade uranium ore) from Niger for its nuclear program. Secretary of State Colin Powell forever ruined his reputation by, knowingly or not, presenting false CIA-prepared evidence of Iraqi possession of WMD to the United Nations Security Council. This was not intelligence failure, rather intelligence subordinated to the political priorities of the Bush administration. Based on a series of false claims, both houses of Congress, under Republican control but with significant Democratic support, voted to grant the president authority to invade Iraq. Not surprisingly then, a 2003 Gallup Poll reported that over 76 percent of Americans "expressed 'a great deal' or 'quite a lot' of confidence in their nation's military." Among a poll of 1,200 students conducted by Harvard University, 75 percent believed that the military most of the time would "do the right thing." In addition, the students "characterized themselves as hawks over doves by a ratio of two to one."[17]

The absence of genuine debate in mainstream media on the initiation of what was predictably an immoral and costly war is a strong sign of the militarism of the United States. Mainstream media outlets were an "echo chamber" for a very conservative administration, whose policies, when fully disclosed, only enjoyed the approval of a minority of the people. The majority of the mainstream media ignored their obligation to raise questions and report.[18] At the time, there were news writers "outside the Washington beltway," like the reporters of the Knight Ridder chain, who reported the doubts that Hussein actually had WMDs, based on United Nations records of the inspection and disarmament process. Even the objections of the 23 members of the Senate and 123 members of the House of Representatives who opposed the Iraq War resolution in October 2002 received little attention.[19] Of course, many commentators in the subterranean world of the critical press and internet media, magazines such as *Z*, the *Nation*, the *Progressive*, and *Mother Jones*, knew from the beginning that this was based on lies,[20] and the war also encouraged the rise of the New Blue Media, such as MoveOn.org, Jon Stewart's *Daily Show*, *The Colbert Report*, Amy Goodman and Juan Gonzalez on *Democracy Now!* and a good deal of the blogosphere.[21] Record-breaking, but undercovered, protests in the United States and around the world also indicated significant numbers of people who did not believe what they were being told, and were taking action even before the war began.

Pop Goes the War

In order to sell a war to the American public, cultural institutions also play an important role in supporting the effort and convincing people to enlist or otherwise support it. Popular culture is a particularly effective propaganda tool because when people are participating in entertainment activities, they are often less suspicious or skeptical of political agendas than when reacting to news media or government. There is a strong sense, supported by the entertainment industries, that one shouldn't read too much into cultural products that are "just entertainment." Nevertheless, powerful ideological messages of militarism are communicated through popular culture, sometimes through unconscious reproduction of negative stereotypes and values, and sometimes as part of orchestrated agendas.

As media outlets think in global terms, some things like action violence translate well across cultures without worrying about cultural sensitivities. Inspired by George Gerbner and his colleagues, Marc Edge points out that "Unlike comedy, violence translated well into other languages and cultures, making it a cheap industrial ingredient to be packaged and sold to a global audience." Using an "ice age" analogy, even if the individual effects of militaristic presentations on the media are very small, "they all tend to move glacier-like in one direction and thus add up over time."[22] Militaristic popular culture can lay the basis for receptivity to militarism over the long-term, in addition to advocating for specific actions in the present.

There is a well-established pattern in which an administration that wants to start a war can count on powerful allies in the media, private industry, and think tanks to support this using increasingly sophisticated techniques of propaganda and persuasion including popular culture. The administration builds support for war by constructing a palatable rationale that is then repeated, independently or in concert with, the powerful engines of the news media and popular culture. Equally, popular culture has shown itself to be an effective medium of dissent and opposition to war. In the *Cultural Resistance Reader*, activist and scholar Stephen Duncombe explains that cultural resistance can be an attractive and nonthreatening way for people to engage in political dissent.[23] By creating cultural products and activities that protest war, activists can express their resistance through the content of their messages such as the explicit lyrics of an antiwar song or the theme of a novel or film. Cultural resistance is also communicated through the form that cultural opposition takes. Thus, producing a cultural protest independently, free from the pressures of owners and advertisers of the mainstream entertainment industries, can itself be part of the message of change. Sometimes preexisting forms of popular culture can be reinterpreted from neutral or conservative meanings and transformed into antiestablishment anthems or icons. The historical record provides us with a plethora of examples of the way culture has been used as a tool in the service of both war and peace.

Ancient Times

Historically, support for war has always been accompanied by some forms of cultural expression whether through songs of patriotism or protest, cartoons of valorization or ridicule, and theater to rally the troops or the pacifists. In ancient Rome, political leaders offered their people entertainment as a way to gain popularity and win support for their imperial agendas. The Roman poet Juvenal coined the phrase "bread and circuses," to mean that as long as the public was provided with the essentials (bread) for human survival and entertainment (circuses), they would comply with the wishes of the elite or would be distracted from the implications of their agendas, and thus a ruling elite could effectively manipulate the public. In his play *Lysistrata*, Greek dramatist Aristophanes used the tool of culture to alternatively make fun of war as a dangerous and bloody game among men that women sought to put to an end by withholding their sexual favors. In the lead-up to the invasion of Iraq, Kathryn Blume and Sharron Bower organized the Lysistrata Project in which over one thousand simultaneous productions of this ancient play were performed in fifty-nine countries as part of a global peace action.

The War of 1812

"The Star-Spangled Banner," which would become the American national anthem, was written as a patriotic poem by Francis Scott Key depicting a battle in the War of 1812 and was immediately embraced by militarists. During the nineteenth century, "The Star-Spangled Banner" became one of the nation's best-loved patriotic songs, and was adopted by the military, which required that it be played at the raising and lowering of the colors. In 1917, both the army and the navy designated the song the "national anthem" for ceremonial purposes, and patriotic organizations launched a campaign to have Congress recognize "The Star-Spangled Banner" as *the* U.S. national anthem. After several decades of attempts, a bill making "The Star-Spangled Banner" the official national anthem was passed by Congress and signed into law by President Herbert Hoover on March 3, 1931. The militarism of the anthem has raised debate for many years and was the subject of Jimi Hendrix's famous protest rendition at Woodstock in 1969, which incorporated sonic effects to emphasize the martial lyrics "rockets' red glare," and "bombs bursting in air." Charles Shaar Murray makes a case that Hendrix's performance articulated the complexities of the Vietnam problem more acutely than any other artistic expression:

> The "Star Spangled Banner" is probably the most complex and powerful work of American art to deal with the Vietnam war and its corrupting, distorting effect on successive generations of the American psyche. One man with one guitar said more in three and a half minutes about that peculiarly disgusting war and its reverberations than all the novels, memoirs and movies put together. It is an interpretation of history which permits no space for either the gung-ho revisionism of Sylvester Stallone and Chuck Norris or the solipsistic angst of Coppola and Oliver Stone; it depicts, as graphically as a piece of music can possibly do, both what the Americans did to the Vietnamese and what they did to themselves.[24]

World War I

In World War I, American publishers of juvenile literature produced over two hundred books detailing the fictional adventures of boys helping to win the Great War. Howard Zinn recalls his own first impressions of war being shaped by these books which he read at the age of ten: "I read with excitement a series of books about 'the boy allies'—a French boy, an English boy, an American boy, and a Russian boy, who became friends, united in the wonderful cause to defeat Germany in World War I. It was an adventure, a romance, told in a group of stories about comradeship and heroism. It was war cleansed of death and suffering."[25] Ernest Hemingway, on the other hand, sought to reveal the death and suffering in his WWI epic, *A Farewell to Arms*, in which he graphically demonstrates the futility and horror of war: "[A]bstract words such as glory, honor, courage, or hallow were obscene beside the concrete names of villages, the numbers of roads, the names of rivers, the numbers of regiments, and the dates."[26]

World War II

The use of popular culture to sell war reached new heights during World War II. Once the United States declared war on Japan and Germany after

Pearl Harbor, President Roosevelt established the Office of War Information (OWI), which was designed to "formulate and carry out, through the use of press, radio, motion pictures and other facilities the development of an informed and intelligent understanding, at home and abroad, of the status and progress of the war effort and of the war policies, activities, and aims of the government."[27] The government encouraged musical composers in New York's "Tin Pan Alley" to compose anti-Japanese music, songs such as "You're a Sap, Mr. Jap" (1941), "The Sun Will Soon Be Setting for the Land of the Rising Son" (1941), and many others. As Krystyn Moon says, these songs were commercial disappointments for the composers and OWI, however, because stylistically they took the form of marches rather than the more popular "swing" style, and as for the words, listeners were more interested in sentimental lyrics or positive patriotic messages.[28]

While not as abundant, antiwar songs also existed in WWII including Wingie Manone's 1941 release, "Stop the War," which in "hip" terms told the listener not to pick up guns and bombs or fight the other side.[29] From the very first days of training, however, the most popular of all soldier songs in World War II was "Gee, But I Want to Go Home,"[30] which focused on the bad food, inhumane treatment, and the sense that the army had its ways of fleecing soldiers of their pay.[31]

Walt Disney was one of the culture industry leaders who came to attention and saluted in support of WWII. Donald Duck appears in films such as *Der Fuehrer's Face* (1942), presenting life under the Nazi regime,[32] and *Commando Duck* (1944), in which Donald destroys a Japanese air base.[33] Disney characters also appeared in newspaper comic strips in service to the war effort.[34] As Gerald Raiti notes, in addition to ideological motives, animators had commercial interests. In the case of Disney, the company almost went bankrupt from its failed 1940 presentation of *Fantasia*, so reliable government payments for propaganda work was its war-time bread and butter.[35] At the same time, Warner Brothers produced twenty-six cartoon series between 1943 and 1945 portraying "Private Snafu." Snafu was the "everyman soldier," the little guy, the common army grunt caught up in a global conflict that is beyond his understanding and, seemingly, beyond his power to cope with. The cartoons portray Snafu as "the worst soldier in the army, the one who does everything wrong," providing comic relief but also conveying to the audience the way to do everything right.[36] Warner Brothers also created cartoon shorts such as *Any Bonds Today?*, *The Ducktators*, and *Confusions of a Nutzy Spy*.[37]

The most famous antiwar cartoon is *Peace on Earth*, which was apparently the only cartoon ever to be nominated for a Nobel Peace Prize.[38] Released during the Christmas season, after war had broken out in Europe, this acclaimed pacifist cartoon told a grim story about humanity's final days. Directed by

Hugh Harman, the short shows a postapocalyptic world populated by animals picking up the pieces after a war kills every human on earth. The surviving animals decide to rebuild a society dedicated to peace and nonviolence and use the helmets of soldiers to construct their houses.[39]

While the 1940s was an ambiguous time for women, caught between traditional and modern values, it was vitally important for the state to get women's support for the war at home, in factories or agricultural labor, and in any of the women's corps that were created in the British, U.S., and Canadian militaries. Patriotic femininity was communicated through a multitude of popular culture forms. Betty Crocker provided advice on how to prepare meals based on wartime shortages and the rationing system,[40] while "Rosie the Riveter" was used to promote women in industry.[41] Colorful posters, often borrowing from the Soviet "socialist realist" style of art, encouraged women to work in nontraditional jobs to support the war effort, and depicted happy and heroic female workers proud of their achievements.[42] The radio "soap opera," a new form of entertainment, incorporated war themes and propaganda to build support for U.S. participation in the war. A soap opera entitled *Against the Storm* was broadcast in the United States, beginning in the fall of 1939, featuring two young central European refugees who had fled Nazi aggression and were adjusting to life in a small U.S. college town. The series, which won a Peabody award in 1942, disseminated propaganda against the Axis Powers and made the case for U.S. entry into the war. President Roosevelt was scheduled to appear on the program but canceled because of Pearl Harbor.[43] Marilyn Hegarty also chronicles the sexual mobilization of women that took place during the war to maintain soldiers' morale through dances and parties. She documents the role of popular culture in enlisting these women's help but then turning on them, eventually representing these women as "patriotutes," part patriot, part prostitute, who were characterized as a dangerous source of sexually transmitted diseases.[44]

The paper crane became a well-known symbol of the movement for a world without nuclear weapons after several postwar children's books popularized the true story of a Japanese girl who was two years old when the United States dropped the atomic bomb on Hiroshima. Sadako Sasaki developed leukemia as a result of exposure to the nuclear radiation, and at the age of twelve attempted to fold one thousand paper cranes in the hopes that, according to a Japanese legend, she would be granted her wish of good health. Only able to complete 648 cranes before she died, her friends completed the remaining ones for her. A statute of Sadako was erected in 1958 at the Hiroshima Peace Park and every year thousands of children across the globe fold paper cranes to honor the children who died in the atomic bombings of Hiroshima and Nagasaki. Contemporary peace movement activists have continued this tradition, organizing four hundred participants in eighteen countries to fold over one million paper cranes for peace.

The Cold War

The cultural support and opposition to militarism continued after World War II in the period known as the Cold War. World War II had been won but as the United States returned to militarism, cultural forms such as the movies and other entertainment products were called back into service. The focus in the 1940s and 1950s was the new red menace, the seeming spread of communism in Europe and Asia. While the House Un-American Activities Committee (HUAC) had been established in 1938, this era has been named for Senator Joe McCarthy, who claimed there were "card-carrying" Communists working in the federal government, the entertainment industry, and even the U.S. Army. McCarthy's claims were ultimately dismissed and he was personally rebuked by the political establishment, but in the meantime his "zealous campaigning" ruined the careers of many Americans in the entertainment industry, education, and government service. Prominent entertainers, including Dashiell Hammett, Waldo Salt, Lillian Hellman, Lena Horne, Paul Robeson, Elia Kazan, Arthur Miller, Aaron Copland, Dalton Trumbo, Leonard Bernstein, Charlie Chaplin, and Group Theatre members Clifford Odets and Stella Adler, were called before the committee, accused of being Communists, and asked to "name names." All told, 320 artists were blacklisted, and many would not work again.[45] The message to entertainers was clear: subordinate yourselves to government values and priorities or be prepared to live with the consequences.

Even among the studio owners this service to the state agenda was starting to chafe. Most studios made anti-Nazi films with conviction, but who could blame the studios by the end of the war if they felt they had done their share? By 1946 it was peace time and the studio movie moguls were convinced that audiences wanted "Technicolor musical escapism or film noir romantic agonies" rather than propagandistic war stories. Yes, Hollywood would "mop up after World War II," by making pictures in which Nazi war criminals were tracked down (*The Stranger*, Orson Welles, 1946) or reflecting on the disappointments of the returning veterans (*The Best Years of Our Lives*, William Wyler, 1946). Young directors released a new wave of films that "dealt with heroic black, Jewish, or even Nisei soldiers suffering from bigotry or racial assault, including murder," including *Crossfire* (Edward Dmytryk, 1947), *Gentleman's Agreement* (Elia Kazan, 1947), *Home of the Brave* (Mark Robson, 1949), and *Bad Day at Black Rock* (1955) by

John Sturges. For their honesty and their trouble some of these directors, like Elia Kazan, ended up before HUAC. In response to the pressure of the McCarthy period the studios made some quick anti-Communist films with little artistic merit, such as *I Married a Communist*, in which a labor leader was the main villain, and *Big Jim McClain*, starring John Wayne, in which Hawaiian communists were exposed. In *Trial* (Mark Robson, 1955), a lawyer and his client discover that Communist assistance in a criminal defense is designed not to help the client but provoke opportunistically an uprising over an unjust conviction.[46]

But there was also cultural resistance to the patriotic fervor demanded by the McCarthy period, where filmmakers critiqued American militarism and presented cautionary tales of mutually assured destruction if the cold war continued unabated. In the classic 1951 science fiction film *The Day the Earth Stood Still*, an extra-terrestrial ambassador named Klaatu comes to earth bearing the message that humankind's militarism has been ignored by the rest of the galaxy's residents as long as it was restricted to Earth, but now that the humans were on the brink of entering space, their homicidal behavior can no longer be tolerated. Explaining that robot enforcers will wipe them out if they continue with their warlike way, Klaatu tells the humans that they must choose either to live in peace with each other and the galaxy, or the extra-terrestrials will be forced to wipe out humanity to protect themselves. The antiwar sentiment of *The Day the Earth Stood Still* is credited with representing and inspiring the peace movement that was building in response to the Korean War and which would achieve new heights in the Vietnam era.[47]

The Vietnam War

Not many "movie pitches" have been initiated through a letter to the president, but history tells of one that was. In December 1965, President Lyndon B. Johnson received a letter which began as follows: "Dear Mr. President. When I was a little boy, my father always told me that if you want to get anything done see the top man—so I am addressing this letter to you." This was written by none other than John Wayne, the fifty-eight-year-old actor who had worked in over 140 films, mostly westerns and war movies. He suggested the American people needed a patriotic movie about the country's involvement in the Vietnam War, focusing on a military unit of recent vintage. The result was *The Green Berets* (1968) directed by, and starring, Wayne. It featured the U.S. Army Special Forces, formed only during the Kennedy era as a response to the new demand for "counterinsurgency warfare." As Philip Taylor says, it "was the most blatantly propagandist contemporaneous American feature film made about the Vietnam War."[48]

Some of the other cultural support for the war in Vietnam came after the war, as history was being revised to reinterpret the loss and humiliation of that invasion and instead to characterize it a new light. The film *First Blood*, which introduced Sylvester Stallone's character Rambo, was released in 1982, seven years after the end of the Vietnam War. The movie is an ultraviolent story about a supersoldier re-fighting the Vietnam War, implying that the American military could have won in Vietnam if squeamish liberals hadn't "cut and run." The film and its sequels introduced the word "Rambo" into daily language, in phrases like "Rambo foreign policy" and "ramboid" (adjective), and in "Shock and awe? That was ramboid, man!"[49] Douglas Kellner has also linked the success of Rambo to the film's role as propaganda for Ronald Reagan's domestic and foreign policy. For Kellner, Rambo is an articulation of important elements of Reaganism including unilateral military intervention.[50] Ronald Reagan apparently joked at the end of a TWA hostage crisis that "After seeing Rambo last night, I know what to do the next time this happens."[51] A Vietnam War vet, Gustav Hasford, author of the book that became *Full Metal Jacket*, compared *First Blood* to a German propaganda classic when he called it "Triumph of the Will for American Nazis."[52]

Other filmmakers also constructed their cultural representation of the Vietnam War after the fact but with a different message. Carl Boggs and Tom Pollard state that the best-received Vietnam films captured the intense antiwar feeling of a generation influenced by the lengthy military debacle, the radicalism of the new left, and the experimental sensibilities of the counter-culture.[53] Considered to be among the most significant anti–Vietnam War films, *The Deer Hunter* (1978), *Apocalypse Now* (1978), *Platoon* (1986), and *Full Metal Jacket* (1987) all abandoned the "good war" script and instead explored the dark consequences of war on the perpetrators and their enemies. The attack on the seacoast village in *Apocalypse Now* is considered to be one of the ultimate surrealistic depictions of the horror, the madness, the sensuousness of war.[54] In a now-famous scene, speaking to a soldier in his platoon, a deranged and raspy-voiced U.S. colonel extols the virtue and scent of napalm, claiming that to him it smells like victory. According to film scholar Lawrence Suid, after Vietnam "film makers will never be able to show the United States winning glorious victories and making the world a safer place as they could with the nation's earlier wars."[55] This historical overview highlights only a few of the multiple examples that reveal the powerful impact of popular cultural engagement with war.

Understanding Popular Culture

Culture consists of the values that the members of a given group hold, the norms they follow, and the material goods they create.[56] Culture is often divided into three categories: high culture, folk culture, and popular culture. High culture, sometimes called elite culture, is considered by its supporters to be the "best that is known and thought in the world."[57] It includes fine art, literature, and music that has been identified by social elites as enhancing human experience by elevating the mind and spirit. High culture is not intended to be accessible to the public and requires education to be fully appreciated. Historically, high culture was reserved for the elite but at various times, there has been an effort to "civilize" the masses by bringing elite culture to them through visits to museums or public presentations of "classics" such as Shakespearean plays. Folk culture is the traditional cultural expression of the public and consists of folk music, folk art, folk tales, folk dance, folk costumes, local humor, oral literature and history, and superstitions. It is usually understood that folk culture is made by the people for the consumption and pleasure of the people. The rise of nineteenth- and twentieth-century urbanization and industrialization is associated with the decline of both high and folk culture in favor of the development of a culture which is mass produced by culture industries and which is passively consumed by many people. Labeled as "popular culture," this form of culture includes mainstream movies, best-selling books, video games, toys and collectibles, sports, and all forms of popular entertainments. Something is considered to be popular when it is created to respond to the values of the majority, and when it has mass appeal. The public can appreciate popular culture without the aid of special knowledge or experience. Many critics see popular culture as a reflection of the vulgarity and poor taste of a mass of nondiscriminating consumers. Others reject the notion that popular culture is an authentic expression of the values or desires of the public, but rather focus their analysis on the fact that popular culture in a contemporary capitalist society is produced in a top-down manner by industrial elites with ideological and financial ties to those in power.

In the 1930s and 1940s Theodor Adorno and Max Horkheimer, who both lived under Nazi German rule for a time and were concerned about the power of the state and private actors to manipulate the masses, developed a critical analysis of the culture industry. For them, culture was at one time a more-or-less autonomous realm of human activity, in which creative people interpreted their world in a relatively independent fashion using both "low culture," such as craft, and "high culture," such as fine art. Political, economic, and social forces have always influenced or interfered with this creativity, but Adorno and Horkheimer noted that it has become much more systematic with the development of mass culture. Whereas historical cultures were created to a significant extent "from below," based on the lived experience of diverse communities, the industries that produce culture and entertainment for the masses, create culture from above.[58] This tends to create conformity of thought because the same culture is being pumped out to entire countries, and in the contemporary period, even globally, through the reach of Western television broadcasters. Culture in the age of mass society is thus produced industrially because its products are manufactured on a massive scale, involving thousands of workers in a highly specialized division of labor.[59] They argued that mass culture was a way of distracting the working classes from the real causes of their problems in capitalist society such as low wages, exploitation, lack of power and status, and so on. The development of a mass culture that encouraged passive consumption of the prepackaged products of big business not only destroyed vital, communal aspects of folk culture, but also provided the working classes with an illusory sense of happiness, togetherness, and well-being.

Culture studies scholar John Fiske argues that for a cultural product to be popular, it must meet contradictory needs. On the one hand, the product must be sold in sufficient volume to bring the investors a return, which means that it must appeal to what people have in common. A leading candidate for this common trait is subordination to the social system, or disempowerment. On the other hand, it is also true that the public are not always merely consumers of culture. Despite the evidence of the narcotizing and conservative effects of popular culture, the people are also active creators of culture. Thus the cultural commodity is also potentially a cultural resource, offering plural pleasures and meanings. Popular culture is a place of struggle, because the significance and meaning of its products is open to interpretation and change.[60] Popular culture thus can also be understood as a contested site where the public can use the products of mass culture to create their own meanings, some of which may serve as a powerful critique of the dominant culture.

The Significance of Gramscian Hegemony in Explaining and Undermining Militarism

In the last thirty-five years, students of society and culture in the English-speaking world have also found important insights in the work of Antonio Gramsci. Gramsci, a journalist, trade unionist, and leader of the Italian Communist Party in Italy in the 1920s and 1930s, provided some key intellectual tools to help people understand both the durability of systems of domination as well as the means for undermining and transforming them. This is the concept of *hegemony*, which Gramsci referred to as a political-economic-social-cultural order in which the existing political, economic, social, and cultural ideas and institutions seem universally valid and natural. "Universally valid and natural" means that most people look at the form of organization in the state, society, and economy as valid for all places and all times, and as the result of a natural process rather than human decision. Of course, our state-society complex is the product of human decisions, though a popular recognition of that on a daily basis might give the masses the idea that the majority of people could change it. Gramsci pointed out that, even at the best of times, these ideas and institutions are periodically in crisis, and that at these moments a counter-hegemonic movement has the potential to successfully challenge the existing dominant forces and overthrow them and transform the state-society. The lesson taken from Gramsci by social critics in Western Europe and North America, and indeed around the world, is that transformation requires not just change at the surface level of electoral politics, or other realms like the economy, but rather genuine transformation can only happen when more thoroughgoing change challenges the exercise of power in the economy, society, *and* culture.[61]

From this perspective, militaristic culture in the United States is a form of hegemonic culture that, over time, is more or less dominant and occasionally subject to challenges from counter-hegemonic social movements that emphasize their own version of peace, equality, and fairness, both globally and domestically. Each of the hegemonic and counter-hegemonic movements must continually remake itself to meet the challenge posed by the other. The idea of a *hegemonic* militaristic culture is that, at certain moments, a large majority of the U.S. population lives within a "bubble," in which everything they see confirms the militaristic understanding of the world. The leaders they follow, the media and entertainment that they listen to, watch and read, the people they know and work with, the church they attend, all largely confirm the same, dominant understanding of domestic and global affairs.

The idea of the "bubble" is similar to the role of the bubble in economic terms, such as the recently much-discussed "housing bubble." In economics, a bubble is a period of growth and/or price increases which most people are led to believe will be sustainable over the medium- to long-term, even though by definition such things can only be temporary. The institutions of society, such as the media, political leaders, investment advisors, and others, encourage a situation in which no prominent person raises the possibility of collapse, for as long as possible. When they do raise misgivings, they use terms like "correction" ("there will be a correction") to express the reality that nothing can rise forever (or as central bankers will say obliquely, "things that cannot go on forever will not go on forever"). Despite the abundant and early signs of decline, when the bubble collapses most people are surprised.

So too a hegemonic militaristic culture is a "bubble," in which those who believe in it find that the ideas are reinforced by political leaders, the media and culture industry, other economic forces, the education system, and religious institutions. The two major political parties become a duopoly—two uncompetitive, colluding sellers of similar ideas—in which the party leaderships will not challenge the basic assumptions of militarism. This describes the situation of the United States at many times in its history, most recently in the three years or so after 9/11, and still to some degree today. It is important when thinking about hegemony to recognize that a hegemonic order may be dominant but it is never universally successful or total. This is even true in totalitarian states (like North Korea), let alone in more liberal states in the Western world. There is always dissent from hegemonic militarism, and this was the case from 9/11 through to the reelection of George W. Bush in November 2004. But all of that dissent, available online at Tomdispatch .com, Znet, DailyKos, *The Daily Show*, DemocracyNow.org, the *Onion*, Alter Net, and so many others sources, remained largely subterranean for a time. It was subterranean because it was driven underground by both major political parties, which signaled with the Patriot Act, passed in the fall of 2001, that domestic political dissent could easily be criminalized, just as it was back in World War I and during the Cold War. As Bush said, "you're either with us or you're with the terrorists," and the message was understood. So long as the dissenters were kept off the front pages of the national press and the TV networks, unable to impact or "infect" the moderate suburban majority, they could be tolerated as ultimately ineffectual, a minority opinion that confirmed the legitimacy of U.S. liberal democracy. It goes without saying that the country would be much better off, from a medium- to long-term perspective, had it fully engaged with its dissenters of all stripes in those years after 9/11, since the dissenters were largely correct while the establishment was largely wrong.

One can see a parallel picture in the early 1960s, when New York folk singers like Bob Dylan, Phil Ochs, Tom Paxton, and Joan Baez, to name only a few, were, along with a small number of journalists and academics, a source of counter-hegemonic dissent even before major U.S. escalation in Vietnam. But they were part of a subculture, in particular a counterculture, that would need a lot of organizing effort and several years to break through to the mainstream of U.S. life. But like in the late 1960s and early 1970s, by 2005 and 2006 U.S. militarism was in a hegemonic crisis, because the counter-hegemonic movement picked up a great deal of strength in those years, as indicated by Bush's plummeting approval ratings and growing domestic opposition to the U.S. wars in Afghanistan and Iraq. The greater the domestic dissent, the less able the dominant forces are to intimidate to maintain their rule. During Bush's second term, the military-corporate establishment had every reason to believe, from past experience, that a Republican loss would not be very threatening. The election of the Democrats would harness the dissent in 2006 and then in 2008, but there would be no fundamental reduction of militarism. The cultural products and activities discussed in this book are a means of reinforcing or undermining people's belief in militaristic or alternative solutions to human problems; they are part of the struggle between hegemonic versus counter-hegemonic responses to militarism. The battle over militaristic culture will be fundamental to whether the state can promise militarism and implement it (Bush), whether the state will promise a peaceful alternative but implement militarism (Obama), or the creation of a third option, the promise and implementation of a peaceful alternative to militarism.

Conclusion

The United States became more democratic over the last sixty years, and as a result of this the "manufacturing of consent" has become more important in whipping up enthusiasm to go to war. In previous eras, unaccountable rulers went to war and if necessary they governed largely by coercion. However, as should be clear from this chapter, as time has passed the decision-making elite has increasingly found it difficult to win consent for militaristic policies. The need to manufacture consent was particularly important in the decisions to go to war against Iraq in 1991 and 2003, for in fact militarists were forced to resort to outright lying in both cases. The Afghanistan war was not so difficult to engineer since the United States was attacked, after all, even if it was not the Afghani government that did the attacking, and even if the United States had ulterior motives for the invasion.

However, culture has been used for a long time to prepare people to support the war just beyond the horizon, in cases from the ancient world and U.S. wars in the nineteenth and twentieth centuries. This support used the media of drama, music, literature, cartoons, and, since the 1940s, the movies. It is also important to have some tools to understand the plethora of cases and examples that are available to the curious person. Popular culture itself is significant, as is the fact that today it is largely produced by the culture industry. Importantly, recent history shows that not all social orders are "hegemonic"; on the contrary, not only does culture play a role in creating a hegemonic social order, but it has also played a major role in undermining the hegemonic militarism of the early Bush era, and can be used for the same purposes in the present and future.

Notes

1. Miriam Pemberton, "Poll: Fewer Guns, More Talk," *Foreign Policy in Focus*, October 27, 2006, www.fpif.org/fpiftxt/3649 (accessed August 10, 2009).

2. "An Interview with Khomeini (Man of the Year)," *Time*, January 7, 1980, www.time.com/time/magazine/article/0,9171,923858-1,00.html (accessed August 10, 2009).

3. For the official inquiry into this, see John Tower, *The Tower Commission Report* (New York: Bantam Books / Times Books, 1987).

4. Wendell Bell, "The American Invasion of Grenada: A Note on False Prophecy," *The Yale Review* 75, no. 4 (1986): 564–86.

5. John M. Barry, *Rising Tide: The Great Mississippi Flood of 1927 and How It Changed America* (New York: Simon and Schuster, 1997), 137.

6. Gabriel Kolko, "Mechanistic Destruction: American Foreign Policy at Point Zero," *Antiwar*, August 10, 2007, www.antiwar.com/orig/kolko.php?articleid=11426 (accessed June 11, 2009).

7. Garth S. Jowett and Victoria O'Donnell, *Readings in Propaganda and Persuasion: New and Classic Essays* (Thousand Oaks, CA: Sage, 2005), 31.

8. Quoted at Holocaust Education & Archive Research Team, "Joseph Goebbels: 'The Poison Dwarf,'" Early Nazi Leaders, www.holocaustresearchproject.org/holo prelude/goebbels.html (accessed June 10, 2009).

9. Quoted at Holocaust Education & Archive Research Team, "Hermann Göring: 'The Iron Knight,'" Early Nazi Leaders, www.holocaustresearchproject.org/holo prelude/goering.html (accessed June 10, 2009).

10. Edward S. Herman and Noam Chomsky, *Manufacturing Consent: The Political Economy of the Mass Media*, updated ed. (New York: Pantheon Books, 2002).

11. John Stauber and Sheldon Rampton, *Toxic Sludge Is Good for You: Lies, Damn Lies, and the Public Relations Industry* (Monroe, ME: Common Courage Press, 2002).

12. Stauber and Rampton, *Toxic Sludge*, 173.

13. Stuart Croft, *Culture, Crisis and America's War on Terror* (Cambridge: Cambridge University Press, 2006), 271.

14. Naomi Klein, *The Shock Doctrine: The Rise of Disaster Capitalism* (Toronto, ON: Alfred A. Knopf Canada, 2007).

15. Richard A. Clarke, *Against All Enemies: Inside America's War on Terror* (New York: Free Press, 2004).

16. "The Man Who Sold the Iraq War: John Rendon, Bush's General in the Propaganda War," *Democracy Now: The War and Peace Report*, November 21, 2005, www.democracynow.org/2005/11/21/the_man_who_sold_the_iraq (accessed June 9, 2009).

17. Kevin Baker, "We're in the Army Now: The G.O.P.'s Plan to Militarize Our Culture," *Harper's Magazine*, October 2003, 37.

18. For an excellent, brief critique of the U.S. media, see Douglas Kellner, "Spectacle and Media Propaganda in the War on Iraq: A Critique of U.S. Broadcasting Networks," Graduate School of Education and Information Studies, UCLA, www.gseis .ucla.edu/faculty/kellner/papers/mediapropaganda.htm (accessed June 9, 2009).

19. "Iraq War Vote in 2002: 156 Congress Members Who Voted NO," About.com, http://usliberals.about.com/od/liberalleadership/a/IraqNayVote.htm (accessed June 9, 2009).

20. There is now an outpouring of books and articles on this subject, but see "50 False News Stories by Bush Propaganda Machine: A Strategy of Lies: How the White House Fed the Public a Steady Diet of Falsehoods," Earth Island, November 10, 2003, www.rense.com/general44/50.htm (accessed June 9, 2009).

21. Theodore Hamm, *The New Blue Media: How Michael Moore, MoveOn.org, John Stewart and Company are Transforming Progressive Politics* (New York and London: The New Press, 2008).

22. Marc Edge, *Asper Nation: Canada's Most Dangerous Media Company* (Vancouver: New Star Books, 2007), 92.

23. Stephen Duncombe, *Cultural Resistance Reader* (New York: Verso, 2002).

24. Charles Shaar Murray cited in Andy Bennett, ed., *Remembering Woodstock* (Aldershot, England, and Burlington, VT: Ashgate, 2004), 24.

25. Howard Zinn, *Howard Zinn on War* (New York: Seven Stories Press, 2001).

26. Ernest Hemingway, *A Farewell to Arms* (New York: Scribner, 1978), 185.

27. Barkin quoted in Christopher Dow, "Private Snafu's Hidden War," *Bright Lights Film Journal,* November 2003, www.brightlightsfilm.com/42/snafu.htm (accessed August 18, 2008).

28. Krystyn R. Moon, "'There's No Yellow in the Red, White and Blue': The Creation of Anti-Japanese Music during World War II," *Pacific Historical Review* 72, no. 3 (2003): 333–52.

29. The Authentic History Center, www.authentichistory.com/ww2/music/19410319_Stop_The_War_The_Cats_Are_Killing_Themselves-Wingie_Manone.html (accessed August 1, 2009).

30. Gina Buchanan, "Songs of War and Peace: Smithsonian Folkways," Smithsonian Channel Blog, May 1, 2009, http://blog.smithsonianchannel.com/2009/05/01/songs-of-war-and-peace-smithsonian-folkways/ (accessed August 1, 2009).

31. Buchanan, "Songs of War and Peace."

32. *Der Fuehrer's Face*, film, directed by Jack Kinney (Los Angeles: Walt Disney Productions, 1942). See "*Der Fuehrer's Face,*" IMDB, www.imdb.com/title/tt0035794/ (accessed August 15, 2008).

33. *Commando Duck*, film, directed by Jack King (Los Angeles: Walt Disney Productions, 1944). See "*Commando Duck,*" IMDB, www.imdb.com/title/tt0036718/ (accessed August 15, 2008).

34. DisneyDave, "Toons at War: Exploring and Sharing the History of Walt Disney Studio during World War II," Toons at War Blog, 2006–2008, http://toonsatwar.blogspot.com/ (accessed August 15, 2008).

35. Gerald C. Raiti, "The Disappearance of Disney Animated Propaganda: A Globalization Perspective," *Animation: An Interdisciplinary Journal* 2, no. 2 (2007): 157.

36. Dow, "Private Snafu's Hidden War."

37. "Goopey Geer's Rare Cartoon Page," Goopey Geer website, http://members.fortunecity.com/goopygeer2/ (accessed August 18, 2008).

38. According to Hugh Harman's obituary in the *New York Times*, the cartoon was nominated for a Nobel Peace Prize. However, it is not listed in the official Nobel Prize nomination database. See "Hugh Harman, 79, Creator of 'Looney Tunes' Cartoons," obituary, *New York Times*, November 30, 1982, www.nytimes.com/1982/11/30/obituaries/hugh-harman-79-creator-of-looney-tunes-cartoons.html (accessed August 1, 2009).

39. Joseph Barbera, *My Life in "Toons": From Flatbush to Bedrock in Under a Century* (Atlanta: Turner Publishing, 1994), 72–73.

40. Pauline Adema, "Betty Crocker," in *American Icons: An Encyclopedia of the People, Places, and Things That Have Shaped Our Culture*, ed. Dennis Hall and Susan Grove Hall (Santa Barbara, CA: Greenwood, 2006), 73–81.

41. Maureen Honey, *Creating Rosie the Riverter: Class, Gender and Propaganda during World War Two* (Amherst: University of Massachusetts Press, 1984).

42. R. J. Evans, "Fighting Females: Women and Propaganda in World War Two," Socyberty, October 18, 2008, www.socyberty.com/History/Fighting-Females-Women-and-Propaganda-in-World-War-Two.301841 (accessed July 10, 2009).

43. J. Fred MacDonald, "Soap Operas Go to War," in *Don't Touch That Dial! Radio Programming in American Life, 1920–1960* (Chicago: Nelson-Hall, 1979), see http://jfredmacdonald.com/war.htm (accessed July 10, 2009).

44. Marilyn E. Hegarty, *Victory Girls, Khaki-Wackies, and Patriotutes: The Regulation of Female Sexuality during World War* (New York: New York University Press, 2007), ii.

45. Cyndy Hendershot, *Anti-Communism and Popular Culture in Mid-century America* (Jefferson, NC: McFarland, 2003).

46. Dan Georgakas, "The Hollywood Blacklist," in *Encyclopedia of the American Left*, ed. Mari Jo Buhle, Paul Buhle, and Dan Georgakas (Urbana: University of Illinois Press, 1992).

47. Tony Shaw, *Hollywood's Cold War* (Amherst: University of Massachusetts Press, 2007), 140.

48. Philip Taylor, "The Green Berets," *History Today* 45 (March 1995).

49. "Ramboid," Urban Dictionary, www.urbandictionary.com/define.php?term=ramboid.

50. Edwin A. Martini, *Invisible Enemies: The American War on Vietnam, 1975–2000* (Amherst: University of Massachusetts Press, 2007), 126.

51. Gil Troy, *Morning in America: How Ronald Reagan Invented the 1980s* (Princeton, NJ: Princeton University Press, 2005), 192.

52. Jesse Walker, "The Ghost of Rambo," *Reason Online*, January 28, 2008, www.reason.com/news/show/124630.html (accessed August 10, 2009).

53. Carl Boggs and Tom Pollard, *The Hollywood War Machine: U.S. Militarism and Popular Culture* (Boulder, CO: Paradigm Publishers, 2006), 90.

54. Gilbert Adair, *Vietnam on Film: From "The Green Berets" to "Apocalypse Now"* (New York: Proteus, 1981), 151.

55. Lawrence H. Suid, "Hollywood and Vietnam," *Air University Review* 34, no. 2 (1983): 127.

56. Anthony Giddens, *Sociology* (Cambridge: Polity Press, 1993).

57. Matthew Arnold cited in John Storey, *Cultural Theory and Popular Culture: An Introduction*, 3rd ed. (Athens: University of Georgia Press, 2001), 18.

58. See Theodor W. Adorno, "Culture Industry Reconsidered," trans. Anson G. Rabinbach, *New German Critique* 6 (Fall 1975): 12–19, www.why-war.com/news/1975/09/01/culturei.html (accessed July 11, 2009).

59. Douglas Kellner, "The Frankfurt School and British Cultural Studies: The Missed Articulation," Cultural Studies and FS: McGuigan Reader, Graduate School of Education and Information Studies, UCLA, January 1, 2007, www.gseis.ucla.edu/courses/ed253a/MCkellner/CSFS.html (accessed July 11, 2009).

60. John Fiske, "The Commodities of Culture," in *The Consumer Society Reader*, ed. Martyn J. Lee (Oxford and Malden, MA: Blackwell, 2000), 284.

61. There has been an outpouring of analysis and applications of Gramsci's thought, but the fundamental translation of Gramsci's work is found in Q. Hoare and G. Nowell Smith, eds. and trans., *Selections from the Prison Notebooks of Antonio Gramsci* (New York: International Publishers, 1971).

3

Toying with War

Conscripting Children through War Games

M Y VERY FIRST RECRUITING OFFICER WAS G.I. JOE," says Michael Prysner, an Iraq War veteran who was an aerial intelligence specialist in the U.S. Army Reserve.[1] Toy soldiers and miniature weapons are thought to have taught future generations of warriors the art of war.[2] State actors and their partners in civil society have discovered over the last number of decades that socialization of the youth is important as part of militarism, to provide both the recruits and political supporters for war. Socialization is the process of taking individuals and imbuing them with social values, so that what is normal and natural for the society seems so for each individual. As Wendy Varney notes, "It is therefore in the interests of militarists and those who seek to gain advantage from war in any number of direct and peripheral ways, to socialize children into militarism, to make it seem logical, necessary, 'natural', and even fun."[3]

Socialization of young people is arguably more important now than it was in the past, because in the past militarists could count on military conscription, which ended in the United States in 1975, as a means of getting access to a broad sampling of young men. Like the socialization process generally, in this case the purpose is to enable people to function in the society in an approved way. As Andrew Martin says, "popular narratives are ideological, but not just because they are fabrications or because they dupe and distract. They also work to transform real social and political desires and insecurities into manageable narratives in which these can be temporarily articulated, displaced or resolved."[4]

This promotion of the militarist version of childhood is not purely a "top-down" process however, in which state and corporate leaders provide strict directions and people blindly follow. The promotion of militaristic toys and activities for young people waxes and wanes over time. Take the case of the G.I. Joe doll, for example. G.I. Joe is a military doll that has been marketed off and on, in different versions, since 1964. As Karen Hall notes in her excellent study, the doll maker Hasbro's approach to G.I. Joe varied significantly based on the public mood toward the military and militarism. G.I. Joe started in the mid-1960s as a clean-cut, white, male member of the regular military, but with public opposition to the U.S. war in Vietnam growing in the late 1960s, sales plummeted. Hasbro then retooled Joe as part of the "Adventure Team," a departure from the regular military. Joe still had guns, but the increasing focus was on nonmilitary adventures with many nonmilitary accessories, such as civilian helicopters, dune buggies, jeeps, boats and so on. For example, whereas in the 1960s Joe drove what was clearly a military, olive-drab army jeep (with mounted machine gun), as part of the Adventure Team in the early 1970s Joe drove a tan, civilian-oriented jeep *sans* 50-cal. Adventure Team Joe himself also came in an African American version, and all the dolls had fuzzy hair and beards, which definitely did not meet the accepted military grooming standard. By the 1980s, the age of Reagan, however, G.I. Joe was remilitarized and redesigned.[5] Predictably, following 9/11 G.I. Joe was back in style. Hasbro reports that between 2001 and 2002, sales of G.I. Joe increased by 46 percent.[6] G.I. Joe hit the big screen in 2009 with a feature film in which a pair of U.S. soldiers abandon their original allegiances in favor of membership in a secret international military organization "that gives them cool toys and lets them chase after hot babes."[7] Alyssa Rosenberg writing in *The Atlantic* observes that, like other propagandistic war movies, *GI Joe: The Rise of Cobra* communicates the message that "in war only the bad or extraneous people die, and that the military best operates without oversight or checks from the outside world."[8]

Toys and Militarism

The rise of conservatism and militarism over the last thirty-five years has led to a renewed effort to promote militaristic toys and activities to young people. While we can see a reduction in this militarism during the Clinton era, in which the focus was on liberal free trade and the erasure of borders for trade and investment, the last ten years have seen a renewed rise in militaristic toys and games owing both to the mood of the Bush administration, but more importantly, to the attacks on the United States on 9/11, and the choice by the U.S. state to go to war in Afghanistan and in Iraq. A 1943 study of Hawaiian schoolchildren showed that shortly after the bombing of Pearl Harbor children began to play more war games and make more toy weapons. Girls, too, took part in this play, making buildings to be bombed and playing the roles of military nurses.[9] The proliferation of war toys in society has a tremendous effect on socialization, and the way children learn how to act within their social environment. Toys have a profound effect on the way children understand their role in society. When so many of the toys that are sold to children all carry the same militaristic theme, and depict values associated with war, it follows that acceptance of violence and fears about security are transferred to youngsters in early development. As Margaret Higonnet notes, war toys "domesticate war . . . and remind us that war is not something that happens far away on a neatly contained 'battlefront' but part of the everyday; war is not simply an isolated event but an eruption within a continuum that runs through what we call peacetime."[10]

Killing Is Learned Behavior

Why is it so important to militarists that militarism and violence be promoted among the population, especially to the youth? A key answer comes from Lt. Col. Dave Grossman (ret.), an expert in "killology," or the science of killing. Grossman argues that both the United States and world is suffering from a rise in violence. He notes that from 1957 to 1992, the per capita rate of violent crime increased, and so too did the population of people imprisoned for violent crime. Yet he argues that killing is unnatural for humans, and must be taught. "Children don't naturally kill; they learn it from violence in the home and most pervasively, from violence as entertainment in television, movies, and interactive video games."[11] Barbara Ehrenreich observes that the male appetite for battle has always been far less voracious than either biologically inclined theorists of war or army commanders might like. "In traditional societies, warriors often had to be taunted, intoxicated, or ritually 'transformed' into animal form before battle. Throughout Western history, individual men have gone to near-suicidal lengths to avoid participating in wars—cutting off limbs or fingers or risking execution by deserting."[12] It should be no surprise that this has been a concern for militaries, including in the United States. Historical research and military studies show that in wars such as the U.S. Civil War, World War I, and World War II, only a minority of U.S. soldiers were willing to shoot to kill. As a result of new psychological approaches to training, by the Korean Conflict this rose to 55 percent, and in Vietnam 90 percent were willing to kill.[13]

How was this achieved? Grossman identifies four techniques: brutalization, classical conditioning, operant conditioning, and role modeling. Brutalization refers to the desensitization that happens in military training, in which individuality is undermined and the trainees take on a new set of military values in place of their old, humanistic ones. Classic conditioning refers to the creation of an association between killing and pleasure, which Grossman says is less evident in military training but more evident in civilian video games, which themselves have military spillover, as we will see later. Operant conditioning is "stimulus-response," in which a soldier (or police officer) is trained to respond in certain ways (such as by using deadly force) when faced with certain conditions. Hopefully he or she doesn't kill in the absence of the stimulus. Finally, the military provides numerous role models, such as the drill sergeant, and later the experienced, noncommissioned (e.g., the corporals and sergeants) and commissioned officers.[14]

Certainly one of Grossman's concerns is about the long-term damage that is done to members of the military, but his greatest concern is that *these techniques now permeate society*, through television, video games, and for some, events in the neighborhoods they live in. Having seen so much simulated death, and having reveled in killing even if only in video games, young people in particular have become desensitized. This can contribute to domestic violence, such as school shootings, and willingness to join violent gangs, but can also contribute to militaristic culture in the society. Grossman notes that unlike the military, there is no command structure among civilians to regulate how and when they commit violence. Humans are not naturally violent or militaristic, but experience shows that they can be trained to shed their restraints and participate in both.

Bang, Bang, You're Dead

Military-themed and violence-oriented toys appear in abundant proportions on the shelf, visible in many different forms. Jeffrey Goldstein, in *Why We Watch: The Attractions of Violent Entertainment*, notes that even though they may be regarded as universal, the popularity of war toys changes with changing circumstances. They are to be found especially in cultures where war and aggression are prevalent. War and war play reflects the prevailing values of the culture in which they flourish, values that stress aggression, assertion, and dominance.[15] In the 1950s, American children got Western-style six-shooters and holsters, Dick Tracy or other detective guns, police guns, toy hunting rifles, and futuristic ray guns. In the case of the Western-style cowboy outfits, the kids got to rehearse the historical script of "how the West was won." From the perspective of an "American Indian" (or "aboriginal" or "First Nations" person), the sets of molded, plastic cowboys and Indians still call up, bring into the present, and normalize unresolved issues of white supremacy and genocide against the American Indian in the United States and the Americas.[16]

Regarding these historical scripts, Tom Englehardt says: "I already knew how such stories turned out, for I had practiced them many times with my friends, my six-guns strapped to my waist, or alone with toy soldiers in my room."[17] Often these guns simulate gun shots by using caps of various kinds, or they are long guns that, when cocked, release air and sound when fired to simulate shooting. From there kids can graduate to pellet or BB guns and then later real hand guns and long guns. The first BB gun was created in 1886. Made for children, it concerned many parents because it was actually a working gun that could cause injury. The BB gun was a descendant of the cap gun, which was invented soon after the U.S. Civil War, when some shotgun manufacturers converted their factories to make toys. Penny pistols and other authentic-looking toy guns also began to appear in the 1880s. Toy guns of one type or another have been popular in the toy market ever since.

In the most violent countries in the world it should be no surprise that legislators see the existence of toy guns as part of the problem. It is already common for governments to ban toy replicas of real weapons, because they can be used in armed robberies, or lead to accidental shootings by the police or army. But in some countries legislators seek to ban toy guns altogether. In Iraq, the penchant for such dangerous toys stem from children living among scenes of violence that are all too readily imitated. Indeed, "A recent study by the Association of Psychologists of Iraq (API) found that violence was profoundly affecting the Iraqi children, being preoccupied with guns, bullets, death and fears." However, despite this, when asked about the toy guns, many Iraqi children view them as innocuous. For example, when asked, a child answered, "I like holding it and going outside to kill evildoers. I like to go outside at night like my uncle (a member of the Mahdi Army)."[18]

The implications of this have recently been examined, evidenced in a new bill proposed in Iraq to ban toy guns. The *International Herald Tribute* reported in April 2008 that the ban attempts to "curb increasingly aggressive behavior among children who have grown up amid real war." The bill would introduce fines and jail time to individuals importing guns and fireworks. The action comes with a comment by Samira al-Moussaqi, head of the parliamentary committee on children and women: "The culture of violence has prevailed in our society and controlled the Iraqi family and it has affected the culture of children." While there is no indication that this bill has become law country-wide, in particular parts of the country military administrators have banned toy guns. In the city of Mahmoudiyah, south of Baghdad, the U.S. and Iraqi militaries jointly banned toy guns and collected them from children.[19] On the other side of the world, legislation was also introduced in Mexico in 2009 to try to demilitarize that society in light of the violence connected to the country's drug war.[20]

Sometimes concern over the impact of toy guns may be contrived, or only selectively applied. A pro-Israeli nongovernmental organization, based in Gelilot, Israel, has criticized the presence and use of toy guns in "Judea, Samaria and the Gaza Strip" which most of the world refers to as the Occupied Territories, claiming that the toys are "part of the education [children] receive in hatred and violence against Israel."[21] If war toys are seen as teaching hatred and violence to the people we have defined as our enemies, can the same not be said about the socialization of our own children? As we have shown above, toy guns have been common in the Western world for over a century, and in North America children have always simulated fixed, militaristic scripts, whether it was as an "Indian fighter," cops and robbers, or soldiering in the war-of-the-moment, whether World War II, Korea, or later. When this becomes as widespread as it has, all over the world, on all sides of contemporary conflicts, then it becomes strong reinforcement for militarism.

Toy Soldiers

Toy soldiers are among the oldest known toys. In her *History of Toys*, Antonia Fraser notes that in a martial era boys will inevitably turn to soldiers.[22] Toy soldiers became popular in Europe after the introduction of professional standing armies. Kenneth Brown, in his study of the British toy business, asserts that war toys and games contributed to a build up of aggression that resulted in enthusiasm for WWI. He argues that implicit in simulated battles with toy soldiers are the "ideas of enemy and conflict." Children were exposed to war toys as part of a continuum of militaristic influences and toy soldiers helped to reinforce a particular view of the nature of war.[23] Research shows that interest in war toys is correlated with heightened public support for military expenditures. Offerings of war toys rise and fall with militarization, perhaps reflecting the attitude of people who choose them or those who choose to produce them.[24]

The contemporary form of the toy soldier is the action figure. Playing with action figures can transfer the militaristic value of the heroism of the soldiers in Iraq to children as they play with smaller versions of real life heroes. According to a Reuters report, "toy makers in the United States and around the world are rushing to cash in on the growing appeal for action figures that embody heroic sentiments since the Sept. 11 attacks on the United States."[25] These heroic incarnations foster support for the war effort, as young children exposed to toys that promote militarism and patriotism can experience similar facets of the war effort from the relative safety of their own homes. Anthony Chin, the vice president of California-based Marco Polo Imports, has said, "A lot of people are aware of the military aspect of our country in Afghanistan, so through these action figures we hope to get them close to the action, in a safe way."[26] The preference for action figures imbued with military associations was illustrated in 2007 when Jazwares, Inc., a Florida-based toy manufacturer, released "America's Army Real Heroes." Based on the computer game of the same name, the Real Heroes have been touted as "[h]ighlight[ing] heroic Soldiers and their stories in this line of action figures." Additionally, the soldiers' likenesses and biographies are also featured in the army's exceptionally popular computer game, *America's Army*, and on the America's Army website.[27] Bringing the war even closer to home, "Jazwares, Inc. worked closely with the U.S. Army to ensure authenticity." Clearly, Jazwares has ensured that their action figures are closely aligned with all-too-real examples of the war, evidenced in their manufacturing and design as their accurate toys support the war efforts by encouraging the values of heroism and ultrapatriotism.

Although there are action toys that glorify the heroism of the U.S. Army soldiers, there are also those that are aimed at buyers who want a representation of our enemies, or even our allegedly weak-kneed allies. For example, the "Talking Double-Headed Uday" is available for online order:

> A specialty doll with a two-sided head that spins 360 degrees . . . transforming Saddam Hussein's son Uday from a smiling face into the bloody mangled one popularized in U.S.-issued photographs. . . . In an unabashedly Orientalist faux-Middle-Eastern accent, the doll cries out: "Someone must help me. I . . . I am still alive only I am very badly burned. Anyone! Can someone please call my father? I am in a lot of pain, I am very badly burned so if you could just . . . (gunshot). You shot me!! Why did you . . . (3 gun shots)?"[28]

There was a "captured Saddam" action figure with long hair and beard and wearing an Ace of Spades T-shirt, a French president Jacques Chirac doll with "le worm" T-shirt and optional pink dress as an accessory, and a doll of the American Taliban, John Walker Lindh, described as "the dumbest American every born."[29] Contempt and triumph also come through in pro-war merchandise. As Steuter and Wills say, this explains, throughout the Bush era, the production and consumption of Osama "Pin" Laden voodoo dolls and genocide-oriented T-shirts and postcards picturing "Lake Afghanistan" or "Lake Iraq," or picturing parking lot grids or mushroom clouds where the countries now are.[30] Ironically, these wars were justified as necessary to prevent nuclear attack on the United States, and the radical militaristic fringe in the United States wears T-shirts contemplating the same thing in a rather light-hearted fashion.

When it comes to militaristic toys, life can imitate art. For instance, in 2005, a group operating under the name of the Al Mujahedeen Brigade, posted a photograph on an Islamist website of a man they claimed to be captured U.S. soldier John Adam. The group had threatened to kill Adam unless the Iraqis held in U.S.-run prisons were freed within seventy-two hours. However, after the release of the photograph, Liam Cusack, the marketing coordinator for Dragon Models USA, said the figure pictured on the website is believed to be "Special Ops Cody," a military action figure the company manufactured in late 2003. Cusack's company had "produced 4,000 of the Cody action figures in 2003, for sale at U.S. military bases in Kuwait and the Middle East."[31]

The attraction of the action figures drew consumers at the start of the war and continue to this day. When toy retailer Small Blue Planet launched a series of figures called "Special Forces: Showdown with Iraq," two of the four models sold out immediately.[32] In May 2009, Britain's Character Options toy company announced the launch of the "HM Armed Forces Collection," thirty-two figures and accessories of action figures and equipment from the British military, designed with government cooperation. A spokesman for the British Ministry of Defence said: "These toys showcase our people and equipment and this commercial recognition proves the high level support for our forces among the British public."[33] The Ministry of Defence denied the initiative was a recruitment ploy, but hopes the toys will help to burnish the armed forces' reputation, as well as generating a stipend in licensing revenues. The action figures are advertised as providing "positive strong role models" and would help moral development by identifying good and bad characters.[34] Howard Zinn notes that "the government and the media want to raise a new generation to believe that the highest form of heroism is military."[35]

Barbie Goes to War

Playing with dolls has never been a wholly innocent occupation, for there has always been a political background to this phenomenon. In Miriam Formanek-Brunell's *Made to Play House: Dolls and the Commercialization of American Girlhood*, she documents how during World War I American doll manufacturers initiated boycotts of German toy makers and stimulated anti-German sentiments by encouraging the public to destroy their German dolls.

Thousands of customers closed their accounts at FAO Schwartz, founded by German immigrants. Capitalizing on the war climate, American manufacturers characterized German dolls as dirty dolls made by a dirty enemy. They imbued their own dolls with patriotic values as in the Maiden Toy Company's "Maiden America" doll whose name was a pun implying that the moral superiority of American feminine innocence derived from native manufacture.[36] During WWII, girls played war games with their paper dolls featuring the Wacs (Women's Army Corps) and Waves (Women Accepted for Volunteer Emergency Service).[37] Currently, the hugely popular American Girl series of dolls features Molly, who is a patriotic historical doll being raised on the home front in 1944. In the late 1990s and early 2000s the Precious Moments Doll Company produced cute he-and-she army, navy, and air force dolls as decorator items.[38] Toy stores sold out of camo-wearing plush hamsters that dance to military music, and managers at KB Toys stores were instructed "to feature military toys in the front of their stores."[39]

Barbie had also signed up for action. Barbie, the ubiquitous girl's doll with the thin waist, full bosom, and arched feet, joined the army in 1989, the air force in 1990, and the navy in 1991, all in time for the first Gulf War. In 1992 she joined the marines. There are more military Barbies than any other profession. Shirley Steinberg in *Kinderculture: The Corporate Construction of Childhood* notes that

> As sergeants and majors, these booted girls march to the beat of proud, patriotic America Desert Storm Barbie, wearing authentic desert battle dress uniforms of camouflage material—Sergeant Barbie is a medic, and she's ready for duty! Staff Sergeant Ken is ready too! Their berets bear the distinctive 101st Airborne unit insignia with the motto: Rendezvous with Destiny. Both are proud, patriotic Americans serving their country wherever they are needed.[40]

The military series of Barbie dolls went through approvals by the Pentagon to ensure the most realistic costumes. As a pro-military website puts it, "her presence in the U.S. Armed Forces validates the acceptance and the importance of women in the military to millions of young women."[41] In the Middle East, Barbie has been displaced by dolls representing, or manifesting, the rise of more conservative Islamic values in the past ten years. In November 2003, NewBoy Design Studio, based in Syria, introduced Fulla, a new alternative to Barbie, a dark-eyed doll with "Moslem values." She comes with either a white head scarf or black *abaya* (full body covering), plus a prayer rug. Maan Abdul Salam, a Syrian women's rights advocate, said Fulla is emblematic of a trend toward Islamic conservatism sweeping the Middle East. "If this doll had come out 10 years ago, I don't think it would have been very popular," he said. "Fulla is part of this great cultural shift."[42]

In the 2002 Christmas season, the J. C. Penney catalogue advertised a product named the "Forward Command Post" for children ages five and up. Krista Foss, journalist for Toronto's *Globe and Mail*, offers a description of the dollhouse after stumbling across it in the catalogue: "It looks like Barbie went ballistic. The bombed out dollhouse has a busted balustrade, crumbling bricks, bullet holes pockmarking its pretty pastel walls and, what's worse, it has been commandeered by fatigue-clad soldiers toting assault rifles."[43] Eric Garris of the California-based Antiwar.com, started a campaign in opposition to the toy. He says:

> War toys have been around forever, but the problem here is the change in focus. Before such toys were more in line with the ideas of self-defense. . . . This is not just another war toy—it's a total paradigm shift in the war toy industry. It's setting up the young people for this new kind of war, where soldiers come into your house and take it over when they need to.[44]

As feminist scholar Lois Ann Lorentzen notes, Forward Command Post illustrates that U.S. militarism has intruded into the sphere of domestic life, just as it has impacted so many other countries in the world.[45] Although children may play using their imagination, the bombed out dollhouse calls forth the context of war, whether it's the war in Afghanistan, Iraq, or somewhere else.

We say *may play using their imagination* because one of the new developments in militaristic toys, as Karen Hall points out, is that the toys, especially those arising from television programs, provide a fixed script for how they will be played with.[46] The medium is the message. Children are immersed within a violent play-world under the pretense of make-believe, which serves to normalize the violence. Another example of this type of toy is "Scan-It," an airport scanner machine that is billed as an educational tool to assist in "acclimatizing kids with airport security checks."[47] However much the toy is billed as educational, it still functions to normalize, for children at an early age, increased airport security in a post-9/11 world, just as the toy cash register of yesteryear trained children to function within the price system of the retail world, as both customer and employee. It is a tool of socializing children to a new world in which security is defined in us-versus-them terms.

Militarizing Teddy Bears

Militarized teddy bears are for sale in stores and across the Internet, each sporting unique additions to their familiar shape, size, and description. Once the teddy bear is militarized, all is subject to militarization. Dressed in the outfits corresponding to their title, bears come adorned as "Marine

Corps Camouflage Desert Sand Uniform" and "Air Force in Dress Uniform." Another brand of bears has the insignia of the U.S. Army, Air Force, Coast Guard, Navy, and Marine Corps.[48] In Canada, the Heinsight company produces custom military dolls in which a photo of mom's or dad's face is transferred to the doll's head, as a comfort for children while the parent is deployed in Afghanistan. More active children can play with the doll roughly, while sensitive types can use the doll like a teddy bear, *The Maple Leaf*, the weekly magazine of the Canadian Forces, reports.[49]

As Marita Sturken argues in her remarkable study of post-9/11 consumerism and U.S. popular culture, teddy bears are more important than they seem. Sturken and many other authors agree that a central theme in U.S. culture is the self-proclaimed innocence of the country, beginning in the seventeenth century with "captivity narratives," which as Susan Faludi says is "the only genre indigenous to American literature."[50] The teddy bear is the embodiment of innocence, the child's comfort increasingly given to adults as a "commodity of grief" to help them cope with trauma, whether personal or societal. (As author John M. Barry tells it, the "teddy bear" originated from a story in which President Teddy Roosevelt, on a bear-hunting expedition in the Mississippi delta, refused to shoot a bear as part of an easy kill.)[51] The teddy bear also has an "infantilizing" effect on adults, allowing them to maintain some distance from their own society and culture.[52] As Sturken states:

> An American public can acquiesce to its government's aggressive political and military policies, such as the war in Iraq, when that public is constantly reassured by the comfort offered by the consumption of patriotic objects, comfort commodities, and security consumerism.[53]

Another popular application of the military theme is in Halloween costumes. Rather than engaging with playing with toys, children actively assume a combat identity when they dress up for the night. Halloween websites promote costumes such as "Operation Rapid Recon Child Costume" that advertise props such as "Special Ops Combat Knife" marketed directly to youth. The fact that the costume comes only in children's sizes between four and eight makes clear the target audience for the military guise. Advertised as "new for 2008," the "Operation Stealth Commando Child Costume" follows in much the same fashion, decking out children from head to toe in army gear. Assuming the identity of soldier and acting out a reality, even for one night, provides the wearer and all who witness this a false sense of military life and contemporary warfare. Children and their parents, through these costumes, demonstrate that they simply accept war as the way of the world.[54]

Adults and children also have the opportunity to assume military identities when playing a board game. Following in the tradition of the popular game

Risk, war-oriented board games allow individuals to enact battle-like strategies as part of a fun and entertaining way to spend time. However, a new game, "War on Terror: The Boardgame," brings the contemporary wartime atmosphere much closer to home, as there seems to be no end in sight to the wars in Afghanistan, Iraq, and the self-proclaimed War on Terror. London's *Daily Mail* newspaper describes the game as "pit[ting] terrorists and empire-builders against each other, with players using game cards to launch suicide attacks and dirty bombs to win." Jacqui Putnam, a survivor of the 2005 London terrorist bombings, commented on the game, stating, "It is so inappropriate at this time. . . . That distance in time makes it quite an abstract subject, but the London terror attacks happened just last year and we are still living with the threat." Designed by two friends running a design company in Cambridge, the game has generated controversy. But Andrew Sheerin, cocreator of the game, said "My mom said we must be quite sick to make money from the War on Terror. But how can this be sick, when there are companies all over the world making a lot of money directly out of the conflict?"[55]

During an era of war with no end in sight, manufacturers have increased their production of militaristic and violence-oriented toys, making it clear that consumers need to be aware when operating under the altered societal conditions. Action heroes based on Army design sit side-by-side on a shelf next to a "bombed-out doll house" at stores across North America like Toys 'R' Us, and the culture of child's play has been clearly altered in the beginning of the twenty-first century.

Joystick Soldiers

Video games have become a major cultural force, and a striking number of games focus on violence and warfare, both historical and contemporary. These games, and the hardware needed to run them, are increasingly common in United States and global homes. By 2006, the global stock of PlayStation 2s and Xboxes exceeded over 100 million units. In the United States, video games generate more revenue than movie box offices, and the Yankee Group estimated in 2007 that the industry would top $8.3 billion in sales by 2008.[56] The industry and the games themselves have become important agents of socialization, and they have also proven to be significant agents of militarization. The rest of this chapter will discuss the tendency to see war as a video game, and then increasingly, to see the video game as a simulation of war. The growth and militarization of video games are good examples of what Roger Stahl calls "militainment," in his 2007 documentary and 2010 book of the same name.[57] He argues that the integration of the military and entertainment industries has led to a transformation of the civilian spectator to the citizen-participant, who is distant from war but more vicariously engaged than in the past. Video games are one of the mechanisms that make this possible.

The video game industry and the U.S. military have been long entangled—war was a central theme in early games like the 1962 *Spacewar!* and the "first commercial home video console," the Magnavox Odyssey, was developed by a military contracting firm, Sanders Associates. Digitized war-gaming and simulation burst onto the scene in the 1980s, culminating in 1990 in SIMNET, the military's "distributed simulator network project" that "sought to explore more cost-effective forms of simulation," particularly in the computer and video game industries. It was adopted by General Norman Schwarzkopf, who used the war game *Operation Internal Look* to prepare his staff at U.S. Central Command for a "potential conflict in the Middle East." That simulation ultimately shaped the defensive strategy for Operation Desert Shield.[58]

The first Gulf War of 1991–1992 mirrored the simulation in many ways, being dubbed the "Nintendo War." It was the first fully televised war, and CNN provided twenty-four-hour coverage that was described by Michael Deaver, image-maker and advisor to President Reagan, as a "combination of Lawrence of Arabia and Star Wars."[59] Tight military control restricted reporting, and public-relations officials used aerial warfare to "create the impression of a 'clean' techno-war, almost devoid of human suffering and death."[60] Indeed, as articulated by author Tom Engelhardt, "weapons counts" and the destruction of "inanimate things" like bridges replaced images of dead bodies, hiding the war's human impact.[61] In true video game fashion, war coverage was dominated by images that glorified the technological superiority of the U.S. military, including by focusing on the exceptional case in which the "smart bomb" actually went down the target chimney as it was supposed to, which was replayed again and again on CNN if only to suggest this was the norm. So distant from the actual violence, there was room for humor, such as when an Iraqi vehicle passed through the crosshairs of a bomb sight, and General Schwarzkopf remarked, "I am now going to show you the luckiest man in Iraq on this particular day."[62] These images of a "clean" war permeated the media, and viewers were inclined to believe that "the war was being fought cleanly and efficiently with smart bombs that were damaging only buildings." In reality, 70 percent of the 88,500 tons of bombs dropped missed their targets.[63]

As if on cue, the intertwining of war and the video game industry took off at this point. The navy commissioned *Fleet Command* and the army issued Tom Clancy's *Rogue Spear*. In 1994 Sega and military contractor Martin Marietta released *Desert Tank*. In 1996, the PC game *Doom* was modified to create *Marine Doom*, first as a training tool and later for popular consumption.

Then, the establishment of the $45-million Institute for Creative Technologies (ICT) at the University of Southern California in 1999 truly solidified the links between military simulations and the entertainment industry.[64]

With the creation of war-oriented video games art imitated life; now we are on the cusp of a world in which life imitates art. The generation that grew up on remote killing with video games can now apply these skills in the military. Eric Stoner reports that in 2007 the first unmanned infantry unit was stationed in Iraq, with plans to deploy more. These units, the SWORD, are three feet high and run on two tank-style treads, and can be mounted with a M-249 SAW machine gun, a 40 mm grenade launcher, or an M-202 rocket launcher.[65] Even more newsworthy is the rise of the unmanned Predator drones currently in service over the "Af-Pak border," the frontier area between Afghanistan and Pakistan. The Reaper is armed with four Hellfire missiles and two five-hundred-pound bombs, can stay aloft for twenty-two hours, and is flown by shifts of military personnel in Arizona, Nevada, and perhaps elsewhere, sitting at terminals looking for targets.[66] Current research is designed to increase the sophistication of these weapons and to move toward "complete autonomy." No one can be blamed if this brings dystopic science fiction to mind, such as the *Terminator* movie franchise.

The intersections between popular militarism and video games intensified after September 11, 2001. After the attacks were attributed to Osama bin Laden, many amateur internet games appeared, "giving players the chance to maim and manhandle the terrorist leader,"[67] like a form of high-tech dart board. Moreover, modifications were made for video games like *Quake* and *Sims*—the bin Laden character was inserted into the games for players to shoot.[68] The "military-entertainment complex" was taken to new levels on July 4, 2002: the army launched *America's Army*, an "engaging computer video game that quickly became a gold standard of 'advergames.'"[69] It cost tax payers $6 to $8 million, and as heralded by one video trailer, it was the first commercial game project "created by the Army, designed by the Army, developed by the Army . . . because no one gets the Army like the Army!"[70]

America's Army is a first-person-shooter game that gives civilians a taste of military life, and provides soldiers with off-hours reinforcement of the same lessons. Players advance through stages of military life, marching and drilling in basic training, mastering their M-16 rifles in target practice, learning basic emergency medicine, and finally, experiencing combat. They cooperate online in combat scenarios set in virtual Mideast cities, oil rigs, and hospitals, using weapons that replicate those used by the army.[71] The game is wrought with ideology, as articulated by Zhan Li: "[T]he advertising slogan 'Citizens. Countries. Video Games. The U.S. Army keeps them all free,' succinctly extols the equivalence made between individual freedom, military guarantees of national and international freedoms, and economic freedoms." Furthermore, *America's Army*'s "Army Values"—"Teamwork & Loyalty, Duty, Respect, Selfless Service, Honor, Integrity, Personal Courage (L.D.R.S.H.I.P.)"—are central to the game, as the player's progress is linked to these values and the honor score system, which "[punish] player actions such as attacking team-mates and cheating, whilst rewarding leadership, teamplay, and the achieving of mission objectives."[72] Realism is said to be a central goal of the game's pro-ducers, whether it is the sights and sounds of basic training, barracks life, or combat. Many of the game's missions are based on actual combat experiences in Iraq and Afghanistan, and the game website features "America's Army's Real Heroes," where visitors can explore the stories of celebrated combat veterans. Ubisoft, the publisher of the console version of the game, wrote in a 2005 press release that *America's Army* is the "deepest and most realistic military game ever to hit consoles," giving players a "realistic, action-packed, military experience."[73]

America's Army, however, is not just a "realistic" game that socializes peo-ple with desirable values; it is an explicit recruitment tool. The game's website links directly to the army's recruitment page. It records players' data and sta-tistics in a database, "tracking overall kills, kills per hour, a player's virtual ca-reer path, and other statistics," and game creator Col. Casey Wardynski stated that frequent and successful players may "get an e-mail seeing if [they'd] like any additional information on the Army." Furthermore, the PC game is often bundled together with gaming magazines and given away at NASCAR events, game centers are set up at state fairs and public festivals, and recruiters stage area tournaments at high schools and community centers.[74] Lt.-Col. John Gillette led one such recruiting tournament in New York in 2004, at which he stated: "This is a fantastic recruiting opportunity. . . . We would like to sign up as many as possible."[75] These events have been controversial—in August 2007, ninety veterans and active-duty service members of Iraq Veterans Against the War protested a game booth in St. Louis, chanting "war is not a game."[76]

While the game declares that it is devoted to realism in graphics, sounds, and play, the violence is unrealistically minimized: "[B]ullet wounds resemble puffs of red smoke, and players can take up to four hits before being killed." Unlike real combat, parental controls can even further reduce the gore. This means that *America's Army* received the equivalent of a PG rating from the Entertainment Software Rating Board, allowing children as young as thirteen to play. In 2008, a report by the American Civil Liberties Union (ACLU) found the army's recruitment strategies in violation of international law, stressing that the armed services "regularly target children under 17 for military recruit-ment." It specifically emphasized the role of *America's Army*, saying the army uses the game to "explicitly target boys 13 and older." Significantly, this is indeed a primary military objective—as articulated by Col. Wardynski, marketing the game to children "[puts] the Army within the immediate decision-making environment of young Americans."[77]

All indications are that with these games the military is achieving its objectives. Michael B. Reagan reports that by 2006, the results of these video games were visible for all to see. In Mosul, Iraq, Sgt. Sinque Swales reported that when he fired his .50 caliber machine gun at "so-called insurgents" for only the second time, it "felt like I was in a big video game. It didn't even faze me, shooting back. It was just natural instinct. Boom! Boom! Boom! Boom!" Other soldiers, like Pvt. Doug Stanbro, said that he "never really thought about the military at all before I started playing this game." The army's own study indicated that four out of one hundred new recruits in Ft. Benning, Georgia, credit *America's Army* as the "primary factor" in convincing them to join the military. This may not seem like a high percentage but when recruiting short falls are a few percent, then every recruiting edge is important. Further, the same study indicated that 60 percent of surveyed recruits played the game more than five times a week.[78]

America's Army has clearly been an effective recruitment tool. One year after its release, it was one of the five most popular online video games.[79] In 2004, an army survey found that nearly a third of Americans aged sixteen to twenty-four had "some contact with the game in the previous six months,"[80] and a poll by *i to i research* showed that "30 percent of a group of young people with a favorable view of the military said they had developed that view from playing *America's Army*."[81] As of 2007, more than 7 million users had registered with 10,000 to 50,000 new downloads daily, and 20 percent to 40 percent of new army recruits had played the game.[82]

America's Army is only the tip of the iceberg, for since 2003 there has been an outpouring of militaristic video games. *Six Days in Fallujah* is a controversial "survival horror" video game due to be released in 2010 that has been developed in collaboration with a handful of Iraq veteran U.S. Marines—who have lent their videos, photos, and diaries to the designers. The Xbox 360 and PlayStation 3 game takes inspiration from the Second Battle of Fallujah—also known as Operation Phantom Fury—which took place between November 7 and December 23, 2004. An estimated 1,500 Iraqi insurgents were killed, reportedly in white phosphorus attacks, along with 38 U.S. troops during the battle. The game's maker said, "For us, the challenge was how to present the horrors of war in a game that is entertaining." Some military families have called the game "crass and insensitive" and called for it to be banned. Reg Keys, whose son Thomas was killed by an Iraqi mob in June 2003, stated, "Considering the enormous loss of life in the Iraq War, glorifying it in a video game demonstrates very poor judgment and bad taste."[83]

In 2004, Sony released *SOCOM II: U.S. Navy SEALs*, produced with the assistance of the U.S. Naval Special Warfare Command, and the Department of Defense and ICT. They also collaborated to revamp a version of *Full Spectrum Command*, a "PC-game/combat simulator" and training tool, and the result was *Full Spectrum Warrior*.[84] In 2004, Kuma Reality Games developed *Kuma War* in cooperation with the Department of Defense. According to its website, "*Kuma War* is a series of playable re-creations of real events in the War on Terror. Nearly 100 playable missions bring our soldiers' heroic stories to life, and you can get them all right now, for free. Stop watching the news and get in the game!"[85] While these games are "breeding grounds for war propaganda," they also serve as training devices for both military tactics and weapons.[86] *America's Army*, *Full Spectrum Warrior*, and the marine's *Close Combat: First to Fight* are all designed to simulate real battlefield missions.

One of the themes that arises repeatedly in this book is the degree to which militarism permeates culture and society in the United States. No better example can be found than developments in the area of video games over the last ten or twenty years. A strong case can be made that violent and militaristic video games have desensitized people, especially young people, to violence and killing. These games, made with the cooperation and sometimes direct participation of the military, present an unrealistically rosy picture of military life. Further, they blur the line between civilian and military for both the civilian and the military member. Militarism occupies more time of the civilian, and civilian concerns occupy less time of the active-duty service member. Despite the absence of conscription, and even if the individual does not serve in Junior ROTC, the military uses video games to get access to young minds. As Nick Turse says very well:

> Certainly, the day is not far off when most potential U.S. troops will have grown up playing commercial video games that were created by the military as training simulators; will be recruited, at least in part, though video games; will be tested, postenlistment, on advanced video games systems; will be trained using simulators, which will later be turned into video games . . . [and] will be taught to pilot vehicles using devices resembling commercial video game controllers.[87]

Conclusion

It is certainly a sign of a militaristic society when violence and warfare are allowed—even urged—to invade the children's world of play. In Roland Barthes view, toys are a major way in which children are prepared to become consumers of both meanings and products, so a society with militaristic toys and amusements is preparing its children for just that fate. Walter Benjamin believed that a society with authoritarian and colonialist values would see these impulses seep into children's play life. As a toy collector himself, "he regarded play with toys as a site where the intimate exchanges between the child and object produced and communicated culture, since play with toys concerns the child's negotiations with representations of an adult world."[88] As this chapter indicates, this has been the case in the United States for decades, with the tolerance for children's culture that sets up warriors of various types as role models, and then encourages a play world in which children act out violence both in times of peace and war. Human beings are not born to kill other humans, a basic fact that may be news to us in a society so permeated by scenes of internal violence and external permanent war. The military recognized after World War II that this was a "problem," and they have been quite successful in inculcating the willingness among soldiers to kill.

The country's toy stores have always been awash with toy guns, which have facilitated children's play as cowboys vanquishing the American Indian, as good-guy cops fighting robbers, and as soldiers in various war scenarios. As this chapter also shows, this violent and war-oriented play culture also seems to have intensified in the last ten to twenty years. In the last twenty years the U.S. state learned that military recruiting and support for U.S. military policies have cultural roots. So blurring the dividing line between civilian and military life has been in the interests of militarists, and using cultural products as propaganda to present the military in a positive light has become a significant goal. Joining the military is like starting a war—it's easier to join/start than it is to get out. Militarism also reinforces the idea of the sanctity of "following orders" and the "chain of command," and it converts an elected, civilian president to a de facto military leader. To sum up, as Nick Turse says, "By co-opting the civilian 'culture of cool,' the military-corporate complex is able to create positive associations with the armed forces, immerse the young in an alluring militarized world of fun, and make intersection with the military second nature to today's Americans."[89]

This intensification of militarist culture can be attributed to the intertwining of video-game producers with the military, but also the intertwining of cultural products generally, based in part on the high concentration of ownership in the economy. A multiplicity of products, including a movie, novelization of the movie in book form, action figures, video and/or board game, are all released at the same time. Each product reinforces the others and children, and adults, live in a highly saturated media environment. This works for those products with violent and militaristic themes as well as it does for other products.

Notes

1. Dahr Jamail and Jason Coppola, "Militarizing the Homeland with G.I. Joe," *Truthout*, August 9, 2009, www.truthout.org/080609A (accessed August 10, 2009).

2. Antonia Fraser, *A History of Toys* (London and New York: Spring Books, 1972).

3. Wendy Varney, "Playing with 'War Fare,'" *Peace Review* 12, no. 3 (2000): 385.

4. Andrew Martin, "Popular Culture and Narratives of Insecurity," in *Rethinking Global Security: Media, Popular Culture and the "War on Terror,"* ed. Andrew Martin and Patrice Petro (New Brunswick, NJ, and London: Rutgers University Press, 2006), 110.

5. Karen J. Hall, "A Soldier's Body: GI Joe, Hasbro's Great American Hero, and the Symptoms of Empire," *Journal of Popular Culture* 38, no. 1 (2004): 34–54.

6. Henry A. Giroux, *Against the New Authoritarianism: Politics after Abu Ghraib* (Winnipeg, MB: Arbeiter Ring Pub., 2005), 80.

7. Alyssa Rosenberg, "G.I. Joe & Company," *The Atlantic*, August 7, 2009.

8. Rosenberg, "G.I. Joe & Company."

9. Bronte and Musgrove cited in Jeffrey Goldstein, *Why We Watch: The Attractions of Violent Entertainment* (New York: Oxford University Press, 1998), 58.

10. Margaret R. Higonnet, "War Toys: Breaking and Remaking in Great War Narratives," *The Lion and the Unicorn* 31, no. 2 (2007): 118.

11. Dave Grossman, "Trained to Kill: Are We Conditioning Our Children to Commit Murder?" *Christianity Today*, August 10, 1998, in www.killology.com/article_trainedtokill.htm (accessed June 18, 2009).

12. Barbara Ehrenreich and Katha Pollitt, "Fukuyama's Follies: So What If Women Ruled the World?" *Foreign Affairs*, January/February 1999.

13. For a corroborating account of the difficulty of training contemporary soldiers to kill see Gwynne Dyer, "Anybody's Son Will Do," in *War* (Toronto, ON: Stoddart, 1987).

14. Grossman, "Trained to Kill."

15. Goldstein, *Why We Watch*, 67.

16. Michael Yellow Bird, "Cowboys and Indians: Toys of Genocide, Icons of American Colonialism," *Wicazo Sa Review*, Fall 2004, 33–47.

17. Tom Engelhardt, *The End of Victory Culture: Cold War America and the Disillusioning of a Generation*, rev. ed. (Amherst: University of Massachusetts Press, 2007), 70.

18. IslamOnline.net & News Agencies, "Iraq Children Obsessed with Toy Guns," Islam Online, October 19, 2007, www.islamonline.net/servlet/Satellite?c=Article_C&cid=1190886487847&pagename=Zone-English-News%2FNWELayout (accessed July 22, 2008).

19. Associated Press, "Toy Guns Aren't Child's Play for Iraq's Military: Confiscation Aims to Reduce Risk of Being Mistaken for Real Thing," *Washington Times*, December 17, 2008, www.washingtontimes.com/news/2008/dec/17/toy-guns-arent-childs-play-for-iraqs-military/ (accessed June 22, 2009).

20. Jo Tuckman, "Mexico Considers Banning Toy Guns to Cut Child Aggression," *Guardian*, January 12, 2009, http://aftermathnews.wordpress.com/2009/01/12/mexico-considers-banning-toy-guns-to-cut-child-aggression/ (accessed June 2, 2009).

21. Intelligence and Terrorism Information Center at the Israel Heritage & Commemoration Center, "Palestinian Children Playing with Plastic Weapons . . . ," Intelligence and Terrorism Information Center, www.terrorism-info.org.il/malam_multi media/English/eng_n/html/h_i_1107.htm (accessed June 22, 2009).

22. Fraser, *History of Toys.*

23. Kenneth Douglas Brown, *The British Toy Business: A History since 1700* (London: Hambledon Press, 1996).

24. Goldstein, *Why We Watch*, 58.

25. Cited in Bill Berkowitz, "War Toys for Tots," *AlterNet*, April 24, 2002, www.alternet.org/911oneyearlater/12951/ (accessed July 8, 2008).

26. Berkowitz, "War Toys for Tots."

27. Michael McWhertor, "*America's Army* Deployed to Toy Aisles," *Kotaku*, November 15, 2007, http://kotaku.com/gaming/bureau-of-licensing/americas-army -deployed-to-toy-aisles-323416.php (accessed July 8, 2008).

28. Nick Turse, "Bringing the War Home: The New Military-Industrial-Entertain ment Complex at War and Play," *Common Dreams*, October 17, 2003, www.common-dreams.org/cgi-bin/print.cgi?file=/views03/1017-09.htm (accessed July 8, 2008).

29. Dar Haddix, "Companies Cash in with War-Inspired Toys," *United Press International*, December 30, 2003.

30. Erin Steuter and Deborah Wills, *At War with Metaphor: Media, Propaganda, and Racism in the War on Terror* (Lanham, MD: Lexington Books, 2008), 105–6.

31. "So-Called U.S. Hostage Appears to Be Toy," *CNN*, February 1, 2005, http://edition.cnn.com/2005/WORLD/meast/02/01/iraq.hostage/ (accessed July 8, 2008); "U.S. Hostage Photo 'Is Doll Hoax,'" *BBC News*, February 2, 2005, http://news.bbc.co.uk/2/hi/middle_east/4229347.stm (accessed July 8, 2008).

32. Amy C. Sims, "Just Child's Play," *Fox News*, August 21, 2003, www.wmsa.net/news/FoxNews/fn-030822_childs_play.htm (accessed August 15, 2009).

33. "Military Dolls to Promote Forces Careers to Children," ArmyDomain, www.army.com/forum/showthread.php?t=9220 (accessed July 12, 2009).

34. David Teather, "Ministry of Defence Hopes New Toy Action Figures Will Help Image," *Guardian*, May 7, 2009.

35. Howard Zinn, interview with Ian Svenonious, *Index Magazine*, 2002, www.indexmagazine.com/interviews/howard_zinn.shtml (accessed August 12, 2009).

36. Miriam Formanek-Brunell, *Made to Play House: Dolls and the Commercialization of American Girlhood, 1830–1930* (Baltimore: Johns Hopkins University Press, 1998), 145.

37. William M. Tuttle, *Daddy's Gone to War: The Second World War in the Lives of America's Children* (New York: Oxford University Press, 1995), 140.

38. Precious Moments Company, "Military Dolls," Precious Moments Museum, www.pmcdolls.com/museum/military.html (accessed July 12, 2009).

39. Maureen Tkacik, "Military Toys Spark Conflict on Home Front," *Wall Street Journal*, March 31, 2003, B1.

40. Shirley R. Steinberg and Joe L. Kincheloe, *Kinderculture: The Corporate Construction of Childhood* (Boulder, CO: Westview Press, 1997), 212.

41. For photos and quotes, see, Women in Military Service for America Memorial Foundation, Inc., "Collections Archive—Mattel's Barbie® Joins the Military," History & Collections, www.womensmemorial.org/H&C/Collections/barbie.html (accessed July 12, 2009).

42. Katherine Zoepf, "Bestseller in Mideast: Barbie with a Prayer Mat," *New York Times*, September 22, 2005, www.nytimes.com/2005/09/22/international/middleeast/22doll.html?_r=2 (accessed July 12, 2009).

43. Krista Foss, "All I Want for Christmas Is a Bombed-Out Dollhouse," *Common Dreams*, November 23, 2003, www.commondreams.org/views02/1123-01.htm (July 8, 2008).

44. Foss, "All I Want for Christmas."

45. Lois Ann Lorentzen, "Feminists and Forward Command Posts," *The Scholar and Feminist Online* 2, no. 2 (Winter 2004), www.barnard.edu/sfonline/reverb/printllo.htm (accessed July 12, 2009).

46. Karen Hall, "'For Real Life?' War Toys in the Peace-Loving Household," Syracuse Peace Council, www.peacecouncil.net/pnl/02/715/715WarToys.htm (accessed June 16, 2009).

47. Addy Dugdale, "Scan-It X-Ray Machine the Ugly Face of 21st-Century Toys," Gizmodo, February 20, 2008, http://gizmodo.com/358524/scan+it-x+ray-machine-the-ugly-face-of-21st+century-toys (accessed July 8, 2008).

48. Vanguard, search for product "Bears," www.vanguardmil.com/store/index.php?main_page=advanced_search_result&search_in_description=1&keyword=bear&x=0&y=0 (accessed July 8, 2008); "Military Teddy Bears," Prior Service, www.priorservice.com/mitebe.html (accessed July 8, 2008).

49. Sgt. Dennis Power, "Personalized Dolls to Comfort Military Families," *The Maple Leaf* 11, no. 10 (2008), www.dnd.ca/site/Commun/ml-fe/article-eng.asp?id=4213 (accessed July 12, 2009).

50. Susan Faludi, *The Terror Dream: Fear and Fantasy in Post-9/11 America* (New York: Metropolitan Books / Henry Holt and Company, 2007), 214.

51. John M. Barry, *Rising Tide: The Great Mississippi Flood of 1927 and How It Changed America* (New York: Simon and Schuster, 1998), 110–11.

52. Marita Sturken, *Tourists of History: Memory, Kitsch, and Consumerism from Oklahoma City to Ground Zero* (Durham, NC, and London: Duke University Press, 2007), 6.

53. Sturken, *Tourists of History*, 6.

54. "Operation Rapid Recon Child Costume," Halloween Express, www.halloweenexpress.com/operation-rapid-recon-child-costume-p-15724.html (accessed July 20, 2008), and "Operation Stealth Commando Child Costume," Halloween Express, www.halloweenexpress.com/operation-stealth-commando-child-costume-p-15725.html (accessed July 20, 2008).

55. "Fury over 'War on Terror' Board Game," *Daily Mail*, September 18, 2006, www.dailymail.co.uk/news/article-405801/Fury-war-terror-board-game.html (accessed July 8, 2008).

56. David Verklin and Bernice Kanner, "Why a Killer Video Game Is the Army's Best Recruitment Tool," *Chiefmarketer Report*, April 29, 2007, http://chiefmarketer

.com/disciplines/branding/video-game-recruitment-04292007/ (accessed January 27, 2009).

57. Roger Stahl, *Militainment, Inc. War, Media and Popular Culture* (New York: Routledge, 2010).

58. Mark J. P. Wolf, "A Brief Timeline of Video Game History," in *The Video Game Explosion: A History from Pong to PlayStation and Beyond,* ed. Mark J. P. Wolf (Westport, CT: Greenwood Press, 2008), xvii; Marcus Power, "Digitized Virtuosity: Video War Games and Post-9/11 Cyber-Deterrence," *Security Dialogue* 38 (2007): 271–88.

59. Michael Deaver, as cited in Ann Marie Barry, *Visual Intelligence: Perception, Image, and Manipulation in Visual Communication* (Albany: State University of New York Press, 1997), 283.

60. H. B. Franklin as cited in Eric P. Louw, "The 'War against Terrorism': A Public Relations Challenge for the Pentagon," *Gazette* 65 (2003): 211–30.

61. Tom Engelhardt, as cited in Louw, "The 'War against Terrorism,'" 211–30.

62. Kevin Robins, *Into the Image: Culture and Politics in the Field of Vision* (New York: Routledge, 1997), 65.

63. Material in this paragraph was drawn from Stig A. Nohrstedt, "Ruling by Pooling," in *Triumph of the Image: The Media's War in the Persian Gulf—a Global Perspective,* ed. Hamid Mowlana, George Gerbner, and Herbert I. Schiller (Boulder, CO: Westview Press, 1992), 126; Barry, *Visual Intelligence,* 283.

64. Power, "Digitized Virtuosity," 277–78.

65. Eric Stoner, "Attack of the Killer Robots: Pentagon Plans to Deploy Autonomous Robots in War Zones," *In These Times,* February 18, 2009, www.alternet.org/story/127484/ (accessed July 12, 2009).

66. Tom Engelhardt, "Filling the Skies with Robot Assassins: The Drone Wars Have Begun," *TomDispatch,* April 8, 2009, www.alternet.org/story/135594/filling_the_skies_with_robot_assassins:_the_drone_wars_have_begun/ (accessed July 12, 2009).

67. Henry Jenkins, "A War of Words over Iraq Video Games," *Guardian,* November 15, 2003, www.guardian.co.uk/technology/2003/nov/15/games.iraq (accessed January 28, 2009).

68. Anne-Marie Schleiner, "Velvet-Strike: War Times and Reality Games," Velvet-Strike: Counter-Military Graffiti for CS, February 3, 2002, www.opensorcery.net/velvet-strike/about.html (accessed January 28, 2009).

69. Verklin and Kanner, "Killer Video Game."

70. Zhan Li, "The Potential of *America's Army* the Video Game as Civilian-Military Public Sphere" (master's thesis, Massachusetts Institute of Technology, 2003), www.gamasutra.com/education/theses/20040725/ZLITHESIS.pdf, 7 (accessed August 15, 2009).

71. Verklin and Kanner, "Killer Video Game"; Michael B. Reagan, "U.S. Military Recruits Children: 'America's Army' Video Game Violates International Law," *Truthout,* July 23, 2008, www.truthout.org/article/us-military-recruits-children (accessed January 27, 2009).

72. Li, "Potential of *America's Army,*" 44–49.

73. Ubisoft as cited by Reagan, "U.S. Military Recruits Children."

74. This material comes from Reagan, "U.S. Military Recruits Children"; Power, "Digitized Virtuosity," 279.

75. "Army Recruits Video Gamers," *CBS News*, March 30, 2004, www.cbsnews .com/stories/2004/03/30/eveningnews/main609489.shtml (accessed January 27, 2009).

76. "War Is NOT a Game," Iraq Veterans Against the War, September 7, 2007, http://ivaw.org/node/1654 (accessed January 26, 2009).

77. Reagan, "U.S. Military Recruits Children."

78. This paragraph relies on Reagan, "U.S. Military Recruits Children."

79. Turse, "Bringing the War Home."

80. Reagan, "U.S. Military Recruits Children."

81. Clive Thomson, "The Making of an X Box Warrior," *New York Times*, August 22, 2004, http://query.nytimes.com/gst/fullpage.html?res=9C02EEDD133FF931A157 5BC0A9629C8B63&sec=&spon=&pagewanted=2 (accessed January 29, 2009).

82. Verklin and Kanner, "Killer Video Game."

83. "Iraq War Video Game Branded 'Crass and Insensitive' by Father of Red Cap Killed in Action," *Daily Mail*, April 7, 2009, www.dailymail.co.uk/news/article -1168235/Iraq-War-video-game-branded-crass-insensitive-father-Red-Cap-killed -action.html##ixzz0Nris1bIa (accessed August 13, 2009).

84. Turse, "Bringing the War Home."

85. Kumagames, *Kuma/War* website, www.kumawar.com/.

86. Rune Ottosen, "The Military-Industrial Complex Revisited: Computer Games as War Propaganda," *Television New Media* 10, no. 1 (2009): 122–25.

87. Nick Turse, *The Complex: How the Military Invades Our Everyday Lives* (New York: Henry Holt and Company / Metropolitan Books, 2008), 140.

88. Jonathan Bignell, *Postmodern Media Culture* (Edinburgh: Edinburgh University Press, 2000), 117.

89. Turse, *The Complex*, 101.

4

War Fever

Hollywood Mobilizes Support for the War on Terror

I N TIMES OF CRISIS, CULTURAL INSTITUTIONS CAN MOBILIZE SUPPORT for retaliation and acts of aggression. The power of popular culture to dramatize the immediacy of a threat and build a sense of urgency for a heroic and decisive response is only further enhanced by a massive entertainment industry that can produce militarist merchandise overnight. Immediately after 9/11 there was a frenzy of production to memorialize the attacks through souvenirs and collectibles. The Patent and Trademark Office was flooded with applications to corner the market on phrases such as "lest we forget," and "remember the Twin Towers," and by 2003, "shock and awe." The rush to make a quick buck from the attacks attracted widespread criticism from people concerned that companies were profiting from the tragedy. At the time applications were also filed for products inscribed with the phrases "Osama, can you see the bombs bursting in the air?" and "Osama, Yo' Mama."[1]

Expressions of revenge against Osama bin Laden, al-Qaeda, the Taliban, the country of Afghanistan, and later Saddam Hussein and the country of Iraq, were communicated through a plethora of pop culture items such as toilet paper ("Help wipe out terrorism!"), golf balls and piñatas ("Take a whack at the enemy"), and even condoms ("Shock and Awe" and "Screw you bin Laden"). There was also Bunker Buster Shock 'N' Awe Hot Sauce (complete with Saddam Hussein cartoon) and even Shock and Awe "infant action crib toys."[2]

Violent merchandise, porn, and video games proliferated on websites such as blowshitup.com, kissmyUSbutt.com, makempay.com, and nukeafghanistan .com.[3] American gamers created a number of game modifications for games such as *Quake*, *Unreal*, and *The Sims* in which they inserted Osama bin Laden skins and characters to shoot at and annihilate. Anne-Marie Schleiner notes that "One Osama skins distributor suggested feeding *The Sims* Osama poison potato chips. If you can't shoot him, then force him to overeat American junk food, to binge, death by over-consumption, death by capitalism."[4] On display in October 2001 at a commercial game industry exhibit in Barcelona called "Arte Futura," Osama is represented as an Arab corner grocery store owner and the goal of the modification is to enter the corner liquor grocery store and kill the Arab owner.[5] At boardwalk arcades people were invited to play a "Wack the Iraq" game in which contestants fire paint balls at live targets dressed as Iraqis.[6] Henry Giroux notes that "ongoing and largely uncritical depictions of war injected a constant military presence in American life . . . and help to create a civil society that has become more aggressive in its warlike enthusiasms."[7] The line between hostility toward specific enemies and entire countries and religions was quickly blurred as seen in the T-shirts and coffee mugs showing all-American boy Calvin, from the comic strip *Calvin and Hobbes*, peeing on the word "terrorists" on a map of Iraq and on the Islamic symbol of the star and crescent. In animated Web games such as *Beat the Shit Out of Bin Laden Yourself*, many of the images do not distinguish between "terrorists" and "Arabs" and are overtly racist, depicting Afghans as primitive, tribal, "uncivilized" people.

These conservative and militarist products have not disappeared with the Obama administration, addressing both the home front and foreign lands. There are new bumper stickers with slogans like "Bomb Iran Now,"[8] "Impeach Pelosi," "Jack Bauer 2012," "Don't Blame Me, I didn't Vote for Him!" "USA Liberal Hunting Permit," "Jihad Works Both Ways" (with Airborne, CIA, Army Rangers, or 10th Mountain Division decal), "I [heart] Torturing Terrorists," and "The Only Good Terrorist Regime is a Glowing Terrorist Regime" with nuked Iran pictured.[9]

Kenneth Cloke, conflict resolution mediator, cautions,

> As a nation, we need to re-examine how we responded to the conflicts that occurred, and are still occurring, as a result of the September 11th tragedy. . . . This response has led to increased suffering, including grief, fear, divisiveness, and confusion—not only for us, but those whose lives we have similarly shattered by violence. . . . By responding to violence with violence, we not only lost a unique opportunity to unite people and governments around the world in opposition to terror, we helped strengthen a culture of war rather than peace, bullying rather than compassion, revenge rather than forgiveness, and isolation rather than collaboration. By our aggressive statements and unilateral actions, we have deprecated the importance and prestige of peace-making, conflict resolution, international partnership, and public dialogue, thereby contributing to

future conflicts, making them more serious, and constricting opportunities for settlement and resolution.[10]

United We Go Shopping

As the United States prepared for war after the attacks of September 11, 2001, concerns arose that decreases in consumer spending and investment would incite a severe economic downturn, a downturn that would cut into corporate profitability and depress necessary revenues for the War on Terror.[11] While the political leadership, particularly President Bush, urged the country to shop and spend as virtually a patriotic act, the advertising industry was recruited for the task of supporting consumerism and nationalistic patriotism as well. As Chuck Kelly said, "as marketers, we have the responsibility to keep the economy rolling. . . . Our job is to create customers during one of the more difficult times in our history."[12]

Advertising agencies responded with patriotic fervor, frequently adorning their clients in the flag. The New York Stock Exchange ran commercials that associated the bell ending daily market speculation with the civil rights movement, declaring "Let Freedom Ring," and radio spots by Toys 'R' Us encouraged families to come to the store and color a flag.[13] This consumer-as-patriot mentality was captured by a mall sign which read: "Ask not what your country can do for you, ask 'Can I get this shoe in size seven?'" underwritten by the declaration that "It's time for you to do your part to stimulate the economy. And there's no better way to kick the economy up a notch than with a really great pair of pumps. . . . Or whatever you've been dying to get your hands on!"[14]

The automobile industry was particularly explicit in their efforts to promote patriotic consumerism. Ford linked its TV ads to the events of 9/11: "In an instant everything can change. Yet everywhere you look the spirit of America is alive. . . . We at Ford want to celebrate that spirit with the Ford Drives America Program, to help America move forward with interest-free financing on all new Fords."[15] Furthermore, a General Motors television advertisement declared "The American Dream: We refuse to let anyone take it away from us"—implying Americans could defy "the terrorists" by purchasing GM cars.[16] In other commercials, GM evoked the phrase "let's roll"—the last words of Flight 93 passenger Todd Beamer—"visit your Saturn retailer and 'Keep America Rolling.'"[17]

Association with 9/11 and the military also became major advertising themes. The "official nutrition bar of the U.S. military," the Hooah! bar, exploded in popularity, even though its main contents are found in most nutrition bars.

Indeed, the military association and accompanying "support the troops" ribbons are but "a good marketing ploy," according to Bonnie Liebman, director of nutrition for the Center for Science in the Public Interest.[18] In January 2009, Disney announced a free admission ticket for military members, and cut rates for family members and for hotel rooms, though of course this was in a period of economic difficulty in which the entire travel industry was offering discounts.[19] Both the military and defense contractors also produce videos and advertise in their own interest. In support of its "Future Combat Systems," a high-tech system of drone tanks, helicopters, and other vehicles, the Defense Department created a seven minute video with a final tag line that says "Future Combat Systems: One Team—the Army/Defense/Industry." The video portrays a U.S. Army response to a domestic U.S. earthquake, using equipment that in reality is being used in Iraq and the Af-Pak border region.[20]

Many consumers took the militaristic, consumerist message to heart, which may explain in 2009 the explosion of public and private debt and the wave of bankruptcies. A condominium manager who was planning to save further before buying a new roof, a car, and thousands of dollars worth of new furniture, purchased them all in October 2001: "We bought now because we don't want the terrorists to think they won." In response to a California television station's question "Are you reluctant to spend money after the attack on America?" one watcher declared, "Let's not give into the terrorists at all . . . shop till you drop."

Enlisting Superheroes

Since their conception prior to World War II, comic books have become an interesting site for the discussion of contemporary social issues. The United States enjoyed a "Golden Age" of superheroes between the years of 1938 and the end of World War II, at a time when America seemed most in need of powerful and enduring heroes.[21] Comic book content developed to reflect evolving values and tumultuous social changes, and their popularity ensured that their messages were transmuted through gripping illustrations. Indeed, from 1938 on the superheroes enjoyed great popularity. So successful were some of them that they quite frequently outsold news stand magazines like *Time* and *Newsweek*. Comic book historians note that the superheroes "express in today's idiom the ancient longing of mankind for a mighty protector, a helper, a guide, or guardian angel who offers miraculous deliverance to mortals."[22]

When World War II began, comics chipped in to the war effort and fought the Nazis and the Japanese fleets on their pages.[23] Joe Simon and Jack Kirby invented the famous "Captain America" in 1941, just as the United States was entering into the war.[24] In its first publication, "the cover featured Captain America socking Hitler in the jaw!"[25] "Cap," as he is affectionately named, was explicitly a product and agent of the U.S. military, and remained America's most powerful piece of wartime comic-book propaganda. Wearing the symbols of America all over himself, Cap became the ultimate patriotic hero and a national figure.[26] Clearly, the heroes introduced to the American public through early comic books embodied the characteristics of a consistently "good" archetypal hero defeating evil, a depiction reflecting a common desire within the United States to beat the fascist powers. Comic books were able to skillfully weave aspects of WWII within their plots, to entertain through illustration, and to also bolster patriotism and hope in the United States.

After 9/11, DC and Marvel, two Manhattan-based companies, published comic books to raise money for the relief effort as "our way of lifting bricks and mortar."[27] Marvel comics published *A Moment of Silence*, wordless stories of experience on September 11, 2001, while DC Comics united with Dark Horse, Image, Chaos! and Oni to produce two reflective volumes, *9-11: The World's Finest Comic Book Writers & Artists Tell Stories to Remember* and *9-11: Artists Respond*.[28] In a more retaliatory mode, the Hulk, "his green muscles bulging, waving an American flag as fighter jets fly overhead," headed for Afghanistan, with the slogan, "Strongest One There Is."[29] Frank Miller proposed a Batman versus bin Laden showdown. Miller, who penned *The Dark Knight Returns, Sin City*, and *300*, told the press that there was once again a need for the archetypal satisfactions of the classic 1940s wartime propaganda comic:[30] "These terrorists are worse than any villain I can come up with, and I think it's ridiculous that people in entertainment are not showing what we are up against here. . . . I'm ready for my fatwa."[31] Marvel published *Combat Zone*, based on the journalistic experiences of Bush's domestic policy adviser, Karl Zinsmeister. Zinsmeister wrote a graphic novel that showed "his GI subjects in a uniformly heroic light, with one member of the central platoon eventually making the ultimate sacrifice for his buddies."[32] Henry Jenkins notes that these comics represent "a developing trend toward comics with a 'superpatriotic' theme, setting square-jawed American heroes and superheroes on the trail of Osama bin Laden and other terrorists."[33]

The conservative response by many comic publishers may well be connected to the allegiances of their parent companies. DC Comics, for example, is owned by Time Warner, which also owns CNN. Paul Gambaccini, the DJ and comics connoisseur, observed, "It's tough for DC and Marvel, because they don't want to damage their relationships with the government . . . the failure of mainstream comics to lead on this issue is just a symptom of the extent to which the American media were co-opted into supporting the war. Now, of course, they all look stupid. But that's because they were stupid."[34]

Back the Attack

In the run up to the U.S. invasion of Iraq, many people who might otherwise be independent-minded and humanitarian suspended their powers of critical thought as they lined up to back the attack, including journalists such as Dan Rather and media tycoon Oprah Winfrey.[35] Oprah, as she is known, owns a media and publishing empire, centered around her daily, one-hour afternoon talk show. In terms of its significance, 26 million people each week watch Oprah's show, an audience which is 75 to 80 percent women.[36] In 2008 she ranked at number 155 in Fortune's list of the 400 richest Americans, with net worth of $2.7 billion and an annual income of around $200 million.[37] Her wealth and income are based on her show; her production company (Harpo Productions); her magazine, *O*; and the rest of her business empire. Like others in her position, her "brand" is very important to her success.[38]

On October 9, 2002, as the Bush administration was beating the drums of war, Oprah turned her show over to advocates of a U.S. attack on Iraq. At the time opponents of the war, even those without specialist knowledge, identified the lies and errors on the program, and they turned out to be correct.[39] One of the hawkish guests, Kenneth Pollack, advocated going to war and promoted his recent book *The Threatening Storm: The Case for War in Iraq*. Another, Entifadh Qanbar, the president of Ahmed Chalabi's now-discredited Iraqi National Congress, made a claim tailor-made for Oprah's largely female audience, that Saddam Hussein had men on his payroll whose job was to rape women. Film clips were shown of now-discredited *New York Times* reporter Judith Miller arguing in support of war, and pro-Israeli author Eli Wiesel making an emotional plea for American intervention. Women in the audience who said that this show made them overcome their reluctance for a war against Iraq were applauded, while another who dared to suggest that it seemed like "propaganda" was verbally chastised by Oprah herself.

One day after Oprah's October 9 program, the House of Representatives voted in favor of war in Iraq at the executive branch's discretion, and two days after the Senate voted the same way. Oprah's producers would have been well aware of the importance of the content of the show broadcast on that day. Those were contested votes in which last-minute emails and calls to members of Congress may have made a difference, and Oprah did her part. Second, once the Republicans captured the Senate majority (which they did) and held the House of Representatives in November, Bush and the Republicans would have a free hand for two years. (And the Republican Party paid a steep price for that free hand in the 2006 and 2008 elections.) In fact, the saber-rattling against Iraq in the fall of 2002 was specifically designed with the midterm elections in mind, in the first instance, and some incumbent Democrats, like disabled veteran and genuine war hero Senator Max Cleland (Georgia) were attacked and defeated as "soft on defense." By February and March 2003, given the ongoing cheerleading by Fox News, CNN, and others, a few skeptics couldn't stop the war juggernaut, and the massive uprising among the rest of the media and the public that it would have required (and maybe would not have made a difference anyway) never happened. Of course, by 2008 some of those Republicans in the House and Senate retired or were defeated, but far too late for the victims of the Iraq War.

Popcorn and Politics

On November 11, 2001, four dozen of the Hollywood power elite met with President Bush's top adviser and strategist, Karl Rove, to explore how the entertainment industry could assist the administration's war on terrorism. Rove went through a list of points and projects that he thought might be addressed by Hollywood such as helping to issue a "call to service" to all Americans, helping the public to see the War on Terror as a fight against evil that requires global participation, and the preparation of public service messages that would help to spread pro-American messages at home and abroad.[40] Culture industry leaders acknowledged their expertise in this area. Film producer Lynda Obst said, "We are already propaganda experts. We are the veritable American Dream Machine. We hardly need any instruction from Karl Rove in this area." Jack Valenti, who as head of the Motion Picture Association of America is Hollywood's most powerful lobbyist, said, "This was about contributing Hollywood's creative imagination and their persuasion skills to help in this war effort." Bryce Zabel, chair and CEO of the Academy of Television Arts and Sciences, said, "We are willing to volunteer to become advocates for the American message." Zabel suggested that Hollywood's best filmmakers could each "do a three-minute piece on the theme 'My Country 'Tis of Thee' and then compile them together on video and airdrop them over areas hostile to us."[41]

Journalist Doug Saunders notes that the summit was largely unnecessary because for many years, Hollywood's most prominent products, its major studio films and TV series, have been almost indistinguishable from government-funded propaganda.

> With rare exceptions, whenever men in uniform appear on-screen, Hollywood has been singing Washington's song from the beginning. The flaws and grave errors in U.S. military and intelligence operations may loom large in history, but 50 years of cinema and TV have painted them in bright and unmottled hues. If Bush were to erect a soundstage on the White House lawn, he could not do a

better job getting the official line across than movies and TV shows have been doing for years.[42]

American poet Carl Sandburg declared in 1961 that "Hollywood is the foremost educational institute on earth [with] an audience that runs into an estimated 800 million to a billion," and he also plumbed the source of its influence: "Anything that brings you to tears by way of drama does something to the deepest roots of your personality."[43] Since entertainment is now the second largest U.S. export (second only to aerospace), this audience and Hollywood's role as an agent of socialization and hegemony have since increased significantly.[44] Unsurprisingly, the industry has also been mobilized as a major agent of militarization. This isn't just an ideological preference but also has commercial roots. As Carl Boggs and Tom Pollard note in their excellent book *The Hollywood War Machine*, in the last twenty years the cost of making movies has exploded, and ownership of film studios has become more concentrated in the hands of major multinational corporations such as General Electric, Gulf and Western, News Corporation, Sony, and Viacom. These corporations need significant returns on their operations and the safest way to get these returns is to produce low-risk militaristic films that are consonant with the militaristic culture.[45]

Central to Hollywood's involvement with militarism is its close relationship with the U.S. military. As explained by legal scholar Jonathan Turley, Hollywood and the Pentagon have long been part of a "symbiotic relationship in which each receives benefits from the others' work."[46] As we will see, combat films, and their often-rosy portrayal of military life, benefit the military by improving morale and facilitating recruitment, while producers and directors benefit from significant cost savings, since cooperation with the military grants them access to equipment, personnel, and technical advice. David Robb, in his book *Operation Hollywood*, notes that senior military officials view their cooperation with the movie industry as a way of turning movies into pro-military "commercials."[47]

The roots of Hollywood's connection to the military go back to World War I. Film played a significant role in rallying American support for involvement in the war, like Thomas Dixon's popular *The Fall of a Nation* (1916), which "ridiculed pacifists." Once the United States declared war on Germany in 1917, the small film industry was "fully mobilized" to support the effort. Along with "heavy censorship," antiwar pictures were banned, cinemas became the focus for patriotic rallies (a war tax was placed on admissions), movie stars sold liberty bonds, and official propaganda films toured the country." Thanks to its wartime role and shifting geopolitical relations in Europe, World War I was the impetus for Hollywood's emergence as the world's preeminent film industry.[48]

Collaboration between the War Department and Hollywood continued during the 1920s, most notably in *Wings* (1927), a story about World War I pilots that featured army aircrafts and soldiers, and the first film to win the Academy Award for Best Picture.[49] Military film production declined in the 1930s because of the Great Depression and public opposition to militaristic engagement in the world (often referred to as "isolationism"), but then militaristic films played a key role in bolstering support for U.S. involvement in World War II. For example, the War Department assisted and fast-tracked the production of *Air Force* (1943), because it was "a special Air Corps recruiting job."[50] The close alignment between Hollywood and the military was best exemplified by Frank Capra's propaganda series *Why We Fight* (1942–1945), produced by the War Department. Wartime films were dominated by "the good-war narrative"—they "dwelled on noble American military triumphs over evil monsters"[51]—themes that were later central to the Cold War militarizing of Hollywood, and the rhetoric of which we are seeing being revived to characterize the renewed attack on Afghanistan in the Obama era. Music made a significant contribution to wartime movies, primarily by aiding in presenting German, Italian and especially Japanese enemies as ruthless and inhuman.[52]

The movies promoted militarism not only by presenting combat as noble and relatively bloodless; they also used humor's tendency to lower the viewer's guard, to use a boxing term. During World War II and in the fifteen years after, comedies helped humanize the military, which assisted with recruiting during both wartime and peacetime. The best known of these were the wartime movies of The Three Stooges, including *Boobs in Arms* (1940) and *G.I. Stooge* (1944), and Abbott and Costello, notably *Buck Privates* (1941), *In the Navy* (1941), and *Buck Privates Come Home* (1947). The Bowery Boys (the successor to the Dead End Boys), a group of Lower East Side New Yorkers, acted in almost fifty comedies from 1946 to 1958, including *Bowery Battalion* (1951), *Let's Go Navy!* (1951), and *Here Comes the Marines* (1952).[53] As for the plot of all these films, the focus was usually on how the stars accidentally join up, by being chased into a recruiting station, plus basic-training antics, like in *Buck Privates*. Another plot was that the stars solve various mysteries or crimes, in which service people are the victims of civilian crooks and swindlers, a common theme in the Bowery Boys films. Finally, on occasion the stars, in spite of themselves, cracked a spy ring or gun runners. As Lawrence Suid says, military comedies can serve to present the military as a institution in which young people will feel positive about joining. This was true about films in the 1940s just as it was in the era of the revival of the military comedy (as part of the rehabilitation of the military) in the 1980s, illustrated by *Private Benjamin* (1980) and *Stripes* (1981).[54]

Early Cold War films were characterized by heavy military involvement—the navy supported *The Frogmen* (1951), the Marine Corps aided *Stars and Stripes Forever* (1952), the army helped *Between Heaven and Hell* (1956), and the air force supported *The Hunters* (1958).[55] As Doug Davis notes, the U.S. Air Force made supporting "sympathetic" films a high priority in the 1950s and early 1960s, as part of its effort to control the sorts of "strategic fictions" that would be shown to the public. Jimmy Stewart was given a citation of honor for acting (as a pilot) in 1955's *Strategic Air Command*, and air force general Curtis LeMay fought congressional attempts to ban Pentagon-military cooperation and also helped rush *A Gathering of Eagles* (1963), a pro-military film featuring B-52 long-range bombers, into theaters in advance of Stanley Kubrick's critical and satirical work *Dr. Strangelove* (1964).[56] Like *Fail-Safe* and *Seven Days in May*, *Strangelove* challenged U.S.-Soviet nuclear weapons doctrines, and did not receive support from the Pentagon. *Dr. Strangelove*, as the most creative and least propagandistic of all these films, has held up the best.

As the United States engaged in Vietnam, cooperation between Hollywood and the military reached a new high. John Wayne's *The Green Berets* (1968) received so much support that Don Baruch, head of the Pentagon's film office, had the official Department of Defense credit taken out of the film. In his own words, Baruch was afraid the association might detract from "propaganda value of the film," and might increase "letters of inquiry on how [the] film received assistance."[57]

Before we go on to look at movies during the 1970s and onward, it should be said that militaristic film in the United States has not focused only on interstate wars of the twentieth century. A major form of militaristic film in the United States occupied itself with the first major case of "pacification" (Vietnam being the second), specifically the genre know as the "Western." Tom Engelhardt notes that it has been estimated that one-quarter of all films made in the United States between 1910 and 1960 were Westerns.[58] Predominantly, these movies presented the American Indian as the internal version of the Japanese and German adversary, incomprehensible, ruthless, and faceless. The same themes were played out—good versus evil, civilization versus barbarism, honesty versus deception—albeit on the western frontier rather than across the seas. Of course, the European-descended Americans were the "good guys" (African Americans were airbrushed out of the picture) and violence and mass killing were presented as "how the West was won." Even more so than war programming, western television series were also dominant on the small screen in the 1950s and early 1960s.[59]

In 1965, early in the era of direct U.S. involvement in Vietnam, the U.S. DoD engaged directly in pro-war propaganda with a short, thirty-one-minute film entitled *Why Viet-Nam*,[60] modeled on the Capra World War II series referenced earlier. It is not clear that the film had much influence, because it is not much remembered and is only rarely discussed.[61] It is important for a number of reasons, however, particularly because its arguments will be familiar to those who lived through the run-up to the U.S. invasion of Iraq. This was a black-and-white documentary that made the case for continuing U.S. involvement and escalation in Vietnam. It excerpts speeches from President Johnson, Defense Secretary Robert McNamara, and Secretary of State Dean Rusk. It is remarkable because it presents the Vietnam issue in the "frame" established by the dominant interpretation of World War II and the Korean Conflict. To wit: the Western powers made a mistake in not standing up to Hitler at Munich, and the consequence was World War II. The U.S. reaction to the outbreak of hostilities in Korea—immediate attack—is the model that should govern the United States in Vietnam. What the world would later regard as a civil war in Vietnam was presented as a war of aggression by the "International Communist Conspiracy" in which the Vietnamese strings were being pulled by "Red China" and "Soviet Russia." It should be no surprise that the United States and South Vietnam are presented as the victims of Northern Vietnamese aggression.

This is classic propaganda particularly because so many of the claims are now known to be false and either were known or should have been known to be false at the time, certainly by government officials. There is discussion of U.S. support for the French military until 1954, but no admission that France was trying to reestablish its colonial domination over Indochina; while it is claimed that South Vietnam was an electoral democracy, there is no admission that the United States sabotaged the provision for unifying elections in the late 1950s under the Geneva Accords because it expected a North Vietnamese victory; while it is claimed North Vietnam violated the Geneva Accords, there was no recognition that the United States did not even sign the Geneva Accords and did not feel bound by them. There was no mention of the assassination of President Diem in 1961 and the succession of military dictators, even though this happened with U.S. knowledge and support; the North Vietnamese "attacks" on the USS *Maddox* and USS *Turner Joy* in the Gulf of Tonkin in 1964 are prominently featured though it is known that these attacks never took place.[62] North Vietnamese leader Ho Chi Minh was presented as a monster who had and would continue to brutalize his own people and threaten international peace and security. They should have known that the two major players in the so-called International Communist Conspiracy had fallen out with each other by the early 1960s.

For Tom Engelhardt, this short film reveals a defensiveness that indicates the disintegration of U.S. "victory culture." For our purposes, these themes— an international conspiracy, the ghost of appeasement of Adolf Hitler, and the United States as the innocent victim—show the deep cultural roots of militarist thinking, as well as a particular pattern of shop-worn thought that is familiar to those who listened to the Bush arguments for the need to invade Iraq. But this also shows the limits of the medium. The lies worked for a time but the Vietnam War became very unpopular in the United States by the late 1960s and early 1970s. That is another parallel with the first decade of this new millennium.

The 1970s was a period of crisis for the relationship between Hollywood and the military, because of "a growing negative impression of the U.S. military brought on by the Vietnam War."[63] Because of that war's unpopularity, audiences were more open to movies that presented a different side of the conflict, such as *Apocalypse Now* (1979) and *The Deer Hunter* (1978), to name two famous ones, often produced without Defense Department support. It should be noted that in almost all cases, notwithstanding the mythology, the flowering of antiwar movies in the late 1970s offered only a limited critique of war and the U.S. war in Vietnam. As Boggs and Pollard note, even these critical films tend to focus on the Vietnam War as primarily an American experience, rather than Vietnamese; they often posit an American innocence, both of the country and the noble grunts who fight its wars; as a new version of the Yellow Peril, the Vietnamese are often either stereotyped or portrayed as one-dimensional or rendered invisible; these films present horrors and atrocities but despite the "asymmetry" of that war, with U.S. advantages in firepower and its highly destructive outcome, all combatants are seen as equally culpable as part of a universal message; and these films often lack depth and provide little historical context of U.S. involvement in the war, as just discussed.[64] Of course, as we will see, for every *Apocalypse Now* and *Deer Hunter* there are cinematic efforts to revive the good war tradition, as in Sylvester Stallone's *Rambo* and Chuck Norris's *MIA* series. To sum up, despite the self-image, self-presentation, and intentions of directors like Michael Cimino, Francis Ford Coppola, and Hal Ashby (*Coming Home*), American antiwar movies only rarely surmount commercial and psychological barriers and get to the real heart of the impact of militarism on the United States and the world. When asked about the possibility of U.S. reparations for Vietnam, President Jimmy Carter said he opposed this, and famously said "The damage was mutual," even though Vietnam never attacked U.S. territory. This same thinking turned up even in "antiwar" film in the Carter era.

But, like in many other branches of culture, the 1980s and 1990s was a period in which militarists fought back, using culture in part to shake the so-called Vietnam Syndrome. The relationship between Hollywood and the military was rebuilt in the 1980s, with a "new cycle of ultrapatriotic, militaristic films," like Tony Scott's *Top Gun* (1986) and the *Rambo* series.[65] It is also worth noting that as the mood of an era changes, as it has numerous times since the 1970s, so too the way that viewers see post-Vietnam films changes. "All history is contemporary history," as Italian philosopher Benedetto Croce put it, in which each generation writes its own version of the past. At the movies, "all film viewing is contemporary," for each new audience will get different things from films, and this can limit the impact of the filmmaker's intentions. Andrew Martin relays the comment of Anthony Swofford, the author of *Jarhead*, which was made into an Iraq war film in 2005. Swofford notes that soldiers about to go to Iraq would watch the post-Vietnam films mentioned above not for the political content but purely for the combat action, as a kind of "war porn."[66]

New technology of the 1990s "reshaped both filmmaking and military action," as well as their relationship with each other, and themes of "patriotism, technological wizardry, and combat heroism" pervaded post–Cold War cinema.[67] The Cold War with the Soviet Union ended in 1989–1990, but militaristic movies did not. The box-office profits on military-assisted movies like *Clear and Present Danger* (1994), *Air Force One* (1997), *Armageddon* (1998), and *Saving Private Ryan* (1998) were high, in part because of the economic benefits to the industry of continued cooperation with the DoD. Arising from this close relationship, during the Clinton era Steven Spielberg was awarded the Department of Defense Medal for Distinguished Public Service in 1998 for *Saving Private Ryan*. In 1999, the association between Hollywood and the military intensified with the establishment of the Institute of Creative Technologies, as we noted in the previous chapter, in which screenwriters collaborate with military experts to create stories and technologies used in action movies, games, and military training simulations.[68]

As a result of 9/11, and the interpretation of the events of that day as an act of war against the United States, the mood in the country shifted from a focus on downplaying borders, increasing trade and economic growth (characteristic of the Clinton era), to a focus more on security and military issues, which tend to trump other concerns when they arise (the Bush era). Hollywood's approach was directed by video store trends, where demand for patriotic action films "skyrocketed." *Pearl Harbor*, which was previously "perceived as a moderate failure at the box office," rapidly became the nation's most rented movie. Terrorism and war films became extremely popular, as Americans wanted vicarious revenge and "bloody retribution." Films like *Black Hawk Down* (2002) and *The Sum of All Fears* (2002)—both granted equipment and technical support by the Pentagon[69]—had their release dates moved up to take advantage of this trend.[70] As Doug Davis says:

> In mass culture, tales of nuclear terrorism have accordingly replaced tales of nuclear wars as popular expressions of the nation's new grand narrative of national

security, one not of strategic defense but of strategic defenselessness, that now accompanies the Bush administration's grand strategy of unilateral preemptive war and homeland defense. It is a tale of future catastrophic attack whose mass telling unites Americans as terrorized subjects in a war on terror.[71]

Between 2003 and 2005, Hollywood's dedication to the war became apparent as revenge, violence, and militarism pervaded the industry. *War of the Worlds*, *Terminator 3*, *Master and Commander*, the *Kill Bill* films, and *Mr. and Mrs. Smith* are all evidence of this trend, as are more recent Pentagon-supported films like *Transformers* (2007) and *Iron Man* (2008). Notably, there are many overt parallels with post-9/11 paranoia and the War on Terror. For example, Carl Boggs suggests that the aliens in Steven Spielberg's military-aided *War of the Worlds* "symbolize an omnipresent threat that is supposed to bring to mind the grave menace of dispersed, elusive Al Qaeda operations," as evidenced by one young girl's question, "Is it the terrorists?"[72] As Doug Davis points out, the Bush 2003 State of the Union address justifying a U.S. war in Iraq could have been drawn from the script of *The Peacemaker* (2002), a film in which preemptive war is justified in order to keep WMDs out of the hands of potential terrorists.[73]

Militarizing the Movies

Although the longstanding collaboration of the military and Hollywood is arguably symbiotic, it is highly unequal. According to Philip Strub, chief of the Pentagon's liaison office, films must satisfy three criteria to be eligible for assistance: They must "depict military life as 'realistically' as possible"; must "inform the public about U.S. military prowess";[74] and must "aid in the retention and recruitment of personnel." During the shooting of an approved film, a military supervisor must be on set, to ensure that the film agreements are met. Finally, assisted films must be prescreened by Pentagon officials before their release to the public.[75] The Pentagon's Phil Strub is quoted as saying that the Pentagon places a high priority on using entertainment to recruit and boost the morale of people in the service, in order to retain them in the all-volunteer military.[76] The military is unique among U.S. government agencies, especially compared to the CIA and other intelligence organizations. This is because the key carrot is the provision of military hardware, which only the Pentagon possesses. The CIA is more likely to be presented negatively because it doesn't have much leverage to influence scripts. "The real money shot in any presentation of the [CIA] is the lobby scene with the seal of the agency on the floor," says CIA film liaison Chase Brandon, and that's it.[77]

Despite these assertions about realism, the record reveals that the Pentagon's first priority is the creation of a positive image for the forces, whether it is justified or "realistic" or not. Boggs has identified several images that they endorse, among them that the U.S. military is "driven by noble ends," that enemy forces are "primitive and barbaric," that Americans "inevitably triumph," that they have "supreme technology," and ultimately that "militarism is associated to heroism."[78] Many directors have self-censored their work to create these images, and Pentagon officials frequently require script changes. For example, David Robb reports that the Pentagon insisted that a joke alluding to the Vietnam War be removed from the James Bond film *Tomorrow Never Dies* (1997),[79] and major revisions were required for *Renaissance Man* (1994)—"an entire scene was rewritten by the army, dialogue was changed," and one character was cut out completely.[80] Historically inaccurate revisions are also often required. In *Black Hawk Down*, the name of a military hero was changed due to his real-life status as a child molester.[81] In *We Were Soldiers* (2002), the Vietnam-era army is portrayed as "a refuge from a divided society where all men are equal," even though discrimination was pervasive in the army at that time.[82] The directors of *Windtalkers* (2002) were forced to remove a number of scenes, including a historically accurate one depicting a marine, "the dentist," taking gold teeth from dead Japanese soldiers because, according to Capt. Matt Morgan, it "displays distinctly un-Marine behavior."[83] Clearly, the goal of the Department of Defense is "first and foremost to produce movies that portray the glory of the U.S." military.[84]

Many films have been denied support for failing Pentagon "positive image" requirements, including *A Few Good Men* (1992), *Independence Day* (1996), and *G.I. Jane* (1997).[85] Dozens of movies did not receive support because movie makers would not alter their scripts sufficiently, like *Thirteen Days* (2000) and many others.[86] Even a script that is significantly revised may not get Pentagon support. For example, the early version of the script for *Forrest Gump* (1994) clearly portrayed Forrest, the main character played by Tom Hanks, and his entire military unit, as part of Defense Secretary Robert McNamara's plan for 350,000 low-intelligence recruits, the so-called Moron Corps. Because of Pentagon objections, the producers made this and many other changes, leaving only Forrest and his friend Bubba as soldiers with subpar intelligence. But these changes were not enough for the military, which refused to provide support for the project, despite all the edits that were made. Unbelievably, the Pentagon remained upset that the script had Forrest Gump refer to his captain as "Captain Dan" (his first name), and this ultimately stayed in the movie.[87] Finally, although Clint Eastwood received assistance for *Heartbreak Ridge* (1986), he failed to omit a scene in which a military officer shoots a defenseless Cuban soldier. Furious, the military withdrew its approval, banned it from military theaters overseas and U.S. bases, and barred Eastwood (a registered Republican) from screening it at a military charity benefit for which he was chair.[88] In another case, Dean Devlin, the maker of *Independence Day*, made many changes to his script but still did not get Pentagon support. Even though he told them that "[i]f this [movie] doesn't make every boy in the country want to fly a fighter jet, I'll eat this script," the Pentagon still shot him down.[89] Numerous directors comment that good drama requires conflict, while the Pentagon frequently calls for the elimination of conflict (and the drama) if in any way the conflict reflects badly on the military. Robb cites evidence that the Pentagon is concerned with the number of viewers who are "exposed" to pro-military movies, with no regard for film quality.[90]

In some cases, film scripts that do not receive support do not get made. One such case is *Countermeasures*, written by Darryl Ponicsan and slated as a major Disney release in the mid 1990s. It was a thriller set on a U.S. aircraft carrier which focused on a secret operation involving the sale of spare jet parts to Iran, modeled on the Iran-Contra scandal of the 1980s, and sabotage, murder, sexual harassment, and cover-up. The U.S. Navy said that it ultimately would not support a movie that presented a negative portrayal of navy life, even though the events portrayed were well documented. Ponsican commented that in a film that he made in the 1970s without navy support (*Cinderella Liberty*), there was even a class element to the navy censorship. "They said that it was okay to show an enlisted man drunk or swearing, but not an officer." *Countermeasures* was never made because it could not be made without an aircraft carrier, the producers said, and no country would provide one.[91]

David Robb argues, correctly, that this abridging of the creative freedom of movie producers has serious implications for U.S. life and the U.S. Constitution. The justifiably celebrated First Amendment to the U.S. Constitution reads as follows:

> Congress shall make no law respecting an establishment of religion, or prohibiting the free exercise thereof; *or abridging the freedom of speech, or of the press*; or the right of the people peaceably to assemble, and to petition the Government for a redress of grievances. (Emphasis added)

This language is 220 years old but its meaning should be clear. The U.S. government or any agency associated with it cannot by the exercise of its discretion favor one form of private speech or media content over another. And yet isn't that what the DoD does in favoring some scripts over others? In 1995, Justice Anthony Kennedy wrote for the U.S. Supreme Court in *Rosenberger v. The University of Virginia* that "[i]t is axiomatic that the government may not regulate speech based on its substantive content or the message it conveys. . . .

In the realm of private speech or expression, government regulation may not favor one speaker over another."[92] In all likelihood, the Pentagon's conditions for use of U.S. military assets and personnel is unconstitutional.

David Robb concludes by arguing that allowing the U.S. military to influence film production is destructive of the U.S. psyche and a free society, and he makes a number of recommendations, including that Pentagon editing of movie scripts should end, and that DoD equipment and personnel should be provided for movie production to all based on a common fee schedule. He notes,

> Even without Pentagon subsidies, Hollywood will still turn out plenty of movies and TV shows about the military. That's because of one simple fact. Hollywood loves heroes and the military has more of them than anyone else.[93]

If David Robb is right, then even in the absence of Pentagon support for militaristic films there will still be such films. This is because militaristic films still sell, especially among young people who disproportionately constitute the moviegoing public, and because of the ideological preferences of some producers and directors. But it would also create a level playing field for directors regardless of their views. As Boggs suggests, "the glorified militarism favored by producers like Jerry Bruckheimer has surely been driven more by ideological than by technical priorities."[94]

Creating Enemies

To the extent that there is an ideological proclivity to support militarism and to scapegoat certain people, in contemporary Hollywood it seems to be directed at Arabs, and secondarily, other brown people, such as "narcoterrorists" from Latin America. Hollywood films have long glorified and justified violence against terrorists—Arab terrorists in particular—who over the last twenty years replaced Communists as the dominant villains. Significantly, as observed by Boggs and Tom Pollard, "homegrown" terrorists like those associated with local militias are never featured in Hollywood films; instead they always present "alien demons," like in *United 93* (2006), in which "cruel, sadistic terrorists filled with irrational hatred attack innocent Americans."[95] As Jack Shaheen, a leading critic of Hollywood's portrayal of Arabs, puts it, post–Cold War military-assisted films such as *True Lies* (1994) and *Executive Decision* (1996) all depicted "rabidly anti-American" Arab terrorists, who represent not just a credible military threat but also a challenge to Western civilization and world order.[96] Boggs and Pollard see these characters presented without historical background or political motivations, as nihilistic and irrational, stereotyped villains characterized by "blind aggression," "suicidal impulses," and "sheer madness." The prevalence of these stereotypes greatly troubles Shaheen, who suggests that "damaging portraits, notably those presenting Arabs as America's enemy, affect all people, influencing world public opinion and policy." Boggs and Pollard also object to these stereotypes, arguing that Hollywood's representations of "good versus evil" and "democracy versus tyranny" legitimize the American foreign policy driven by unilateralism, militarism, and interventionism.[97]

Not only do Hollywood films create and perpetuate Arab-as-terrorist stereotypes, they legitimize vengeful violence toward them, and other people of color. For example, in *Collateral Damage* (2002), Arnold Schwarzenegger undertakes a "crusade for justice" against Colombian terrorists after a bombing kills his family, ultimately promoting violent revenge as the "appropriate responses to terrorist attacks that kill American civilians." This message has particular implications in a post-9/11 world, because U.S. overseas military campaigns in Afghanistan and Iraq are justified as responses to the 9/11 attacks and required to wipe terrorism off the face of the earth. Additionally, a plot twist also reveals the terrorist's wife as a dangerous villain, which suggests that "every Colombian is a potential terrorist." As Joseph Kay says, this rationale reflects that of the "War on Terror"—that "everyone associated with supposed terrorists are also terrorists and deserve the same fate: death."[98]

The appropriateness of violence as a response to Arab terrorists is also central to Pentagon-aided *Rules of Engagement* (2002). Samuel L. Jackson, as Col. Terry Childers, orders his soldiers to fire on a group of civilians outside the American embassy in Yemen, leading to an investigation into his actions and a court-martial. However, in the end the audience witnesses the "wisdom" of Childers's decision. In a re-creation of the scene, the final presentation of *what really happened*, the audience is shown the civilians, including many women and children in full body covering (*burka*), revealing their weapons from under their clothing, in almost comic-book fashion, and shooting at the marines. This is historically inaccurate, in that Yemen was until recently a politically stable country with which the United States has had peaceful relations for decades. Having finished watching *Rules of Engagement*, the viewer might well conclude that when U.S. troops fire on an allegedly civilian mob, the troops should be believed when they or their commander say they saw weapons.

Trickle-Down Patriotism

So far in this chapter we have seen how Hollywood, and other segments of the entertainment industry, have a predominant role in support of militarism. Despite Hollywood's "liberal reputation," many members of the entertainment industry—movies, televisions, sports—also support the military, and militarism, on their own time. Though conservatives have repeated the claim of "liberal Hollywood," there is in fact a large militaristic contingent which helps explain so much of the Hollywood product. In the run-up to the Iraq War there were many conservatives speaking out, if only to nullify what their liberal colleagues were saying. This is a group that includes prominent actors Bruce Willis, Ron Silver, Dennis Miller, Fred Thompson, rapper Kid Rock, and many others.[99] But more importantly, pro-military Hollywood is increasingly organized. By 2008, actors Gary Sinise and Jon Voight, singer Pat Boone, screenwriter Lionet Chetwynd, and producer Craig Hoffman, were openly talking about a group called "Friends of Abe," named for Abraham Lincoln. According to Pat Boone, this is an "underground organization" that has grown from a few dozen people to as many as six hundred, judging from the attendance at a social event at an unnamed billionaire's estate in California.[100] Director David Zucker, a self-identified conservative known for *Airplane!* and *The Naked Gun* series and other comedies, and more recently for *An American Carol*, spoke at length in August 2008 about his perception that both Hollywood and the country are controlled by "the left." While some conservatives no doubt deliberately down play their own historical influence, some seem genuinely unaware of the influence, shown earlier in this chapter, of conservatism and militarism in Hollywood over many decades.[101]

Pro-military Hollywood sometimes supports the cause just by speaking out or working for conservative candidates, but they also do so through the United Service Organizations, better known as the USO. Formed in early 1941, just before the United States entered World War II, the USO's self-proclaimed mission is to strengthen the connections between U.S. military personnel throughout the world and U.S. society. They do this by sending care packages to the troops and operating airport lounges and drop-in centers, sometimes with celebrity help. There is always a strong ideological element to USO activities. For example, in late 2009 Rep. Nancy Pelosi (House Speaker) and Dr. Jill Biden (wife of the vice president) participated in filling care packages for women in the military. Packages customized for women was an innovation, though in this case it played to gender stereotypes, by including lipstick, make-up, and copies of *Cosmopolitan* magazine.[102]

But the USO is best known for its entertainment tours, which also have strong ideological content. In 2009, the USO organized fifty-two tours ranging from a single day and performance to seven to ten days, mainly in Iraq, Afghanistan, Korea, and Okinawa, with performers from movies, television, and sports. The roster of participants reads like a who's who of the entertainment industry. Some, like country performer Toby Keith, are committed conservatives who unabashedly support militarism. Others are liberals, like now-senator

Al Franken, who traveled to perform even with his doubts about the wisdom of the conflict. Some, like Stephen Colbert, make the trip to Iraq, as he did in June 2009, perhaps hoping to get some laughs out of it and maybe make his point as well. In speaking to David Letterman (who, along with his band leader Paul Shaffer, has also entertained for USO), Colbert self-deprecated, said that the standard body armor is "flattering to the middle aged torso," and that he was "issued the helmet of Michael Dukakis." Admittedly, traveling to entertain the troops in Iraq gave Colbert opportunities for anti-militarist comedy before he left and after he returned. Before he left, he made much of the secrecy regarding where he and his *Colbert Nation* crew were actually going. He was also able to deliver some zingers, such as "A country is our ally in between when we give them weapons and when they use them." He also at one point showed a photoshopped picture of an elongated bomber, which he referred to as the "F-88 Overcompensator," a suspiciously long penile aircraft.[103]

In practice, there are obligatory tributes to the "brave" troops and praise "for the great job they are doing." In a time when these missions are controversial at home, militarists know that they need to continually reinforce morale, so that the service people's commitment doesn't weaken. But what do the celebrities get? It is an adventure for them, and for those who are liberal and tend toward antiwar positions (the Al Frankens), it provides them with political cover. But it can also be a form of war tourism. Eva Torres, a WWE (wrestling) RAW Diva who was part of a tour of buff men and attractive women, says that part of the fun for her in going on one of these tours is that she got to shoot a .50 caliber machine gun and ride in the gunner's spot in a mine resistant ambush protected (MRAP) vehicle.[104] The chance to see or meet these celebrities provides soldiers and sailors with a privilege they might not get in civilian life, and makes military life that much more bearable.

But the clearest indication of the ideological nature of USO activities is found in a program which it runs along with the Troops First Foundation called "Operation Proper Exit." This program brings American service people who left Iraq or Afghanistan with wounds back to the country to meet other soldiers and see the area they were in. According to Rick Kell, of the Troops First Foundation, the purpose of the program is to show service people, many of whom have lost limbs, that "Iraq is getting better," and so they can "see that their sacrifices are meaningful." Testimonials from recovering soldiers show them making remarks that the program gave "me an opportunity to leave under my own power," "to leave the right way," and "it goes to show how far this place [Ramadi] has come." No doubt this is intended to reassure serving troops that there is life after the service and after getting wounded, and it also helps spread the gospel at home that U.S. forces are doing good work and that the situation is improving and therefore the sacrifices are worth it.[105]

Conclusion

The broadcast media and film industry largely promoted the U.S. wars of the last decade, in Afghanistan and Iraq. Advertising picked up on militaristic themes after 9/11, and promoted both their products and militarism. Even on the "liberal fringe," when it really counted, before October 10–11 and November 5, 2009, Oprah Winfrey was promoting a U.S. war in Iraq. Only after the damage was done did she, along with so many others, try to shift course somewhat, and that was too little too late. To refer to the concept of hegemony, any cultural product that normalizes or reinforces established practices or goals can be seen as contributing to the continuation of a hegemonic regime.

In the 1970s, in the wake of the disaster of the Vietnam War, the public was more supportive of cultural products that questioned militarism, however limited that questioning might have been. Arguably we are in a similar moment today, after the disaster of the U.S.-led wars in Afghanistan and Iraq, and we may be in a post-hegemonic order, or it may be that there is currently a contest between whether a hegemonic militaristic order can be sustained, or rebuilt. We will examine cultural products that oppose militarism and are playing a role in this struggle in chapters 7 and 8. But it is clear that the dominant trend has been movie and television industries that have catered to militaristic tastes. This has been aided by DoD favoritism toward militaristic films, and regardless of the era film has found an enemy to pillory, whether it was Germans or Japanese, Red Indians, Vietnamese or other communists, or Arab or Latino terrorists more recently. The extent of the efforts to use culture, through advertising, comic books, movies, and other media, to mobilize support for programs like the War on Terror is unknown to most people, and is an indication that such a proposal as unending war seems dubious without this effort. What is remarkable is that despite all the efforts to promote militarism it is always fragile, as we discovered in a previous chapter when we discussed the difficulty of convincing the U.S. population to agree to go to war. Liberal actors and comedians who may want to insulate themselves from McCarthyite charges of disloyalty find that a tour with the USO is good public relations.

Notes

1. Julia Day, "Sony to Cash in on Iraq with 'Shock and Awe' Game," *Guardian*, April 2003, www.guardian.co.uk/technology/2003/apr/10/games.Iraqandthemedia (accessed August 5, 2009).

2. "Drive a Stake into It, OK?" *Los Angeles Times*, November 2, 2003, http://articles.latimes.com/2003/nov/02/opinion/ed-shock2 (accessed February 14, 2010).

3. Kate Silver, "Bin Laden Merchandisers Cash In," *Las Vegas Weekly*, November 9, 2001, www.alternet.org/story/11897/?page=entire (accessed August 4, 2009).

4. Anne-Marie Schleiner, "Velvet-Strike: War Times and Reality Games," *NOEMA*, 2002, www.noemalab.org/sections/ideas/ideas_articles/pdf/schleiner_velvet_strike.pdf (accessed August 13, 2009).

5. Schleiner, "Velvet-Strike."

6. American-Arab Anti-Discrimination Committee, "Protest 'Wack the Iraq' Game in New Jersey," ADC Press Release, August 25, 2004, www.adc.org/index.php?id=2319 (accessed August 4, 2009).

7. Henry A. Giroux, "The Emerging Authoritarianism in the United States: Political Culture under the Bush/Cheney Administration," *symploke* 14, nos. 1–2 (2006): 125.

8. Pro-war bumper stickers, www.bumperart.com/War+(Pro).htm (accessed February 18, 2010).

9. For thousands of products, see Café Press bumper stickers, www.cafepress.ca/+pro-war+bumper-stickers (accessed February 18, 2010).

10. Kenneth Cloke, "Mediating Evil, War, and Terrorism: The Politics of Conflict," Beyond Intractability, www.beyondintractability.org/essay/mediating_evil/ (accessed August 4, 2009).

11. Sheldon Rampton and John Stauber, "Trading on Fear," *Guardian*, July 12, 2003, www.commondreams.org/views03/0712-01.htm (accessed April 15, 2009); Jennifer Scanlon, "'Your Flag Decal Won't Get You into Heaven Anymore': U.S. Consumers, Wal-Mart, and the Commodification of Patriotism," in *The Selling of 9/11: How a National Tragedy Became a Commodity*, ed. Dana Heller (New York: Palgrave Macmillan, 2005), 174.

12. Rampton and Stauber, "Trading on Fear."

13. Sarah Turner, "Cashing in on Patriotism," *CounterPunch*, October 25, 2001, www.counterpunch.org/turner1.html (accessed April 11, 2009).

14. Wendy, "Framing Consumerism as Patriotism," Sociological Images Contexts Blogs, June 13, 2008, http://contexts.org/socimages/2008/06/13/framing-consumerism-as-patriotism/ (accessed April 11, 2009).

15. Sandra Silberstein, *War of Words: Language, Politics, and 9/11* (New York: Routledge, 2002), 125.

16. Dana Heller, "Introduction: Consuming 9/11," in Heller, *Selling of 9/11*, 19.

17. Joe Lockard, "Social Fear and the *Terrorism Survival Guide*," in Heller, *Selling of 9/11*, 221.

18. Amy Chozick, "From Military to Civilians, Hooah! Bar Crosses Front Lines," *Wall Street Journal*, March 7, 2004, B1.

19. CJ, "Disney Offers Free Vacations to Troops," Veterans' Administration Mortgage Center, January 11, 2009, www.vamortgagecenter.com/blog/2009/01/11/disney-offers-free-vacations-to-troops/#comments (accessed February 16, 2010).

20. Nathan Hodge, "Iron Eagle Nominee: The Awesomely Bad 'Future Combat' Mini-Series," *Wired*, March 6, 2009, www.wired.com/dangerroom/2009/03/iron-eagles-the/#previouspost (accessed February 16, 2010).

21. Denise Logsdon, "Comic Book Heros of the Golden Age," History of Comic Books, www.cartage.org.lb/en/themes/Arts/drawings/Comicstrip/HistoryofComics/ComicBookHeros/ComicBookHeros.htm (accessed June 25, 2008).

22. Wolfgang J. Fuchs and R. Reitberger, *Comics: Anatomy of a Mass Medium* (Boston: Little, Brown & Co., 1972), 100.

23. Richard Halegua, "The History of Comics: Part Five," Comic Art and Graffix Gallery, www.comic-art.com/history/history5.htm (accessed June 25, 2008).

24. Larry Holmes, Jonathan O' Beirne, and Glenn Perreira, "Shocking Event for Captain America," *CNN*, March 7, 2007, http://edition.cnn.com/2007/SHOWBIZ/books/03/07/captain.america/index.html (accessed June 26, 2008).

25. Halegua, "History of Comics."

26. Christian Dailly, "Captain America: The United States versus Itself, Through the Eyes of a Wartime Fictional Hero," *American Studies Today* 16 (September 2007), www.americansc.org.uk/Online/ASToday%202007.pdf (accessed August 13, 2009).

27. Henry Jenkins, "Comic Book Foreign Policy? Part One," Confessions of an Aca-Fan: The Official Weblog of Henry Jenkins, July 27, 2006, www.henryjenkins.org/2006/07/comic_book_foreign_policy_part.html (accessed June 17, 2008).

28. Jenkins, "Comic Book Foreign Policy?"

29. Jenkins, "Comic Book Foreign Policy?"

30. Michael Dean, "The New Patriotism: Comics and the War in Iraq Part II," The Comics Journal, May 23, 2006, www.tcj.com/index.php?option=com_content&task=view&id=362&Itemid=48 (accessed June 26, 2008).

31. Scott Thill, "Holy Terror! Frank Miller Is Ready for His Fatwa," *Wired*, April 29, 2007, www.wired.com/underwire/2007/04/holy_terror_fra/ (accessed August 13, 2009).

32. Tim Walker, "Iraq: How a Daring New Generation of Graphic Novelists View the Art of War," *Independent*, June 23, 2008, www.independent.co.uk/news/world/middle-east/iraq-how-a-daring-new-generation-of-graphic-novelists-view-the-art-of-war-852259.html (accessed August 13, 2009).

33. Jenkins, "Comic Book Foreign Policy?"

34. Walker, "Iraq."

35. Robert Jensen, "Dan Rather and the Problem with Patriotism: Steps toward the Redemption of American Journalism and Democracy," *Global Media Journal* 2, no. 3 (Fall 2003), http://uts.cc.utexas.edu/~rjensen/freelance/attack41.htm (accessed August 3, 2009).

36. "Oprah Winfrey," AuditionAgency, www.auditionagency.com/tv/oprah_winfrey.htm (accessed July 13, 2009).

37. "#155 Oprah Winfrey," The Forbes 400 Richest People in America, www.forbes.com/lists/2008/54/400list08_Oprah-Winfrey_O0ZT.html (accessed July 13, 2009).

38. See Oprah.com, www.oprah.com/index (accessed July 13, 2009).

39. David Peterson, "RE: The Oprah Winfrey Show," e-mail to Project-x mailing list, October 9, 2002, https://lists.resist.ca/pipermail/project-x/2002-October/000714.html (accessed July 12, 2009). This is in addition to many dissenting academics and journalists who get little opportunity to speak on television.

40. Rick Lyman "A Nation Challenged: The Entertainment Industry; Hollywood Discusses Role in War Effort," *New York Times*, November 12, 2001; Doug Saunders, "Hollywood, DC," *Globe and Mail*, November 17, 2001.

41. Marc Cooper, "Hollywood Enlists in the War," *Nation*, November 21, 2001, www.thenation.com/doc.mhtml?i=20011210&s=cooper (accessed August 4, 2009).

42. Saunders, "Hollywood, DC."

43. Sandburg as cited in Etienne Augé, "Hollywood Movies: Terrorism 101," *Cercles* 5 (2002): 148, www.cercles.com/n5/auge.pdf.

44. Scott Robert Olson, "Hollywood Planet," in *The Television Studies Reader*, ed. R. C. Allen and A. Hill (London: Routledge, 2003), 115.

45. Carl Boggs and Tom Pollard, *The Hollywood War Machine: U.S. Militarism and Popular Culture* (Boulder, CO, and London: Paradigm Publishers, 2007), 4–6.

46. Jonathan Turley, foreword in *Operation Hollywood: How the Pentagon Shapes and Censors the Movies* by David L. Robb (Amherst, NY: Prometheus Books, 2004), 13.

47. Robb, *Operation Hollywood*, 37.

48. Andrew Kelly, *Cinema and the Great War* (New York: Routledge, 1997), 15, 19, 27.

49. Tim Dirks, "War and Anti-War Films," AMC Film Site, www.filmsite.org/warfilms.html (accessed February 22, 2009).

50. Nick Turse, "The Golden Age of the Military-Entertainment Complex: Six Degrees of Kevin Bacon, Pentagon Style," *TomDispatch*, March 20, 2008, www.tomdispatch.com/post/174908 (accessed February 21, 2009).

51. Carl Boggs, "Pentagon Strategy, Hollywood, and Technowar," *New Politics* 6, no. 1 (2006), www.wpunj.edu/newpol/issue41/Boggs41.htm (accessed August 15, 2009).

52. W. Anthony Sheppard, "An Exotic Enemy: Anti-Japanese Musical Propaganda in World War II Hollywood," *Journal of the American Musicological Society* 54, no. 2 (2001): 303–57.

53. See Timeshredder, "Bowery Boys," Everything2, February 19, 2004, http://everything2.com/title/Bowery%2520Boys (accessed June 29, 2009). See also Robert W. Finnan, Bowery Boys Pages, http://boweryboys.bobfinnan.com/ (accessed June 29, 2009).

54. Lawrence H. Suid, introduction in *Guts & Glory: The Making of the American Military Image*, 2nd ed. (Lexington: University of Kentucky Press, 2002).

55. Turse, "Golden Age of the Military-Entertainment Complex."

56. Doug Davis, "Future-War Storytelling: National Security and Popular Film," in *Rethinking Global Security: Media, Popular Culture and the "War on Terror*," ed. Andrew Martin and Patrice Petro (New Brunswick, NJ, and London: Rutgers University Press, 2006), 19–21.

57. Don Baruch, as cited in Robb, *Operation Hollywood*, 277.

58. J. Hoberman, cited in Engelhardt, *End of Victory Culture*, 34.

59. This analysis is similar in spirit to that provided by Stanley Corkin, *Cowboys as Cold Warriors: The Western and U.S. History* (Philadelphia: Temple University Press, 2004).

60. *Why Viet-Nam? A Gov't Film Outlining American Policy*. The film can be watched in two parts at www.realmilitaryflix.com/public/291.cfm (accessed June 25, 2009).

61. One brief discussion is found in Engelhardt, *End of Victory Culture*, 11–14.

62. The definitive work on Vietnam is still found in *The Pentagon Papers: The Defense Department History of United States Deicsionmaking on Vietnam*, 4 vols., Senator Gravel Edition (Boston: Beacon Press, 1971).

63. Turse, "Golden Age of the Military-Entertainment Complex."

64. Boggs and Pollard, *Hollywood War Machine*, 90–91.

65. Boggs, "Pentagon Strategy, Hollywood, and Technowar."

66. Swofford, cited in Andrew Martin, "Popular Culture and Narratives of Insecurity," in Martin and Petro, *Rethinking Global Security*, 111.

67. Boggs, "Pentagon Strategy, Hollywood, and Technowar."

68. This paragraph also relies on Linda D. Kozaryn, "DoD Honors 'Private Ryan' Director Spielberg," American Forces Press Service, n.d., www.defenselink.mil/news/newsarticle.aspx?id=42941 (accessed March 1, 2009); Laura Gabriele, "Pentagon–Hollywood: Who Runs the Show?" *France 24 International News*, June 21, 2008, www.france24.com/en/20080621-beyond-business-pentagon-cinema-collaboration-defense-propaganda (accessed February 21, 2009).

69. Turse, "Golden Age of the Military-Entertainment Complex."

70. The quotes in this paragraph come from the London *Independent*, "Hollywood Sends in the Troops," December 10, 2001, www.independent.co.uk/arts-entertainment/films/news/hollywood-sends-in-the-troops-619633.html (accessed February 22, 2009).

71. Davis, "Future-War Storytelling," 22.

72. *War of the Worlds* as cited in Boggs, "Pentagon Strategy, Hollywood, and Technowar."

73. Davis, "Future-War Storytelling," 38.

74. Boggs, "Pentagon Strategy, Hollywood, and Technowar."

75. Jeff Fleischer, "Operation Hollywood," Phil Taylor's Website, The Institute of Communications Studies, University of Leeds, September 20, 2004, http://ics.leeds.ac.uk/papers/vp01.cfm?outfit=pmt&requesttimeout=500&folder=933&paper=1783 (accessed February 22, 2009).

76. Robb, *Operation Hollywood*, 178.

77. Robb, *Operation Hollywood*, 149–50.

78. Boggs cited in Jeff Smith, "Popcorn and Propaganda: Movies, Militarism and Mad Mel," *Media Mouse*, January 29, 2007, www.mediamouse.org/news/2007/01/popcorn-and-pro.php (accessed June 25, 2009).

79. Robb, *Operation Hollywood*, 30.

80. Robb, *Operation Hollywood*, 81.

81. Robb, *Operation Hollywood*, 91.

82. Joseph Kay, "Hollywood's Ideological War," World Socialist Website, March 23, 2002, www.wsws.org/articles/2002/mar2002/war-m23.shtml (accessed June 25, 2009).

83. Robb, *Operation Hollywood*, 59.

84. Gabriele, "Pentagon–Hollywood."

85. Robb, *Operation Hollywood*, 67–70, 71–72, 185.

86. Robb, *Operation Hollywood*, 121.

87. Robb, *Operation Hollywood*, 77–80.

88. Robb, *Operation Hollywood*, 232–40.

89. Robb, *Operation Hollywood*, 65–69.

90. Robb, *Operation Hollywood*, 88.

91. Robb, *Operation Hollywood*, 45–47.

92. Cited in Robb, *Operation Hollywood*, 48.

93. Robb, *Operation Hollywood*, 365–67. The direct quote is found on p. 367.

94. Boggs, "Pentagon Strategy, Hollywood, and Technowar."

95. Carl Boggs and Tom Pollard, "Hollywood and the Spectacle of Terrorism," *New Political Science* 9 (2006), www.ocnus.net/cgi-bin/exec/view.cgi?archive=103&num=26261 (accessed June 25, 2009).

96. Jack G. Shaheen, *Reel Bad Arabs: How Hollywood Vilifies a People* (New York: Olive Branch Press, 2001), 15.

97. Boggs and Pollard, "Spectacle of Terrorism"; Shaheen, *Reel Bad Arabs*, 29.

98. This paragraph relies on Kay, "Hollywood's Ideological War."

99. "Pro-war Celebs Making Voices Heard," *CBC News*, March 11, 2003, www.cbc.ca/arts/story/2003/03/10/celeb100303.html (accessed February 16, 2010).

100. Amy Fagan, "Hollywood's Conservative Underground: 'Friends of Abe' Group Meets Quietly," *Washington Times*, July 23, 2008, www.washingtontimes.com/news/2008/jul/23/hollywoods-conservative-underground/ (accessed February 16, 2010).

101. Stephen F. Hayes, "Hollywood Takes on the Left: David Zucker, the Director Who Brought Us 'Airplane!' and 'The Naked Gun,' Turns His Sights on Anti-Americanism," *Weekly Standard* 13, no. 45 (August 11–18, 2008), www.weeklystandard.com/Content/Public/Articles/000/000/015/385rlkfy.asp (accessed February 18, 2010).

102. LilyBixler, "USO Sends Female Soldiers Make Up, Cosmo-Feministing," Current: News, http://current.com/items/91849004_uso-sends-female-soldiers-make-up-cosmo-feministing.htm (accessed January 31, 2010).

103. For the interview with Letterman, see "Colbert on 'Letterman': Obama Is Meryl Streep of Presidents" (video), *Huffington Post*, www.huffingtonpost.com/2009/11/20/colbert-on-letterman-obam_n_365032.html (accessed February 2, 2010). Other references are found on Colbert's website at www.colbertnation.com.

104. Matt Fowler, "Eva Torres Pays Tribute to the Troops: The WWE RAW Diva Talks to IGN about Her Time in Iraq," IGN, December 17, 2009, http://tv.ign.com/articles/105/1056150p1.html (accessed January 31, 2010).

105. See "Operation Proper Exit," including YouTube videos, http://blog.uso.org/2009/12/26/operation-proper-exit/ (accessed January 31, 2010).

5

The War Must Go On

How Pop Culture Legitimates the Sacrifices of War

W E HAVE EXPLORED THE ROLE OF POPULAR CULTURE in laying the ground for
the state's decision to go to war. Popular cultural products, such as
toys, video games, film, and television prepare the population for the possibility of war and then the decision to go to war. But what is the role of popular
culture once the war begins? As Lee Cooper argues, in a democratic society,
for military activity to be sustained, people must accept that there is a "just
cause" as a basis for the effort. Songs can provide this sense of the just cause,
and the "propaganda value of oft-repeated tunes understandably exceeds the
influence of singular political speeches, newspaper editorials and magazine
articles."[1] This chapter will focus on the variety of ways in which forces in
popular culture support the continuation of war and reinforce militaristic
ideas. A key role that popular culture plays during war is to reassure the public that the costs of war—in civil liberties, money, and lives—are necessary
costs and must continue to be borne, that the show must go on. We will also
highlight the ways in which human agency is still important, because events
since 9/11 show that people may believe for a time, but there is a limit to how
much they will accept when reality diverges from impression.

Contemporary militarism is highly dependent on cultural supports because
of what we might call, along with Ira Chernus, the "spectacle of war." It has
been sixty years since the U.S. people have been faced with a total or general
war that *really* touches every family and all aspects of life. To the extent that
wars are "limited" most people have little direct experience with them. They
depend on the media and general societal impressions which means that there
is an increasing role for narrative and spectacle. The great temptation—maybe

even the imperative—of the state is to engage in "impression management" to the extent that the impression becomes more important than the reality. Starting the wars in Afghanistan and Iraq required the presentation of a "grand narrative," which was as much about the self-understanding or fondest wishes of the United States, as it was about Afghanistan or Iraq. This explains why the standard account can change so often—because it is just a story to explain the policy choices after 9/11. It does not matter whether these reasons are even real motivations. If they must be used, they will be used.[2]

Scripting Mission Accomplished

Appearances were certainly of great importance in the Bush era, and probably will be for every successive president, because in the short term, at least, these methods work. As David M. Boje noted in an early academic analysis, there is evidence that every detail in Bush public appearances was planned with care, including the "digital wallpaper" that presents graphics (like "Strengthening the Economy") behind presidential appearances, to the carefully selected audiences placed behind the president, and to the careful screening of speech attendees to ensure a loyal Republican crowd. Boje even notes that at an event in Indianapolis men were asked to take off their neck ties and white button-down shirts were distributed to make the crowd look more "hoosier," and in another case the crowd was digitally altered to make it look more diverse.[3]

The more that Bush critics accused him of going AWOL or deserting during his Air National Guard service in the early 1970s, the greater the effort to build him up as a warrior. The best example of the "spectacle of war" was Bush's September 2003 arrival on the USS *Abraham Lincoln* in a four-seat, S3-B Viking jet. The Secret Service opposed Bush arriving in a riskier combat jet, but in this safer jet Bush said "I flew it," having briefly controlled the plane during the flight. The flight itself was short. The Lincoln, which was returning from the Persian Gulf after ten months at sea, was only forty miles from San Diego. At the direction of former TV producer Scott Sforza, Bush's photo-op set-up man, Bush would speak in late-afternoon, "magic hour" light, interrupting popular programming on a Thursday evening, prime time in the Midwest and back east.

Everything about this was a stunt, albeit a very effective one. To grab attention Bush was dressed in a flight suit, and landed on the deck. According to Bush critics, including Tina Fey of NBC's *Saturday Night Live*, the president looked like he had an "enhanced package," as though someone had "stuffed socks down the front of the jump suit." The ship was turned so that camera shots would not catch the San Diego skyline. He spoke to cheering service people in front of a "Mission Accomplished!" banner, only 40 days into the war and with only 139 U.S. combat dead, as though claiming meant it would be so. The sailors with whom he appeared in photo ops were preselected and wore uniforms of various colors. The conservative and moderate media and commentators, whether it was Morton Kondracke, Chris Matthews, David Broder, or Robert Novak, still playing the "stenographers to power" role, ate it up. So too did the American people, according to polling and the president's approval rating.[4] George W. Bush's transformation from president to heroic action hero was made complete in September 2003 with the production of a presidential action figure dressed in a flight suit with the requisite pilot's accessories, including a helmet with oxygen mask, survival vest, and parachute harness, as it "recreat[es] . . . the Commander-in-Chief's appearance during his historic Aircraft Carrier landing" on the USS *Abraham Lincoln*.[5] Bush was canonized as both president and ultramilitaristic figure via his inanimate transformation, making patriotism and national unity synonymous with the goals of the presidency. This is a disturbing development because it smacks more of 1970s- and 1980s-era Latin American military dictatorships than it does the traditions of the republic. The idea of the U.S. Constitution is that the president is commander in chief, but not a military figure, even if, like many presidents, he had a distinguished military record. Commander in chief is *a* role of the elected civilian president, not *the* role or *the* identity. The president is directly accountable to the public as an elected official, whereas the generals and admirals are not.

Like so much of militaristic propaganda, there is not much reality behind this presentation of President Bush. Much has been written about the real military record of George W. Bush, but for our purposes, suffice it to say that after graduating from Yale in 1968 the younger Bush went into the Air National Guard, instead of volunteering or being drafted into the regular military during the Vietnam era. He trained as a pilot but there are questions as to whether he even fulfilled his National Guard obligations, despite his 1973 honorable discharge.[6] Even in the pantheon of militarism, Bush fell far short of his two principal presidential rivals, Al Gore and John Kerry, both of whom saw active duty in Vietnam.

The Soundtrack of War

Immediately after the 9/11 attacks, broadcast media interrupted their normal formats for a few days to provide wall-to-wall coverage of the attacks and their aftermath. As they returned to regular schedules some went to music and some to spoken word or talk, but all programming reflected on the events of that day. As James Castonguay notes, some radio stations had contests for the best way to kill Osama bin Laden, the prize for which in one case was to smash an Osama piñata full of prizes. A Memphis radio station produced a mock program entitled "The Huntin' Channel: Baggin' Feral Afghans," and a variety of songs were composed and played, including "Die Osama," "Tali Bon Bon," and "Bombs will be Fallin'."[7]

But as far as radio is concerned the greatest impact was on the hit parade and music play lists. Historically, popular music has been used to support U.S. military policies throughout the twentieth century, and tunes have been used to justify both current wars and past conflict as well. As Lee Cooper says, "American public opinion is more susceptible to popular culture imagery about wars than to critical historical analysis, scholarly reinterpretations, or rapidly changing world conditions."[8] According to *Entertainment Weekly*, just three weeks following the U.S.-led invasion of Iraq in 2003, pro-war songs were climbing the music charts, as Darryl Worley's patriotic tune "Have You Forgotten" soared to No. 1 on the Billboard country singles chart.[9] His call to antiwar activists to remember the September 11 attacks reinforces the idea that the war in Iraq was somehow justified by this, or that the United States should get Osama bin Laden at all costs. Similarly, country singer Clint Black's pro-war song "I Raq and Roll" rapidly climbed the singles charts in early April 2003, as the United States tried to conjure up support for the war.[10] Black's unapologetic pro-war stance ultimately has him threatening opponents of the war, by suggesting that the terrorists are cowards and that anyone who opposes the war in Iraq is a Saddam Hussein supporter and might face the same fate. These songs aren't limited to country music, as Lynyrd Skynyrd's classic patriotic song "Red, White and Blue" reached No. 15 on the rock singles chart during that same week.[11] In Darryl Worley's song "I Just Came Back from the War," he devalues Iraqis and demonstrates frustration with his fellow Americans, by expressing disgust that people don't seem to care anymore.

Clearly there is a strong link between the rise of pro-war songs in popular culture following the September 11 attacks and the War in Iraq. This is particularly true of country music, which is the preponderant music on radio in the United States, is male-dominated in terms of performers, and features socially conservative, traditionalist values.[12] Particularly in the period immediately following the attacks, the country had choices regarding how to respond, and how to conceive of itself. As we have said before, what formed under the leadership of Bush and the Republican-dominated Congress was revitalized neoconservatism, militarism, and aggressive nationalism. The result was also rhetorical valorization of those who worked in the aftermath of the attacks, restoring New York City and the country, the fire fighter, the cop, the construction worker, and the soldier.[13] Country music was well positioned to appeal to the "everyday" American along the lines being promoted by Bush, Fox News, and CNN.[14] Its messages of patriotism, militarism, and justifications for ongoing warfare provide foundation for morale building and mass-mobilizing efforts. But is this production of song in support of the war really a genuine expression of popular culture? The argument is this section is that powerful human agents used their positions to promote one kind of music and discourage others, and for a time they were quite successful. But this sort of success is not permanent, and after a few years there was some change in attitudes in popular culture, as exemplified in the revived career of the Dixie Chicks, and the reassertion of opponents of militarism.

According to the *Denver Westword News*, the answer to the genuineness question is a clear "no." Michael Roberts, in his April 3, 2003, article "The Message," investigates Clear Channel Communications and its pro-war stance.[15] According to its official website, Clear Channel Communications owns approximately 1,200 radio stations across the United States, so it's clear just how big Clear Channel's potential influence is on the people.[16] According to Roberts, aside from the rah-rah chatter, and the George W. Bush lovefest that was heard regularly from the radio hosts on the various Clear Channel outlets, they in fact polled the audience and found out they were positive toward the Beastie Boys' antiwar tune "In a World Gone Mad."[17] With pro-war cheerleaders spinning tunes on the radio stations, it makes sense that they might have a problem with songs that suggest that one war leads to another and that there are corporate campaign contributors acting in the background. While KCTL, a local Denver modern rock station, played the song twenty times in the initial week that it was released, they did this only after they surveyed two thousand listeners about the track. In response to the question "How does the fact the song is a 'protest' song change your opinion about it?" 34 percent said, "It makes me like the song more"; 16 percent answered, "It makes me like the song less"; and 51 percent replied, "It doesn't change my opinion one way or the other."[18] Clint Black's intimidating threat to antiwar activists climbed the charts in 2003, while the Beastie Boys' plea to lose weapons and end war was forced through a gauntlet before it could get *any* airplay. But it also shows that the media echo chamber has only limited success in transforming the opinions of many listeners, who despite all the efforts are still open to dissent.

According to Tim Jones, a *Chicago Tribune* national correspondent, Clear Channel radio stations sponsored well-attended "patriotic" rallies in various American cities during the lead-up to the invasion of Iraq in March

2003.[19] As the state prepared to go to war, the sponsored rallies endorsed George W. Bush's agenda against Iraq and Saddam Hussein, and often drew as many as twenty thousand people.[20] Instead of "grassroots" activity this is referred to as "teflon roots," and is similar to the contrived Spring 2009 "Tea Party" tax revolts organized around the country largely by Fox News and allied neoconservatives. (This "tax revolt" was rather ironic because they were protesting a federal tax code, including two tax cuts, passed by Republican congresses and president.) While the 2003 rallies had been advertised on the corporation's website, Clear Channel spokeswoman Lisa Dollinger denied that there was corporate direction in the organization of the rallies. And yet, perhaps not surprisingly, there were ties between Clear Channel and the Bush administration. Bush connections to senior Clear Channel personnel go back to his time in Texas.[21] More recently, in the 2004 presidential campaign, Clear Channel executives gave $42,200 to George W. Bush, in contrast to the $1,750 that they gave to John Kerry. In addition to a donation of $12,500 to the Republican National Committee, chair and CEO L. Lowry Mays also gave $2,000 to George W. Bush in July 2003, while his two sons, Clear Channel president Mark Mays and chief financial officer Randall Mays, also each gave $2,000 to Bush in the same year.[22] Even with all those personal and political ties between Clear Channel Communications and Bush, Clear Channel continues to say that the sponsored rallies "have been organized locally, and are not 'pro-war', but rather 'pro-troops' and 'non-political.'"[23]

Clear Channel is a self-proclaimed "nonpartisan" corporation, though following the September 11 attacks they banned over 150 songs from radio airplay.[24] The decision to ban songs is a good example of the differential power of human agents. The exercise of this agency by Clear Channel means that millions of agents at the base of society will not be able to choose whether or not to listen to that song. Though they may claim that they were simply being sensitive, many of the banned songs did not even feature themes of violence. Certain songs on the list included vague references to battle, weapons, fire, or to people from the Middle East.[25] Surely, Pat Benatar's "Love Is a Battlefield" can't be a more offensive reminder of the attacks than Darryl Worley's "Have You Forgotten." Rage Against the Machine is known to produce political music, since they sing about issues like justice, poverty, and U.S. foreign policy, and are regularly belittled by conservative pundits such as Ann Coulter. So not surprisingly, Clear Channel banned all Rage Against the Machine songs from airplay.[26] Going even further, they banned John Lennon's "Imagine" and Cat Stevens's "Peace Train," both of which were on Clear Channel's list of "songs with questionable lyrics."[27]

Silencing Dissent

And what happened to singer-songwriters and other entertainers who did dissent from the state? The period after 9/11 was a charged period, in which what people said, particularly through electronic media, was highly scrutinized, and government, owners, and advertisers were not above using their power to silence critics. On the September 17, 2001, edition of his program *Politically Incorrect*, Bill Maher effectively agreed with his conservative guest Dinesh D'Souza of the American Enterprise Institute. On the subject of whether the Bush White House's characterization of the 9/11 attackers as "cowards" was fair, Maher said "We have been the cowards, lobbing cruise missiles from 2,000 miles away. That's cowardly. Staying in the airplane when it hits the building, say what you want about it, it's not cowardly." This led Bush press secretary Ari Fleischer to say that "people have to watch what they say and watch what they do." Federal Express and Sears terminated their sponsorship of the program, which was cancelled shortly after.[28]

Cartoonist Aaron McGruder, author of the syndicated comic strip Boondocks, started addressing 9/11 on September 24, 2001, and also found his cartoon cancelled by certain newspapers, including the *New York Daily News*.[29] Editorial cartoonists were not immune from this either, even though one should expect "political," dissenting opinions from them. Mike Marland drew a cartoon for the *Concord Patriot* using the image of pilot Bush bombing the Twin Towers, labeled with "social" and "security," to criticize President Bush's Social Security proposals. This also drew negative comment from Ari Fleischer, and negativity was so swift and harsh that the paper's editor in chief wrote a follow-up column saying that in retrospect the paper should not have run the cartoon. Speaking in June 2002, cartoonist Mike Konopacki said that since 9/11 editorial cartoons have become "dumber" and the "emphasis is on humor rather than analysis."[30]

But establishment efforts to silence dissent is best illustrated by the experience of the Dixie Chicks. At a Dixie Chicks concert in London, just days before the American-led invasion of Iraq in March 2003, Natalie Maines, a Texas native, asserted her disapproval of the decision to go to war, and more importantly her disapproval of George W. Bush.[31] At that time, she said: "Just so you know, we're on the good side with y'all. We do not want this war, this violence, and we're ashamed that the President of the United States is from Texas."[32] What followed was a heated controversy as well as a significant loss of support for the Dixie Chicks. Their songs disappeared from the airwaves and the music charts, and their CDs were destroyed.[33] According to BBC News, just ten days following the very public remark made by Maines, airplay for the group's music fell 29 percent on country music radio stations and 20 percent on general music radio stations. Rich Meyer, president of Mediabase, a radio monitoring service, explained that radio tends to be a reflection of the "mood" of the country, and that "if radio perceives that its listeners are upset with the Dixie Chicks, they will respond accordingly." One of the core claims of the U.S. state is that war is thrust upon the United States by foreign aggressors, and that the sacrifices that warfare requires, whether in civil liberties, blood, or treasure, is regrettable but necessary. If as a policy maker you can convince people that "there is no alterative," a phrase remembered from the 1990s "free trade" era, then your work is done. Discovering that there are alternatives is the job of human agency, beginning with dissent. The Dixie Chicks would be seen as a necessary casualty of the need to unite the country behind the war effort.

As for the Dixie Chicks' popularity, according to *USA Today* journalist Brian Mansfield, their last single to reach the top twenty on the Billboard country singles chart was their 2002–2003 hit "Travelin' Soldier." With the hegemonic crisis in the United States in recent years, however, the Dixie Chicks have largely recovered from the attacks of 2003 and 2004, showing that persevering has its benefits. As of this writing the band's most recent CD, *Taking the Long Way*, was released in May 2006, won five Grammy Awards, and sold 2 million copies in the first year, having debuted at No. 1 on the Billboard 200.[34] It is accepted that its audience has shifted somewhat from country to mainstream rock, though an audience is still an audience.

With the creation of the To the Fallen record label, there is further evidence that suggests that this pro-war stance in popular song is more a creation of the cultural industry than an authentic expression of popular preferences. According to its official website, To the Fallen Records sells various compilation albums in the rock, hip hop, and country genres.[35] Perhaps more importantly, as the self-proclaimed, nonpartisan label states, "It's not about politics, it's about music."[36] In an interview conducted by the BBC World Service, cofounder and CEO of To the Fallen Records Sean Gilfillan explained that the label "was neither pro or anti-war," and that they'd had "nothing but support" from government.[37] That having been said, not only have they had "support" from the military, but To the Fallen remains as the only all-military record label. While there are a small number of antiwar songs on To the Fallen, written by soldiers questioning their mission, most of To the Fallen songs share themes of pride for their country, as well as ideas that the troops are keeping the people of Iraq and the United States "safe and free."[38] Additionally, on its website there is a direct link to "Hooah Radio," a veteran run, Internet-based radio station complete with Uncle-Sam-like patriotic symbols, "supporting our troops and military families."

As pro-war songs rushed the radio airwaves in the early 2000s, a different style of music was chosen for background music on television news networks. Networks like CNN, CBS, and Fox News commissioned warlike musical themes which included "victorious brass, pounding timpani, and electronic war sounds."[39] While certain news outfits see this as being a way to grab the viewer's attention,[40] it can be also be said that this music is there to heighten the emotional aspects which comes with any newscast about the war or the September 11 attacks.[41] Lawrence Grossman, former president of NBC News, admits that the background music during the broadcasts "tell[s] you what to think."[42] According to the *Philadelphia Tribune*, Eric Shapiro, director of CBS News and CBS special events, commissioned composer Peter Fish to write music that would "convey some idea of mood."[43] With that, Fish produced a variety of music for CBS News intended to convey a "climate of fear."[44] As for Fox News, they had their theme music ready even before the invasion on Iraq had begun, predictably named, "Liberation Iraq Music."[45] This album also conveys warlike qualities with the sound of "war drums,"[46] and French horns, implying a sense of urgency. Bruce Brubaker, a member of the faculty at the Julliard School in New York, refers to this style of music as a "fanfare" sound. "Why is it so fun to march up and down the street? Because we can see how powerful we are, that if there were to be a battle, we would be able to beat our enemy," Brubaker explains.[47] It's plain to see that the theme music used in the war coverage yells "We're at war!" and is indeed meant to produce an emotional reaction.[48] On those particular news stations, TV viewers are being told just "what to think" and "how to feel" about the war on Iraq, before the news has even been broadcast.[49] One can say, however, that the militarist policies in the 2000s went so poorly—or at least were perceived by the large majority of U.S. people to have gone poorly—that political parties and powerful cultural producers have had to shift their focus to maintain support among voters and viewers. The fact that so many of these of these tactics, such as banning songs and keeping dissenters out of the media, have faded from the scene is an indication of the ongoing importance of the mass of human agents—the listener and customer.

Pop Torture

Within the last decade, pop culture has been invaded by "pop torture," a term that has come to describe the frequency of images of torture and violence in mainstream culture.[50] While Clear Channel banned songs from airplay, the U.S. military in Iraq and Guantánamo Bay play many of those same banned songs, and they play them loud. According to U.S. Air Force Lt.-Col. Dan

Kuehl, it was in the battle of Jericho that Joshua's army first used the strategy of "torture by music."[51] While Joshua and his army sounded the trumpets and caused the walls to fall, now years later, the U.S. military continues to use these psychological operations (psyops) to force Iraqi gunmen out.[52] During the siege in Fallujah, U.S. soldiers blasted AC/DC's "Hells Bells," Jimi Hendrix, and other rock and metal music at full volume in order to attract Iraqi gunmen in order for them to be able to attack and advance farther into the city.[53] Marine staff sergeant Coleman Kinzer, whose battalion was situated nearby, says, "They'd play Drowning Pool, Korn, then start taking requests—anything that was hard and loud and totally American. The guys loved it. It was like having a soundtrack to your own war movie."[54]

This music as torture doesn't stop once the Iraqi enemies have been caught either. This carries on into the "interrogation" period. Binyam Mohamed, a British resident who has experienced both the physical and psychological torture in Guantánamo Bay, said in an interview with the *Guardian*'s Clive Stafford Smith: "Imagine you are given a choice, lose your sight or lose your mind," the answer is simple.[55] He explained that being able to anticipate the start and end of physical pain was much different than the experience of turning mad as a result of torture by music.[56] Some songs that are used during interrogation procedures have included David Gray's "Babylon," which was played at the infamous Abu Ghraib jail in Iraq,[57] and Rage Against the Machine's songs were used in Guantánamo Bay, as was Metallica's "Enter Sandman."[58] While these musicians have objected to the use of their music for torture, they have limited options. Lars Ulrich of Metallica sarcastically jokes with *Slate* magazine's David Piesner, "What am I supposed to do about it? Get George Bush on the phone and tell him to get his generals to play some Venom [instead]?"[59] Likewise David Gray explains to Clive Stafford Smith, "Perhaps you could sue [the Bush administration], but let's face it, they're outside the law on the whole thing anyway."[60] So for now, until songwriters are able to make claims against the government for unpaid royalties, music as torture continues. As David Gray pointed out, it's difficult to dissent from the Pentagon's power.

Since 9/11 torture has been particularly common in media in the United States, exemplified by television shows such as *24*, watched over seven seasons by millions of viewers. We would expect broadcast television to be the last medium to accept torture, because it is the form of media most heavily regulated, in this case by the Federal Communications Commission. Indeed, *24* attracts a weekly audience of fifteen million viewers, and generates millions of dollars through DVD sales.[61] The question of torture, or "aggressive interrogation" as the Bush administration called it, is a particularly good case in which the media, along with other aspects of culture, try to rationalize something which centuries of experience have taught us is hard, even impossible, to accept.

One of the ways President Bush justified these techniques was to assert the severity of the stakes in the War on Terror, to downplay the harshness of these techniques, and then to claim that they get results unavailable any other way. In a major speech in September 2006, he characterized the War on Terror as similar in importance to World War II, the latter of which, we might remember, was ended with the dropping of atomic bombs on civilian targets:

> Free nations have faced new enemies and adjusted to new threats before, and we have prevailed. Like the struggles of the last century, today's war on terror is, above all, a struggle for freedom and liberty. The adversaries are different, but the stakes in this war are the same. We're fighting for our way of life and our ability to live in freedom. We're fighting for the cause of humanity against those who seek to impose the darkness of tyranny and terror upon the entire world. And we're fighting for a peaceful future for our children and our grand-children.

(The great military inequality between the Western countries and these terrorists is never mentioned.) He then said that after the attacks of 9/11 he "directed our government's senior national security officials to do everything in their power, within our laws, to prevent another attack," and that "the most important source of information on where the terrorists are hiding and what they are planning is the terrorists themselves." The "procedures were tough and they were safe and lawful and necessary," and the "program has given us information that has saved innocent lives by helping us stop new attacks, here in the United States and across the world."[62] This is certainly a case in which the president is asking citizens to bite the bullet and support what needs to be done, though most of these claims are unverifiable by the public, who can't be blamed for their skepticism, given the lies that were told to get the United States into Iraq. Unpleasant things must be done, though he refuses to go into detail, but these are necessary to achieve larger, good aims.

To see some of the techniques that are used, and to see the media echo the rationale of the president, we should look at the television series *24*, which has now run for seven seasons. Like in comedy, viewers don't necessarily analyze what they're seeing when they watch television dramas or action programs; rather, they let their social and moral guard down simply to enjoy a show. The television program *24* has garnered both praise and controversy for its portrayal of torture as a means to extract vital information from terrorists. Each season of the series covers the events of one twenty-four-hour day, in "real-time," as viewers follow the exploits of U.S. counterterrorism agent Jack Bauer, played by Keifer Sutherland. As a commercial and critical success (*24* won an Emmy Award in 2005 for Outstanding Drama Series), Jack Bauer and his brutal forms of interrogation, including torture, have seeped into the public consciousness. In the show's seven seasons, Bauer has tortured terrorists, criminals, even colleagues who may have crucial information, acting out numerous forms of torture that serve to justify his end of extracting information. For example, this attitude is clearly expressed after Bauer shoots and kills a restrained criminal in front of his superior, George Mason, in an episode that aired during the second season. When Mason condemns Jack's action as unnecessary and extreme, Bauer fires back, "That's the problem with people like you, George. You want results, but you're never willing to get your hands dirty."[63] David Danzig, a project director at Human Rights First observes, "The torturers have changed. It used to be almost exclusively the villains who tortured. Today, torture is perpetuated by the heroes." There has always been torture in popular culture, but in the past it was employed by domestic criminals, such as in *The Sopranos*. More recently, it is employed by government agents.

Jack Bauer represents a growing movement that supports a new definition of patriotism, following the motto "whatever it takes" to preserve the safety of the United States. Joel Surnow, creator of *24*, defines his show as "patriotic." Indeed, interviewer Jane Mayer of the *New Yorker* writes:

> The series, Surnow told me, is "ripped out of the Zeitgeist of what people's fears are—their paranoia that we're going to be attacked," and it "makes people look at what we're dealing with" in terms of threats to national security. "There are not a lot of measures short of extreme measures that will get it done," he said, adding "America wants the war on terror fought by Jack Bauer. He's a patriot."[64]

Pertinent to the controversy surrounding *24* is the consensus that there is no proof that torture is a successful method of extracting accurate information, although Bauer's methods unrealistically continue to draw out the information he is seeking.[65] For example, navy veteran and presidential candidate John McCain confessed that when tortured by his North Vietnamese captors, who were demanding from him the names of the men in his unit, he gave them the names of the Green Bay Packers' offensive line in order to end the pain.[66] Actor Kiefer Sutherland, portraying Jack Bauer of *24*, has also conceded that "You torture someone and they'll basically tell you exactly what you want to hear whether it's true of not, if you put someone in enough pain."[67] Additionally, Tony Lagouranis a former army interrogator in the war in Iraq has stated:

> In Iraq, I never saw pain produce intelligence . . . I used severe hypothermia, dogs and sleep deprivation. I saw suspects after soldiers had gone into their homes and broken their bones, or made them sit on a Humvee's hot exhaust pipes until they got third-degree burns. Nothing happened.[68]

However, the prevalence of torture on television as a means to extract information has helped to justify its widespread use, particularly as seen in the Iraq War. For example, on March 8, 2008, George Bush used his veto power to preserve the right to torture, under his preferred term "enhanced interrogation techniques." Bush expressed his belief that "'hardened terrorists' merit different treatment from captured soldiers."[69] In November 2006, U.S. Army brigadier general Patrick Finnegan, an army lawyer and dean at the United States Military Academy at West Point, New York, arrived in Southern California to meet with the creative team of *24* to voice concern about the premise of the show. Finnegan argued that it is becoming more difficult to convince the students at the Academy (cadets who become battlefield commanders in Iraq and Afghanistan) to respect the rule of law and human rights, even when terrorists do not. He suggests that this is because of the message of torture spread by *24*. "The kids see it, and say, 'If torture is wrong, what about *24*?' The disturbing thing is that although torture may cause Jack Bauer some angst, it is always the patriotic thing to do." The relationship between pop culture and societal actions as it relates to torture is complex but clearly important.[70]

As we might expect, popular culture is not immune from movements in the wider society. Perhaps sensing a change in the wind, the seventh season of *24*, aired in early 2009, presents a stronger counterargument against the will-to-torture that is so dominant in the show. There is FBI agent Larry Moss, who consistently argues against "aggressive interrogation," and there is less torture in this season than in previous ones. In the final episode, Agent Jack Bauer confides in the FBI agent he has been working with, Renée Walker, that his propensity to defend the innocent "at all costs" is what his heart tells him, not his head. He knows the importance of the rule of law, he says, but he just can't help it. This change in tone, however modest, is a sign that the producers and writers on the show have realized that their audience, the same people who gave the Democratic Party a stronger hold in Congress and elected the first African American, a Democrat, to the White House, has changed. They elected a Congress and a president on a "Yes, we can" platform, a symbol that the second age of Republican neoconservatism is over. So the show had to moderate its attitude toward torture as a way of holding its audience, or meeting its audience where it is. In an era in which a law professor is president, this is some progress and a sign that producers will change in response to changing public opinion.

Spectator Sport Warfare

One of the most durable buttresses of militarism is found in the world of sport. In the ancient world track and field events directly prepared participants for military combat. Some, like the javelin, survive in contemporary track and field competition. In Social Darwinist thought, sport was encouraged during industrialism to ensure that "the nation" would remain "vital" and able to flex its military muscle. Military training all over the world had a significant element of sport in it, because of the need for fitness as part of battle. In fascist Italy and Nazi Germany sport was also seen as a sign of the greatness and superiority of the state.[71] In subsequent decades, sport and militarism became tightly intertwined in the United States as well. As articulated by World War II general and U.S. president Dwight D. Eisenhower, "the true mission of American sports is to prepare young people for war."[72] The wartime ritual of playing "The Star-Spangled Banner" before each baseball game's opening pitch began during World War II and was eventually adopted by all professional and intercollegiate sports leagues. In this section it will be clear that the rise of sports, and particularly professional sports, is linked with militarism. Football lends itself to militarism above all others, and football, like auto racing, has been a venue to promote militarism among spectators. We will see that patriotic statements from athletes and commentators are virtually obligatory (the acceptable alternative is silence) and antiwar or peace-oriented statements exact a cost.

It is no coincidence that the modern National Football League as we know it was created during the Vietnam War. As has been suggested by Wanda Wakefield, of all sports, "football seemed to serve cultural needs most effectively." Of popular sports in the United States, football is the most militaristic. Simulating trench warfare, two lines of players do combat with each other for territorial advantage, while players in the "skill positions" try to advance the ball or stop the offence from advancing. Head coaches are sometimes referred to as "generals," the strategic masterminds, and the leader of the offence, the quarterback, is like the officer in command on the battlefield. Football is loaded with militaristic terminology, including terms like "attack, blitz, bombs, flanks, conflicts, and territory."[73] While hockey tolerates thuggery in the form of the occasional one-on-one fight and slashing with the stick, no sport matches football for routine, violent contact. It is ludicrous to claim that golf and baseball lend themselves to militarism to the same extent, because they are much more deliberate and cerebral games in which the action is episodic and one-on-one contact is minimal or nonexistent. Of course, as we will see, golfers and baseball players may promote militarism, but militarism is not in the *structure of the game* to the degree that it is in football. Football players often equate their game with war, as evident by former New York Giant Michael Strahan's description of football players as "violent, bloodthirsty warriors."[74] In collegiate sports, for a century football has been the dominant sport at the military service academies, particularly the U.S. Military Academy (West Point, or army) and the U.S. Naval Academy (navy), which play a famous, annual rival contest (i.e., the army-navy game). Since their inception, the NFL and its annual Super Bowl have been pervaded by "military pageantry," which has escalated in the last twenty years.[75] The Super Bowl has also become a major social event, in which even non-fans watch the game at Super Bowl parties. Knowing that much of her audience doesn't know football, but will be attending a Super Bowl party, U.S. homemaking diva Martha Stewart provided not only Super Bowl recipes and decorative tips, but also a primer on football and the 2008 Giants-Patriots Super Bowl so those who know nothing about the game can watch it a little more informed.[76]

Like in other areas of popular culture, this sport-war complex has been growing along with the rehabilitation of militarism in the 1980s to the present. On the eve of the 1991 Super Bowl, eleven days after the United States attacked Iraq in the first Gulf War, NFL commissioner Paul Tagliabue refused to postpone the event because "we've become the winter version of the Fourth of July celebration."[77] Accordingly, Super Bowl XXV featured a flurry of nationalism including "American flag decals on the players' helmets, images of soldiers in the desert throughout the pregame show, and a halftime address from President George H. W. Bush, who described the Gulf War as *his* Super Bowl."[78] Patriotism and militarism were equated with popular entertainment, and as articulated by academic Varda Burstyn, "the entire five-hour broadcast was one massive infomercial for war."[79]

In response to 9/11, the NFL's community outreach programs emphasized disaster relief and recovery of the tourism industry in league cities. However, after the invasion of Iraq, and at the height of public support for the occupation, the league took on "more explicitly patriotic and militaristic projects carried out in collaboration with the Bush administration."[80] The Super Bowl of 2002, the first after the World Trade Center attacks, both promoted militarism and by so doing made watching the game a patriotic act. Fox held a three-hour pregame show, "Heroes, Hope, and Homeland," which opened with the declaration that this was "a special day where Americans come together to share a common vision." There was a "Tribute to America," during which "former NFL stars read from the Declaration of Independence, and former presidents recited Abraham Lincoln's speeches from an earlier national crisis." Before commercial breaks, "postcards" from American soldiers in Afghanistan were read, and during the halftime show, the names of those who died on September 11 scrolled on the screen.[81]

After the U.S. decision to go to war in Iraq, the NFL worked with the Department of Defense to hold an NFL Kick-off Concert at the National Mall in August 2003.[82] It was broadcast live on ABC along with an hour-long special on "Operation Tribute to Freedom," a program designed to "honor soldiers and give them opportunities to thank the American people for their support."[83] These kinds of links between militarism, sports, and entertainment operate as propaganda which, as articulated by Robert L. Ivie, "normalizes war, rendering it habitual, seemingly rational, and largely immune to challenge."[84] Having gone to war, the state, media, and allied institutions attempt to maintain public support for the effort, a task that has proven more difficult in the late 2000s.

The NFL and the state are not above lying in order to promote militarism through football and football through militarism. Take the case of Pat Tillman. In 2002, at age twenty-seven, Tillman turned down a $3.6 million NFL contract with the Arizona Cardinals to enlist with the United States Army Rangers. Turning down the big salary to enlist was, of course, seen as a great act of patriotism and sacrifice, one that not many making over a million dollars a year have been prepared to emulate. He first served in Iraq, and then in Afghanistan, where he was killed on April 22, 2004. On April 30, an army press release announced his Silver Star citation (the third highest medal for bravery) and stated that he died while he "personally provided suppressive fire with an M-249 Squad Automatic Weapon [SAW] machine gun."[85] On May 3 three thousand people attended his memorial service in his hometown of San José, California, and it was nationally televised on ESPN, the United States' leading sports network. In the weeks that followed, Tillman became a heroic symbol of patriotism—a scholarship was created in his name, and the Cardinals announced the retirement of his jersey and the dedication of an area outside the stadium—the "Pat Tillman Freedom Plaza."[86]

However, on May 29, the army acknowledged that Tillman "probably died of fratricide" and that "there was no one specific finding of fault."[87] Then, in December 2004, a two-part *Washington Post* series by Steve Coll found that the initial investigation into Tillman's death had discovered fratricide, that top commanders in the U.S. military were notified of this days before the memorial service, and that his Ranger body armor was burned shortly after his death.[88] There have since been multiple public inquiries into the cover-up of Tillman's death. Among the many findings, Specialist Bryan O'Neal, the last soldier to see Tillman alive, reported in 2007 that he was warned against revealing the circumstances of his death. O'Neal also explained that the final version of his statement for Tillman's Silver Star commendation "contained false statements that had been inserted by someone else."[89] (The posthumous Silver Star has not been revoked even though facing enemy fire is a condition of its award.) Throughout, Tillman's father has maintained that "the administration clearly was using this case for its own political reasons."[90] No one in the military chain of command has faced a court-martial for these offenses. Ultimately, Pat Tillman's story highlights the ways that professional athletes have become propagandistic symbols of militarism, and how the truth will be violated to promote the sport-military complex.

It is worth noting as well that the employment of individual stories to promote militarism extends well beyond the role played by sports stars and other celebrities. The ordinary person can become an exemplar, illustrated well by the story of Pfc. Jessica Lynch, even if the details are falsified, like in the Tillman case. In the early phases of the U.S. invasion of Iraq, Pfc. Jessica Lynch's unit, the 507th Ordnance Maintenance Company, was ambushed and, according to the early account, she was wounded and also returned fire. She was taken prisoner and kept at a hospital near Nasiriyah, and then was rescued by a U.S. military unit which attacked by helicopter, shot its way into the hospital, rescued Pfc. Lynch, and then shot its way out. These details were provided by the Pentagon and were widely reported, effectively showing U.S. forces as competent, and putting a human face on what the United States was doing. Even if the Iraq war was not a rescue of the Iraqi people, at least it was a rescue of one of the army's own.[91]

Quite a story, but a false one. It turns out that Jessica Lynch was injured, but in an explosion, not by gunfire. She was in an Iraqi hospital, but she was not a prisoner, and her civilian doctor had tried to return her to the U.S. military but was turned back by small arms fire at a checkpoint. She was "rescued" by the U.S. military, but they faced no resistance because there was no Iraqi military presence. She affirmed all this in her public testimony before Congress.[92] So why were these lies told? From the Pentagon's perspective, this was a story to promote the war, which is always a short-term concern. Maybe the truth never comes out, or maybe it comes out and doesn't make the front page, or maybe it comes out too late to have any impact, beyond increasing the new generation's cynicism toward the state and politicians. The story may have been floated to divert attention from the fact that this noncombat unit was left without combat escort, and the attack resulted in eleven dead and six wounded, just over half of the complement.[93]

Another possibility for the dishonesty is that it is a good story, one that serves commercial or cultural purposes. As Ed Wasserman notes, given the concentration of ownership in the media, the people who own CBS television (including the news division) decided to dramatize the Lynch story, so don't expect CBS News to feature truth that undermines the initial story.[94] As Susan Faludi argues, the response of the United States (or at least U.S. conservatives) to 9/11, perpetrated by Islamic traditionalists, was to try to turn back the clock and impose traditional (gender) roles in the United States. So the Jessica Lynch story was a chance to treat a military woman as a "damsel-in-distress," and find a male rescuer who could be a hero. Pfc. Lynch herself wasn't really a strong agent in her own cause. She had relatively little input into her own "autobiography," *I Am a Soldier, Too: The Jessica Lynch Story*, written largely by former *New York Times* reporter Rick Bragg. Despite the title, the book focused on the ways in which Lynch was *not* a soldier, including her ultra-feminine upbringing and values. Bragg even floated the idea that Lynch was sexually assaulted, perhaps to promote book sales, even though she never claimed this and forensic evidence was inconclusive. As Susan Faludi says, the search for male heroes began with Private Patrick Miller, then Sgt. Donald Walters, then Sgt. Robert Dowdy. Finally, an Iraqi man, Mohammed Odeh al-Rehaief, stepped forward to claim credit for tipping off the U.S. military, and despite holes in his story, he got a book deal and a commitment from NBC to produce a made-for-TV movie.[95] This was a case in which the Pentagon sought to use Pfc. Lynch's experience, or a false version of it, to increase support for the war, and media outlets and book publishers were eager to flood the market with ghost-written autobiographies and made-for-TV biopics.

To return to the sports-war complex, links between contemporary Western sport and war are endorsed and perpetuated by sportscasters and sports networks. The many examples include ABC's use of a destroyer, supplied by the U.S. Navy, as the stage for the announcers of the 2003 Super Bowl,[96] and NBC's reference to the Iranian athletes as part of President Bush's "axis of evil" during the Opening Ceremonies for the 2002 Olympics in Salt Lake City.[97] U.S. Memorial Day and Canadian Remembrance Day (November 11) are also occasions for networks' overt support for war. ESPN's *Sportcenter's Top 10* and the Canadian Broadcasting Corporation (CBC)'s *Hockey Night in Canada* both feature annual celebrations of the military on their countries' respective holidays.[98] ESPN has taken its support for war and militarism to new heights with the Bell Helicopter Armed Forces Bowl, an annual college football postseason game that adopted that name in 2006.[99] Viewers frequently hear generic praise for "the troops" and "the great job they do" during sports broadcasts, and never hear the opposite.

North of the border, former NHL coach Don Cherry is featured in "Coach's Corner" during the first intermission on the CBC's weekly Saturday night hockey broadcast. Cherry is well known as a right-wing "pro-Canadian" who is skeptical of the value and work ethic of European hockey players, but he has increasingly used his platform to promote militarism and to support the small Canadian Army contingent that has been in Afghanistan since February 2002, first in the capital city Kabul, but now mainly in the Kandahar district. While this has nothing to do with hockey, CBC brass have permitted Cherry to promote Canada's military mission and "support the troops" on the national public broadcaster during hockey games.[100] Canadian public opinion on the Canadian effort is Afghanistan turned decisively against the war in 2009 and 2010, and like in the United States, militarists must continue to promote militarism lest the people compel their politicians to withdraw the forces.

Another significant sports promoter of militarism is the NASCAR auto racing circuit. For over thirty years the U.S. military has had a close relationship with the stock car racing circuit to build the audience for racing and to use NASCAR and other aspects of the car-enthusiast subculture to recruit military personnel. Each branch of the military sponsors racing teams in both auto and drag racing, at a cost of $38 million in Fiscal Year 2005. One driver, Tony Schumacher, is a past multiple winner as the National Hot Rod Association Top Fuel Champion and an Honorary Sergeant, and actively recruits young people into the military. Catering to another aspect of the car subculture, the armed services tour with souped-up Hummers, pick-ups, and other vehicles, some aimed particularly at Latino youth. The military sends these vehicles to car shows around the country, and in Miami in 2003, they sent the cars with attractive young women from a modeling agency, dressed in camo, to encourage young men to sign up.[101]

Many athletes have also been complicit in the militarization of sport, and the "sportification" of war. Some support war through financial means, like the Strikeouts for Troops program, a national project that has raised over one million dollars since 2005 "from contributions made by over 60 professional baseball and football players, fund raising events, fan donations and corporate partnerships."[102] Others do so by holding events for soldiers and their families. In both 2007 and 2008, Tiger Woods donated thirty thousand tickets to the AT&T National Golf tournament to services members and their families.[103] Woods, whose father, Earl, was in the U.S. Army Special Forces (the "Green Berets"), is known as a strong supporter of the military, saying that he would have joined up if he hadn't made it as a professional golfer. Likewise, the U.S. military is known as a strong supporter of the game of golf, and owns and runs as many as 234 golf courses in the United States and around the world.[104]

Many NHL, MLB, NFL, and NBA teams hold annual Seats for Soldiers events[105] or "Canadian Forces Appreciation Nights."[106] Each of these events feature overt expressions of militarism, like the standing ovation given to soldiers as they entered the Dallas Mavericks arena,[107] and the ceremonial first pitch at a 2008 Boston Red Sox home game, delivered by Bronze Star and Purple Heart recipient Michelle Saunders.[108] Furthermore, as we said earlier, many individuals, teams, and leagues have supported the military by visiting troops abroad.

Conclusion

War has become a spectacle, in which managing impressions is more important than reality, and the entertainment industry provides references that leaders can play on to win acceptance of their policies. The purpose of this chapter has been to show that even once the war is started, the job of militaristic culture and propaganda is not over. Far from it. It should be clear that masculinity is important to militarism, in that popular culture presents music, sports, and other entertainment designed to encourage a certain version of manhood. As O'Toole and Schiffman remark, "The culture normalizes militarism through the celebration of military holidays and heroes and through legitimating the unconscious use of military metaphors in our daily communications: we attack a problem, are under the gun to find a solution and frequently beat an idea to death."[109]

Elites learned from Vietnam that if a war drags on long enough, the public may lose its will to continue to support the effort, particularly if the stakes are unclear or don't seem that high. As was stated previously, the seeming public consensus in favor of militarism must be re-created on an ongoing basis. This apparent consensus is a structure, which only exists because it is the accumulation of individual commitments. A failure to do so, to re-create and reinforce the structure, leads to a "hegemonic crisis," in which, faced with the heavy human, economic, social, and cultural costs, people begin to question the rationale for militarism, beginning with the rationale for specific wars, unless there is an ongoing effort to reinforce these values. The case of music shows how concentrated corporate ownership of the music industry with ideological predispositions will promote militaristic messages, but the case of the Dixie Chicks shows that staying the course as dissenters, without apology or shame, can pay off for an artist, because the conditions under which the intimidation and pressure can happen are not permanent. The normalization of torture on television as a legitimate form of interrogation has become very common in movies and even on network television, particularly in the popular program *24*. But even this case shows that the presentation of culture is not purely a top-down phenomenon. To be sure, in a time in which militaristic sentiment is being whipped up, in the wake of the 9/11 attacks, the producers and writers of *24* are prepared to feed on it, certainly for commercial reasons, and to aggravate it. However, by 2009, with two unpopular wars and a change in partisanship in Congress and the White House, the producers behind *24* can read the writing on the wall. Suddenly there is less torture in the seventh season and a final discussion about it which is more thoughtful than anything in the previous six seasons.

Finally, while all sports have the trappings of militarism on the surface, such as the playing of anthems and tributes to service members, football seems made for a militaristic society, inherent in the very structure of the game. As "America's game," it has risen alongside militarism, however, even it is not and will not be immune from the challenge to militarism. But it has been clear that the military's influence is so pervasive that even a game as serene as golf is not immune. The military promotes golf, and golf promotes the military. Finally, the cases of Pat Tillman and Jessica Lynch indicate that for short-term gain, the hero-seeking military and corporate sector will misrepresent the raw materials of their cases, but in both these instances intrepid journalists have asked the questions for which there were no good answers, and a version closer version to the truth has come out in the open. Militarism is built by thousands, even millions of small acts, but it can be undermined that way as well.

Notes

1. B. Lee Cooper, "Rumours of War: Lyrical Continuities," in *Continuities in Popular Culture: The Present in the Past & the Past in the Present and Future*, ed. Ray Broadus Browne and Ronald J. Ambrosetti (Bowling Green, OH: Bowling Green State University Popular Press, 1993), 138.

2. This paragraph relies on Ira Chernus, "Glued to Our Seats in the Theater of War," *TomDispatch*, September 25, 2007, www.alternet.org/story/63472/glued_to_ our_seats_in_the_theater_of_war/?page=entire (accessed July 17, 2009).

3. David M. Boje, "Deconstructing Visual Theatric Imagery of the Bush Presidency" (paper presented to August 2003 meeting of the Academy of Management in Seattle, pre-conference on visual imagery), http://peaceaware.com/documents/Boje_ essays/Bush_spectacle/boje_Bush_image_handling.htm (accessed July 18, 2009).

4. This account relies chiefly on Frank Rich, *The Greatest Story Ever Sold: The Decline and Fall of Truth from 9/11 to Katrina* (New York: Penguin, 2006), 88–92, as well as Boje, "Deconstructing Visual Theatric Imagery."

5. Jason Glover, "Techno-Fetishism: Making War Cool as Hell," *Thirdeye Magazine*, July 4, 2007, www.thirdeyemag.com/nonfiction/essays/war_is_entertainment/ (accessed July 8, 2008).

6. "George W. Bush's Military Service," Sourcewatch, www.sourcewatch.org/ index.php?title=George_W._Bush%27s_military_service (accessed June 22, 2009).

7. James Castonguay, "Intermedia and the War on Terror," in *Rethinking Global Security: Media, Popular Culture and the "War on Terror,"* ed. Andrew Martin and Patrice Petro (New Brunswick, NJ, and London: Rutgers University Press, 2006), 156.

8. Cooper, "Rumours of War: Lyrical Continuities," 124.

9. Brian Hiatt, "War Drums," *Entertainment Weekly*, April 10, 2003, www .ew.com/ew/article/0,,442160,00.html (accessed August 15, 2009).

10. Hiatt, "War Drums."

11. Hiatt, "War Drums."

12. For an interesting discussion, see Shannon Sampert and Natasja Treiberg, "The Reification of the 'American Soldier': Popular Culture, American Foreign Policy and Country Music" (paper presented at the annual meeting of the International Studies

Association, 48th Annual Convention, Hilton Chicago, Chicago, February 28, 2007), www.allacademic.com/meta/p179176_index.html (accessed July 13, 2009).

13. Charles K. Wolfe and James E. Akenson, eds., *Country Music Goes to War* (Lexington: University Press of Kentucky, 2005), 172.

14. Deborah Jaramillo, "Ugly War, Pretty Package: How the Cable News Network and the Fox News Channel Made the 2003 Invasion of Iraq High Concept" (Ph.D. diss., University of Texas at Austin, 2006), 325.

15. Michael Roberts, "The Message," *Denver Westword News*, April 3, 2003, http://westword.com/2003-04-03/news/the-message/ (accessed July 3, 2009).

16. See the website for Clear Channel Communications, Inc., www.clearchannel.com.

17. Roberts, "The Message."

18. Roberts, "The Message."

19. Tim Jones, "Media Giant's Rally Sponsorship Raises Questions," *Chicago Tribune*, March 19, 2003, http://web.archive.org/web/20030321204732/http://www.chicagotribune.com/news/showcase/ch-0303190157mar19.story (accessed August 15, 2009).

20. Jones, "Media Giant's Rally Sponsorship Raises Questions."

21. Joseph Kay, "The Ties That Bind: Media Giant Headed by Bush Cronies Promotes Iraq War," World Socialist Website, April 17, 2003, http://www.wsws.org/articles/2003/apr2003/media17.shtml (accessed August 15, 2009).

22. Brian Mansfield, "Country Anthem Plays a Drumbeat for War," *USA Today*, February 26, 2003, www.usatoday.com/news/politicselections/2004-03-23-clear_x.htm (accessed August 15, 2009).

23. Kay, "The Ties That Bind."

24. Eliza Truitt, "It's the End of the World as Clear Channel Knows It," *Slate*, September 17, 2001, www.slate.com/id/1008314/ (accessed August 10, 2009).

25. Truitt, "It's the End of the World as Clear Channel Knows It."

26. "Musical Responses to September 11: The list of Allegedly 'Banned' Songs," Freemuse, December 9, 2004, www.freemuse.org/sw21095.asp (accessed August 15, 2009).

27. Truitt, "It's the End of the World as Clear Channel Knows It."

28. Celestine Bohlen, "Think Tank: In the New War on Terrorism, Words Are Weapons, Too," *New York Times*, September 29, 2001, www.nytimes.com/2001/09/29/arts/think-tank-in-new-war-on-terrorism-words-are-weapons-too.html (accessed February 14, 2010).

29. Jennifer A. Carbin, "Boondocks Speaks: An Interview with Aaron McGruder," *City Paper* (Philadelphia), November 5, 2001, www.alternet.org/story/11859 (accessed February 14, 2010).

30. Andrew Buncombe, "U.S. Cartoonists under Pressure to Follow the Patriotic Line," *Independent* (UK), June 23, 2002, http://license.icopyright.net/user/view FreeUse.act?fuid=NDcxNDMzNg%3D%3D (accessed February 14, 2010).

31. One can also add that others have paid the price for dissent, such as former University of Colorado professor Ward Churchill, and former NBC correspondent Peter Arnett, in addition to Bill Maher, whose case was discussed previously. See

Jaclyn Sakow, "The Cancellation of Bill Maher's 'Politically Incorrect,'" Media Crit, October 3, 2007, http://mediacrit.wetpaint.com/page/The+Cancellation+of+Bill+Maher%27s+%22Politically+Incorrect%22 (accessed August 16, 2009).

32. "'Shut Up and Sing': Dixie Chicks' Big Grammy Win Caps Comeback from Backlash over Anti-War Stance," *Democracy Now!* February 15, 2007, www.democracynow.org/2007/2/15/shut_up_and_sing_dixie_chicks.

33. Adam Sweeting, "How the Chicks Survived Their Scrap with Bush," *Telegraph*, June 15, 2006, www.telegraph.co.uk/arts/main.jhtml?xml=/arts/2006/06/15/bmdixie15.xml (accessed August 15, 2009).

34. "Dixie Chicks, Gnarls Barkley Lead the Way," *USA Today*, December 25, 2006, www.usatoday.com/life/music/reviews/2006-15.

35. See To the Fallen Records website, www.tothefallenrecords.com (accessed August 15, 2009).

36. "To the Fallen: Soldiers Sing Their Own Tributes," *BBC*, July 12, 2007, www.bbc.co.uk/worldservice/programmes/outlook/news/story/2007/07/070712_gilfillan_sa.shtml (accessed August 15, 2009).

37. "To the Fallen," *BBC*.

38. To the Fallen Records, artists section, www.tothefallenrecords.com/artists-section.html.

39. Adam Baer, "The Sounds of War," *Slate*, April 17, 2003, www.slate.com/id/2081608/ (accessed August 15, 2009).

40. Nicholas Engstrom, "The Soundtrack for War," *Columbia Journalism Review* 3 (2003), http://cjrarchives.org/issues/2003/3/sound-engstrom.asp (accessed August 15, 2009).

41. Engstrom, "The Soundtrack for War."

42. Engstrom, "The Soundtrack for War."

43. Peter Dobrin, "Media's War Music Carries a Message," *Philadelphia Inquirer*, March 30, 2003.

44. Dobrin, "Media's War Music Carries a Message."

45. Engstrom, "The Soundtrack for War."

46. Engstrom, "The Soundtrack for War."

47. Engstrom, "The Soundtrack for War."

48. Dorbin, "Media's War Music Carries a Message."

49. Dorbin, "Media's War Music Carries a Message."

50. Richard Kim, "Pop Torture," *Huffinton Post*, December 10, 2005, http://huffingtonpost.com/richard-kim/pop-torture_b_11980.html (accessed May 5, 2008).

51. Clive Stafford Smith, "Welcome to 'the Disco,'" *Guardian*, June 19, 2008, www.guardian.co.uk/world/2008/jun/19/usa.guantanamo?gusrc=rss&feed=39 (accessed August 15, 2009).

52. Suzanne G. Cusiak, "Music as Torture/Music as Weapon," *Transcultural Music Review* 10 (2006), www.sibetrans.com/trans/trans10/cusick_eng.htm (accessed August 15, 2009).

53. Associated Press, "U.S. Deploys Loud Music, Insults in Fallujah," *Globe and Mail*, April 16, 2004, www.theglobeandmail.com/servlet/story/RTGAM.20040416.wpsyop0416/BNStory/International (accessed August 15, 2009).

54. David Peisner, "War Is Loud," *Spin Magazine,* December 2006, http://djpeisner .com/articles/War%20Is%20Loud.pdf (accessed August 15, 2009), 92.

55. Smith, "Welcome to 'the Disco.'"

56. Smith, "Welcome to 'the Disco.'"

57. Smith, "Welcome to 'the Disco.'"

58. Peisner, "War Is Loud," 91.

59. Peisner, "War Is Loud," 91.

60. Smith, "Welcome to 'the Disco.'"

61. Jane Mayer, "Whatever It Takes: The Politics of the Man Behind '24,'" *New Yorker,* February 19, 2007, www.newyorker.com/reporting/2007/02/19/070219fa_ fact_mayer?printable=true (accessed May 8, 2008).

62. The text of this speech is reproduced in "President Bush's Speech on Terrorism," transcript, *New York Times,* September 6, 2006, www.nytimes.com/2006/09/06/ washington/06bush_transcript.html?_r=2&ei=5070&en=0a7d2e2edf2ee45&ex=1190 260800&pagewanted=all (accessed July 4, 2009).

63. Nate Knapper, "Jack Bauer, '24' and the Acceptance of Torture in American Culture," *National Ledger,* September 13, 2006, www.nationalledger.com/cgibin/ artman/exec/view.cgi?archive=4&num=8350 (accessed May 7, 2008).

64. Mayer, "Whatever It Takes."

65. Matthew Alexander with John R. Bruning, *How to Break a Terrorist: The U.S. Interrogators Who Used Brains, Not Brutality, to Take Down the Deadliest Man in Iraq* (New York: The Free Press, 2009).

66. Chris Barsanti, "Network Sadism: Is Fox's *24* an Advertisement for Torture?" Pop Matters, March 6, 2006, www.popmatters.com/tv/features/060306-24.shtml (accessed May 8, 2008).

67. Faiz Shaker, "U.S. Military: Television Series '24' Is Promoting Torture in the Ranks," *Think Progress,* February 13, 2007, http://thinkprogress.org/2007/02/13/ torture-on-24/ (accessed May 8, 2008).

68. Mayer, "Whatever It Takes."

69. David Cole, "The Torture Veto," *Nation,* March 13, 2008, www.thenation.com/ doc/20080331/cole (accessed July 5, 2009).

70. Mayer, "Whatever It Takes."

71. Roberta Vescovi, "Children into Soldiers: Sport and Fascist Italy," in *The European Sports History Review: Militarism, Sport, Europe—War Without Weapons,* vol. 5, ed. J. A. Mangan (Portland, OR: Frank Cass, 2003), 166.

72. Varda Burstyn, *The Rites of Men: Manhood, Politics, and the Culture of Sport* (Toronto, ON: University of Toronto Press, 1999), 187.

73. Steven J. Jackson and David L. Andres, *Sport Culture and Advertising: Identities, Commodities, and the Politics of Repression* (New York: Routledge / Taylor and Francis, 2005).

74. Michael Strahan and Jay Glazer, *Inside the Helmet: Life as a Sunday Afternoon Warrior* (New York: Penguin Group, 2007), 216.

75. This paragraph relies on Michael L. Butterworth and Stormi Moskal, "Football, Flags, and Fun: The Bell Helicopter Armed Forces Bowl and the Rhetorical Production of Militarism" (unpublished ms).

76. See "Super Bowl 101," Martha Stewart, www.marthastewart.com/article/super-bowl-101?autonomy_kw=patriotic&rsc=header_5 (accessed July 8, 2009).

77. Paul Tagliabue as cited in Sue Curry Jansen, *Critical Communication Theory: Power, Media, Gender, and Technology* (Lanham, MD: Rowman and Littlefield, 2002), 191.

78. Michael Oriard, *Brand NFL: Making and Selling America's Favorite Sport* (Chapel Hill: University of North Carolina Press, 2007), 23.

79. Burstyn, *The Rites of Men*, 186.

80. Samantha King, "Offensive Lines: Sport-State Synergy in an Era of Perpetual War," *Cultural Studies and Critical Methodologies* 8 (2008): 527–39.

81. Oriard, *Brand NFL*, 24.

82. Army News Service, "NFL and Operation Tribute to Freedom Kick-Off Concert," Military Info—American Military News, August 21, 2003, www.militaryinfo.com/news_story.cfm?textnewsid=508 (accessed January 15, 2009).

83. "Supporting Our Soldiers," Operation Tribute to Freedom, January 18, 2009, www4.army.mil/otf/about.php (accessed January 19, 2009).

84. Ivie as cited in Butterworth and Moskal, "Football, Flags, and Fun," 2.

85. Frank Rich, "The Mysterious Death of Pat Tillman," *New York Times*, November 6, 2005, http://select.nytimes.com/2005/11/06/opinion/06rich.html (accessed January 16, 2009).

86. News Service, "Cardinals Add Tillman to Ring of Honor," *Washington Post*, November 13, 2006, E10, www.washingtonpost.com/wpdyn/content/article/2006/11/12/AR2006111201145.html (accessed January 15, 2009).

87. Kevin Tillman, "Deliberate Acts of Deceit," *Guardian*, April 24, 2007, www.guardian.co.uk/commentisfree/2007/apr/24/deliberateactsofdeceit (accessed January 18, 2009).

88. Steve Coll, "Barrage of Bullets Drowned Out Cries of Comrades," *Washington Post*, December 5, 2004, A01, www.washingtonpost.com/wp-dyn/articles/A35717-2004Dec4.html (accessed January 15, 2009), and Steve Coll, "Army Spun Tale Around Ill-Fated Mission," *Washington Post*, December 6, 2004, A01, www.washingtonpost.com/wp-dyn/articles/A37679-2004Dec5.html (accessed January 15, 2009).

89. "Soldier: Army ordered me not to tell truth about Tillman," CNN, April 25, 2007, www.cnn.com/2007/POLITICS/04/24/tillman.hearing/index.html (accessed January 18, 2009).

90. Rich, "The Mysterious Death of Pat Tillman."

91. For some, the media enthusiasm was the product of the U.S. interest in "captivity narratives." Melani McAlister, "Saving Private Lynch," *New York Times*, April 6, 2003, www.nytimes.com/2003/04/06/opinion/saving-private-lynch.html (accessed July 4, 2009).

92. Norman Solomon, "New Chapter in Jessica Lynch Media Saga," *Creators*, www.creators.com/opinion/norman-solomon/new-chapter-in-jessica-lynch-media-saga.html (accessed July 4, 2009).

93. Susan Faludi provides an excellent account of these events in "Precious Little Jessi," in *The Terror Dream: Fear and Fantasy in Post-9/11 America* (New York: Metropolitan Books, 2007).

94. Edward Wasserman, "Media Monopolies Still Can't Unearth the Truth," *Miami Herald*, June 30, 2003, www.commondreams.org/views03/0630-01.htm (accessed July 4, 2009).

95. Faludi, *Terror Dream*, 177–83.

96. *Militainment, Inc.: Militarism & Pop Culture*, DVD, produced by Roger Stahl (Media Education Foundation, 2007).

97. Duncan MacKay, "Chariots of Ire: Is U.S. Jingoism Tarnishing the Olympic Ideal?" *Guardian*, February 15, 2002, www.guardian.co.uk/world/2002/feb/15/usa.olympicgames (accessed January 18, 2009).

98. For videos, see "Memorial Day ESPN Sportscenter Top Ten Veterans Countdown," YouTube, March 27, 2008, www.youtube.com/watch?v=F6-_EDejG4U&feature=related (accessed January 18, 2009); "Hockey Night in Canada—Don Cherry Salutes Canadian Soldiers," YouTube, November 8, 2008, www.youtube.com/watch?v=wmPnaA1voNA (accessed January 17, 2009).

99. Butterworth and Moskal, "Football, Flags, and Fun," 3.

100. "Coach's Corner" from March 21, 2009, which illustrates this point, can be viewed at www.youtube.com/watch?v=cgtuHzwZtSM (accessed July 3, 2009).

101. Nick Turse, *The Complex: How the Military Invades Our Everyday Lives* (New York: Henry Holt and Company / Metropolitan Books, 2008), 9, 141–46.

102. "Strikeouts for Troops," Strikeouts for Troops, www.strikeoutsfortroops.org/ (accessed January 15, 2009).

103. Tim Hipps, "Tiger Opens Arms for Troops, Families at AT&T National," Army News Service, May 29, 2009, www.army.mil/-news/2008/05/29/9499-tiger opens-arms-for-troops-families-at-att-national/ (accessed January 14, 2009).

104. Turse, *The Complex*, 185–87.

105. Detroit Pistons, "Seats for Soldiers—Giving Back to Those Who Give to You," NBA Media Ventures, www.nba.com/pistons/community/soldiers_071115.html (accessed January 15, 2009); Dallas Mavericks, "Mavs Host Annual Seats for Soldiers," NBA Media Ventures, www.nba.com/mavericks/community/seatsforsoldiers_121308.html (accessed January 15, 2009); Boston Red Sox, "Red Sox Announce Seats for Soldiers Program," MLB Advanced Media, June 6, 2008, http://boston.redsox.mlb.com/news/press_releases/press_release.jsp?ymd=20080606&content_i=2853004&vkey=pr_bos&fext=.jsp&c_id=bos (accessed January 15, 2009).

106. Ottawa Senators, "Bulletin: 5th Annual Canadian Forces Appreciation Night," Capital Sports & Entertainment, Inc., November 3, 2008, http://senators.nhl.com/team/app/?service=page&page=NewsPage&articleid=390288 (accessed January 16, 2009).

107. Dallas Mavericks, "Mavs Host Annual Seats for Soldiers."

108. Boston Red Sox, "Red Sox Announce Seats for Soldiers Program."

109. Laura L. O'Toole and Jessica R. Schiffman, *Gender Violence: Interdisciplinary Perspectives* (New York: New York University Press, 1997), 70.

6

Warrior Nation

When War Becomes a Consumer Lifestyle

I N PREVIOUS CHAPTERS WE HAVE EXAMINED THE ROLE that popular culture played before these wars were started, and how powerful agents in the culture have tried to maintain support for these wars as they drag on. This chapter will examine the forces in culture that are trying to normalize permanent warfare, on an everyday basis. U.S. life is saturated with commercial media, and one of the ways in which Warrior Nation is created is through advertising, both to promote products but also to promote values. One of the values that it has promoted, and used as a selling opportunity, has been the fear-based consumption that in an uncertain and dangerous world there is *one more product* to buy that will increase safety. Fear has spawned new literature, sometimes aimed at children, sometimes in the form of the romance novel, all of which has the effect of helping people adjust to the new reality. There is also the interesting case of "torture chic," in which, ever in search of novelty, fashion designers create new lines of torture- and military-oriented clothing, which triggers a revival of fashion variations of military wear, such as camouflage versions of contemporary clothing, and non-camo or non-desert versions of military clothing. Patriotism, or the militaristic form of patriotism that is the norm in U.S. life, is also manifested in taken-for-granted ways in every day life, such as celebrating the Fourth of July.

In October 2001 the United States invaded Afghanistan, ostensibly because the Taliban government of that country would not or could not hand over Osama bin Laden and other important al-Qaeda leaders, and because that Taliban was an Islamic fundamentalist movement which was said to provide safe haven for anti-Western terrorist organizations. This was easy to sell to

U.S. citizens because memories of 9/11 were very fresh, people were newly inclined to follow the president's leadership, and they sought revenge. To the degree that it was necessary, domestic skeptics were also told that invading and taking over Afghanistan would liberate Afghani women from the grip of Islamic "medievalists." Convincing the people to go to war in Iraq was more difficult, because the purported job in Afghanistan had not been completed (bin Laden was never captured), and as we have seen, and as is now well known, the Bush administration had to tell several lies to gain the necessary minimal domestic consent to go forward. In the fall of 2002 and early 2003 there were massive protests around the world, including within the United States, because a certain segment of the populations understood that this was aggression and that administration claims would probably turn out to be false. Since 2003 there have been protests but the numbers have been small. Perhaps people have relied on elections, like the midterm elections of 2006 and the presidential election of 2008, to change policy fundamentally, just as many thought the 1968 election, one way or another, would spell the end of the U.S. war in Vietnam.[1] However, like in the Vietnam era, elections have not proven as effective as the public expected. In the United States there is a struggle for and against the republic as a warrior nation, in which the reality of permanent war has been or can be normalized through the culture.

Advertising for Recruitment and Propaganda

At the core of day-to-day encouragement of militarism is advertising, both to encourage patriotic consumption and to promote the image of the military in U.S. life. J. M. Flagg's iconic Uncle Sam poster was created for those purposes for World War I and II, and the "Be All You Can Be" campaign, commenced in the years after the end of conscription in the 1970s, was a two decade-long marketing campaign that "publicize[d] the military as a viable alternative to the civilian sector."[2] In the months following 9/11, over two hundred thousand new recruits enlisted in the army, but state planners decided to update their recruiting promotion. Leo Burnett Worldwide, the world's ninth largest advertising agency, was enlisted to promote the army, launching the Army of One campaign. Under Leo Burnett, recruitment campaigns were marketed particularly toward "target" groups. For example, they engaged the Hispanic-owned Cartel Creative with a $380 million contract to help "'penetrate' the Hispanic market." Targeting African Americans, Leo Burnett ran advertisements in magazines like *XXL*; in a 2005 copy, an advertisement depicted a black soldier sitting, showing the ropes to the white soldier.[3] Carl Chery reported:

With help from *The Source* magazine, the U.S. military is targeting hip-hop fans with custom made Hummers, throwback jerseys and trucker hats. The yellow Hummer, spray-painted with two black men in military uniform, is the vehicle of choice for the U.S. Army's "Take It to the Streets campaign"—a sponsored mission aimed at recruiting young African Americans into the military ranks.[4]

Beyond racial groups they also focused on parents, like through the $10 million campaign that urged parents in 2005 to learn more about the services—to "make it a two-way conversation" with their children who want to join the military.[5] With plummeting support for the war in Iraq and increased personnel needs, the military awarded a $1.35 billion contract in December 2005 to McCann Erickson Worldwide, a subsidiary of Interpublic Group, which launched a new campaign, Army Strong, on Veterans' Day, 2006. The prevalence of these advertisements have many concerned, like Mike Doughtry:

> It's perverse to me that we employ ad agencies to attract our soldiers and sailors. How weird is it that on shows skewed young, between the Mountain Dew and the L'Oreal ads, there are exhortations to pick up a gun and serve your country? How did we let this just become noise in the background?[6]

Despite these objections, recruitment advertisements are now everywhere, from billboards, to magazines, to television commercials—and are now unprecedentedly expensive. In 2003, the military's recruiting and advertising budget was $590 million, and they requested $20.5 billion for 2009, aiming to recruit an additional 80,000 enlistees. Significantly, this would cost taxpayers eighty times more than the 1998 budget that enlisted over twice as many.[7] Controversially, there is pressure on school districts and high school principals to let in military recruiters, based in part on a requirement in the federal No Child Left Behind Act that schools that receive federal aid must allow recruiters on campus.[8] It should be no surprise that with the economic crisis of 2008–2010, the U.S. military suddenly had no difficulty meeting its recruiting targets.[9]

Pro-militarist advertising and promotion goes well beyond just recruiting, for all aspects of the development and implementation of policy are geared toward managing public opinion. In the past military operations went by names with seemingly random words, like "Operation Overlord," but today the naming of military missions is "all a matter of branding," as illustrated by carefully chosen labels such as "Operation Enduring Freedom" and "Operation Iraqi Freedom."[10] Notably, Charlotte Beers, former CEO of Ogilvy and Mather Worldwide, was named undersecretary of state for public diplomacy and public affairs following 9/11, and given $520 million to sell U.S. policies abroad in "the largest public relations campaign in the history of foreign policy."[11]

Bush-affiliated organizations, PR and lobbying firms have also played an important role in promoting militaristic policies, including the Project for a New American Century, the Hoover Institution, the Washington Institute, and the American Enterprise Institute. Furthermore, in 2002, the *Times* of London reported that the White House–created Office of Global Communications would spend $200 million on a "PR blitz," using "advertising techniques to persuade crucial target groups that [Saddam Hussein] must be ousted."[12] Freedom's Watch (not to be confused with Freedom House, the human rights organization), another group comprised mostly of former Bush administration officials, launched a $15 million television and radio campaign in twenty states in 2007. Claiming to be "fighting for what is right," these advertisements falsely linked the 9/11 attacks to the War in Iraq, as late as 2007, to bolster public support for the war, and secondarily, for Republican candidates. One of the spots featured a widow who explains, "I lost two family members to al Qaeda . . . my uncle, a firefighter, on 9/11, and my husband, Travis, in Iraq." It also featured an 800-number for the public to urge their representatives "not to surrender to terror." These extremely misleading messages were defended by Freedom's Watch president Bradley Blakeman, who declared that the debate about the War on Terror had been dominated by "those who want to quit while victory is possible," whereas the goal of the Freedom's Watch campaign was "to make clear that when America goes to war, victory is the only outcome."[13] The organization was wrapped up after the 2008 election.

Got Fear? Selling Preparedness

It is said that investors in the stock market are motivated by two emotions—greed and fear—and this applies to the consumer economy as well. For decades, marketing has promoted greed among consumers, but since 9/11 fear has become a major motivator as well. Fear is "one of the most primitive emotions in the human psyche" and it's now being used to sell products and promote militaristic patriotism.[14] As Marita Sturken notes, there has been a rise in "comfort consumerism" in which "domestic contentment" has been marketed as a way of helping people cope with 9/11 and its aftermath.[15] In the 1950s and early 1960s the federal Office of Civil Defense encouraged homeowners to install bomb shelters in their houses, and there is now a wealth of material on the advertising, public service announcements and building plans that were available at the time.[16] In the 2000s, a new market of fear-driven products has emerged, including "urban survival kits," marketed on websites like UrbanSurvivalTools[17] and GetReadyGear,[18] which protect civilians during emergencies, including terrorism. Moreover, Pantheon International published a *Terrorism Survival Guide* as part of an "Operation Enduring Freedom series." Joe Lockard remarks that with a cover crowded with fear-evoking subtitles—"Dangers We Face Now! What You Can Do to Meet the Threats!"—and many advertisements equating consumption with survival, the guide "rel[ies] on reader fear of social threats and general social chaos to promote sales."[19]

The hottest, most recent trend is toward bulletproof clothes, including for civilians. Vexed Generation, a hip clothing store in London, sells what they refer to as "protective daywear," including nylon cargo pants, canvas sailor pants with Velcro closures and padded bulletproof vests. Sale of bulletproof gear amounts to $200 million per year, 5 percent of which goes to civilians. Urban Body Armor in New Jersey sells bulletproof versions of almost everything, including leather pants, baseball caps, and full-length mink coats. This trend, which rappers refer to as "vesting up," can be done in the latest styles.[20]

Less overtly, the exploitation of the post-9/11 fear culture saw the resurgence of the Hummer, the civilian version of the army's standard-issue personnel transport, first popularized following the television coverage of armored Humvees in the first Gulf War. This market was large enough that a smaller, more affordable model was released in 2005.[21] The Hummer craze in the early 1990s helped launch the broader Sports Utility Vehicle (SUV) trend, pushed by urban and suburban Americans' desire for "armored cars for the battlefield," rooted in their "deepest fears of violence and crime," according to a study by psychologist Cloitaire Rapaille.[22] It is a testament to the power of advertising that SUVs are *less* rather than more safe, because they have a higher center of gravity and therefore a greater chance of rollover, and because the driver has less visibility from the windows.[23] Henry Giroux notes that "Humvee ads offer up the fantasy of military glamour and modes of masculinity that seem to guarantee virility for their owners by attempting to induce a mixture of fear and admiration from everyone else."[24] Of course, both General Motors and the U.S. economy are feeling the hangover of this fear- and status-oriented consumerism. In the first four months of 2009, Hummer sales were down 67 percent over the previous year because of the rise in gas prices, particularly in 2008, and because of the economic crisis that began in fall 2008. The economics of fear has turned out to be unsustainable not only for the U.S. government's fiscal position, but also for the consumer. General Motors, as part of its bankruptcy-dictated restructuring, is selling its Hummer division to Sichuan Tengzhong Heavy Industrial Machinery Co. of China, which is making its first foray into auto production.[25] The decline of the SUV, the Big Three's big money maker of the 1990s and early 2000s, may be permanent and is certainly one of the causes of the decline of U.S. auto manufacturing.

Fear has also increased the popularity of other militarized products like "ruggedized" laptops, which are "to ordinary laptops what the Hummer is to the family car." Heavier and more costly, with features like shock absorption and bulletproof plastic, these laptops were initially produced by military suppliers but have since surged in popularity. Dell[26] and Panasonic both now produce a series for popular consumption.[27] Army-navy stores are doing a brisk business selling gas masks, aviator sun glasses, night-vision goggles, and other military equipment. Whether it is fear or comfort or just being with the times, in 2003 sunglass maker Oakley decided to get into the military footwear business, and a consumer version of the "Elite Special Forces Standard-Issue Assault Boot" would be sold to the public at a list price of $225, while the shoe would cost only $195.[28]

Fear is also manifested where consumption and design meet, such as in architecture. The "bollard," originally a strong post to secure boat lines, and now essentially a security barrier, is the new architectural accessory. As Nicolai Ouroussoff notes in the *New York Times*, the security-conscious 2000s have spawned a new approach he refers to as "21st-century medievalism," in which security trumps other concerns such as open concepts and transparency.[29] On the subject of bollards, blogger AO points out on Oslandscape that bollards can be turned into art objects, with decoration on the bollard, or the bollard itself can be designed as an expressive object.[30] Of course this tends to obscure the real purpose of the bollards and make the ubiquity of security-oriented architecture more palatable.

This fascination with security and militarism has created a market for new experiences for adults, ones that they both enjoy and might think will be useful in the real world. Southeast Asia may be better known for its sex tourism, but a lesser known attraction is the chance for a visitor to fire high-end military weapons for a price. A tourist can fire a rocket-propelled grenade, the famous "RPG" of news reports, for fifty U.S. dollars. Closer to home, Tactical Tanks of Sherman, Texas, runs a "military amusement park" in which well-heeled individuals or corporate groups can get the thrill of driving a tank for the day for $8,500.[31] For many years Americans have had access to paint ball for war-gaming purposes, but more recently "airsoft tournaments" have sprung up. In these tournaments, two teams wear "battle dress" and use air guns that are close to perfect replicas of U.S. standard issue M-4 assault rifles and M-60 machine guns. These rifles fire roughly quarter of an inch "biodegradable" rounds as far as two hundred yards and their advocates are referred to as "6 mm Junkies" for the size of the round. The enlightened organizer requires that all participants wear eye protection. In a recent tournament organized by Wayne's World of Paint Ball in Ocala, Florida, many participants, including West Port High School student Arnold Deleon, sixteen, praised the realism of the game.[32]

Henry Giroux notes that popular fears about domestic safety and internal threats, accentuated by endless terror alerts, have created a society that increasingly accepts the notion of a "war without limits" as a normal state of affairs. In the early 2000s, fear and insecurity produced a collective anxiety among Americans, exploited to get them to believe that they should vote Republican as the only way to be protected. In addition to producing manufactured political loyalty, such fears can also be manipulated into a kind of "war fever."[33] The mobilization of war fever carries with it a kind of paranoid edge, stoked by government alerts and repressive laws and used "to create the most extensive national security apparatus in our nation's history."[34]

War Stories

It should be no surprise that in the 2000s, in an environment in which war is a major issue, various aspects of culture including literature would turn their attention to the subject, in some cases as a form of therapy, and in other cases simply picking up on war stories or Middle East settings for story telling. As soldiers from the United States deployed to the wars in Iraq and Afghanistan, opportunities in publishing opened up for military spouses, mainly wives. Authors were most successful writing children's books that focused on easing the separation children had to undergo when their parents and relatives were sent to the Middle East. Carmen R. Hoyt published one such book entitled *Daddy's in Iraq, but I Want Him Back.* She describes her interest in writing this story, stating

> I felt a need for this story to be written when my three year old, Jack, became very insecure upon his father's deployment to the War in Iraq. I wished there was a way to help him "get his little arms around" the situation. It was new for me also and I didn't know how to help him. When my husband returned safely, I wanted to write the story. I wanted to document this time in our family's life; to put parameters around the situation for little people, who have no idea what's going to happen or why.[35]

It seems that, inevitably, the family prays and also helps explain the situation by accepting a white-washed version of the Iraq war and the importance of the military chain of command. From the child's perspective, the mom says that Daddy is following the president's orders to make Iraq safe for its children, and making his family proud, though Iraqis would look at the matter very differently.

After art of a smiling U.S. soldier kneeling with two smiling Iraqi kids, the final line on the page states that even though the child was proud of his father, he still wished his father were at home. This is simply one example in a line of many, with titles like *A Year Without Dad* (2003), *Mommy, You're My Hero* (2005), and *I Miss You! A Military Kid's Book about Deployment* (2007), featuring the experiences of children missing their mothers and fathers serving in the U.S. military. We should not be surprised that these books present the mission in the most noble terms, which itself encourages future missions (and militarism), since this is therapeutic literature and these noble terms make it easier to cope with the absence. These efforts are not limited to book production alone. The long-running children's program *Sesame Street* also cooperated with DoD in introducing war themes into its programs, and it also produced a DVD series and went on the USO tour of domestic military bases.[36] There are also nonfiction works that parents can turn to in order to indoctrinate their children in favor of militaristic patriotism. For example, based on their claim that most media "present a negative view of America," conservatives like Myrna Blyth and Chriss Hinton have written a book entitled *How to Raise an American: 1776 Fun and Easy Tools, Tips and Activities to Help Your Child Love This Country.*[37]

Books centered on Iraq and Afghanistan, yet written for children, appeared early after 9/11, first emerging as a method of encouraging childhood education about the Middle East as references to this part of the world appeared frequently on the news. One of the first of these books was *The Breadwinner* by Canadian writer Deborah Ellis, a novel narrated by young Parvana as she describes life in Kabul, Afghanistan, under Taliban rule. This book, published in November of 2001, was soon followed by two sequels, *Parvana's Journey* (2003) and *Mud City* (2004), clearly filling a void for fictional books set in the Middle East after 9/11. This trio of books provided much-needed information about a way of life foreign to many North American children. The books focus primarily on the story of young Parvana but also highlight the religious and political landscapes of Afghanistan. Of course this truth-telling through fiction can inform the reader but also be raw material in arguments in favor of war for alleged humanitarian reasons. Nine years after the fall of the Taliban, one could still write truthful fiction of Afghanistan, painting an unflattering picture as though little has changed.

While these books serve to ease the heartache of young children upon the deployment of a parent or relative to a war zone, a collection of novels for the wives of deployed soldiers was soon to follow. The ubiquitous *Chicken Soup for the Soul* franchise brought together the stories of military wives in 2005, following the pattern of post-9/11 publications. Numerous publications provided a place for military wives to share their stories of loss and separation, opening up a sphere of communication and a point of connection, including *365 Deployment Days: A Wife's Survival Story* (2007) and *Separated by Duty, United in Love* (2006).

Interestingly, another popular niche of books read by women has unexpectedly adopted a post-9/11 plotline: romance novels. While new novels such as *Sex, Straight Up* (2008) and *Smolder* (2008), portray main characters who have lost their partners in the World Trade Center on 9/11, romance novelist Susan Mallery chose to take a completely different route. A blogger called Not Yet Enlightened remarks that Mallery "began writing romance novels with 'sheik' in the title in November 2001 and is up to eight in her series" and hypothesizes the reasons for frequent depictions of Arab heroes in romance novels: "[R]omance novelists and readers are constantly in search of new diabolical male stereotypes, [and] the recent media coverage of Arab masculinity has sparked an uptick in Arab-male leading roles in romance novels."[38]

Sheikhs and Desert Love, a popular website dedicated to exploring this new subgenre, is complete with a comprehensive listing of romance novels "with a Sheikh (or an Arab or desert prince) as the primary male character." Searching by publication year on the website divulges an impressive increase since 9/11 in romance novels, published mainly by Silhouette and Harlequin, featuring an Arab hero.[39] British author Helen Fielding (famous for her novels about popular character Bridget Jones), published a novel entitled *Olivia Joules and the Overactive Imagination* in 2004 about a terrorist plot and the CIA, while remaining deeply rooted in what is commonly referred to as "chick lit." The integration of terrorist plotlines and handsome Arab men seems to be a means to normalize warrior nation, including bringing women into the fold.

However, another subset of post-9/11 literature has also emerged, written by individuals who have occupied a professional relationship with the U.S. government. For example, Francine Mathews, a former CIA analyst, penned a thrilling espionage novel, *The Cutout*, with a post-9/11 publication date, a book that aids in pioneering a new genre focused on terror. Reviewers describe the book as a "husband-and-wife agent team involved in a terrorist plot, one that results in the kidnapping of the American vice president and a threat to destabilize the entire European continent."[40] Who better to imagine a realistic and intriguing terrorist plot than an ex-CIA analyst once actively involved in foiling the same activities of real terrorists? Romance and fantasy aside, a post-9/11 world in which terror has emerged as a defined fear is also present in contemporary fiction, appearing in more realistic settings and situations. For example, several adult novels engage with 9/11 as a backdrop for character interactions. *Saturday* (2005) by Ian McEwan uses a post-9/11 scene to interact with the changing world after the terrorist attacks. *Extremely Loud and Incredibly Close* (2005) by Jonathon Safran Foer follows young nine-year-old Oscar Schnell as he tries to come to terms with his father's death at the World Trade Center.

Torture Chic

Camo fashion has been growing in popularity since 9/11, to the extent that clothing made in camouflage prints, whether jungle green, desert tan, or futuristic hot pinks and blues, can now be seen from hip hop chic to runway couture. Camo patterns can be found on clothing for adults and children including on bras, underwear, socks, belts, shoes, hoodies, jackets, T-shirts, pants, and dresses. Homes decorated in camo fabric are featured in the interior decorating magazines including bedding sets for children. You can buy camo-designed rubber ducks, magnets, guitars, bike tires, pool table sets, skateboards, purses, dog accessories, chairs, walking canes, cell phone cases, and even have your car or truck detailed in complete camouflage. Francine Parnes, a style writer for *Newsday*, noted that "It's one of the whimsies of the garment industry that Christian Dior created a $5,000 single-shouldered gown in a print that's more typically reserved for the clothing of combat." Camouflage comes from the French word "*camoufler*" meaning "to hide or disguise" and was instituted as a means to hide military vehicles in WWI and eventually soldiers in WWII. Inundated with images of U.S. troops in camouflage uniforms, many fans of the fashion state that they feel powerful and ready to take on the world when they wear their camo gear in daily life.[41] Some wear it with pride as a sign of participation in the military, or as a form of allegiance. As a manufacturer told *Time* magazine, "I think many people wear military clothes because they feel proud of the U.S."[42] In the hip hop community, camo can serve as a statement about inner city living conditions. Ray Newton, a team skate rider for the design firm Choice Casuals, said the camouflage look is hot "because it represents a tough guy thing. We're kids living in the city and the city can sometimes be a war zone, you know."[43]

Even in the age of Obama, the trend toward militaristic fashion is still going strong. In late 2009, pop sensation Rihanna released her latest video, *Hard*, in which she is pictured in sexualized military garb, walking through minefields, firing an assault rifle, wearing a helmet, sitting on a tank barrel, all while oblivious to soldiers running around her.[44] While there is not much political content in the song, one can imagine it may set a fashion trend. The British "pop princess" Cheryl Cole has also launched her 2009 release wearing military-inspired clothes.[45] In early 2010 *Teen Vogue* presented a photo spread for the spring season, under the title "Enchanted Soldier." It appears that military-inspired fashion is making a comeback, in the work of designers and retailers such as Philip Lim, Paul Smith, Clare Tough, Ellen Christine, See by Chloé, Maria La Rosa, Comme des Garçons, Marc by Marc Jacobs, B B Dakota, and American Apparel.[46] Just as President Obama has ratified many of the Bush-era policies, designers may now feel freed to roar back with military designs on the catwalk.

But fashion goes beyond just military inspiration for the runways. In January of 2008, British fashion designer John Galliano debuted his fall men's collection "Delirium" on the Paris runways and sparked a new debate about social commentary in fashion and where the line should be drawn. Midway through his collection, ostensibly modeled after "the frost fairs" of Tudor England, came models who reminded audiences more of Abu Graib than *haute couture*. Viewers of the fashion runway were already accustomed to military-inspired lines, like khaki and camo styles, that had been popular for several years. One designer even "had beefy models in commando gear scramble over tabletops and explode balloons."[47] As Richard Goldstein wrote in the *Village Voice* shortly after the 2003 invasion of Iraq, there *is* a connection between fashion and sex and military conquest, for men at least.[48] But what John Galliano was doing, parading models, bloodied and bruised with large slashes across their chests and hoods or nooses around their necks, wearing not much else but backless underwear, was definitely new. As shocking and appalling as it may have seemed, this was not the first time the fashion world, or John Galliano for that matter, has used the runway as a medium to make a political statement. Back in 2000, his fall line "boho-meets-hobo chic" was inspired by the homeless in a bid to expose the pure decadence of couture by "turning it inside out." He asked us, what's the connection between rich and poor? What's the connection between the person on the street and the person who buys couture clothes? By definition designers design reflecting on the world around them, and the fashion industry focuses on novelty, so political statements can trickle down to the department store rack.

In September of 2006, *Vogue Italia* presented Steven Meisel's photo essay, entitled "State of Emergency," which featured black and white and colored photographs of beautiful women in varying degrees and positions of torture. They feature faceless police officers hassling perfect women in beautiful gowns, in the form of airport strip searches, harassment by dogs, billy clubbing ,and being pushed to the ground with guns pointed at their heads. Just like Galliano's collection, they echo and parody the excess of U.S. policies which at their worst led to situations like Abu Graib.

Meisel uses the same method, demanding that we see the ways in which we are "buying into" the War on Terror. From the plain white T-shirt, to the trench coat, to epaulets, buttons, bell bottoms, safari jackets, lace up boots, shorter hemlines, and camouflage, fashion has drawn inspiration from the military uniform and the war economy so much so that it has become invisible to our eyes. We no longer associate these items of clothing with overseas battles and political agendas but with a set of values, pride, strength, solidarity, patriotism, and masculinity. Galliano and Meisel wish to shift our perspective, shattering the romanticism of war and showing us instead its dark side—the impact on the victims of human cruelty and destruction. Their work creates an opportunity for dialogue, provoking us to question in what ways we are contributing to the United States' and other governments' policies.

Fashion is such a unique forum for this sort of bold statement because "the medium is the message" as Marshall McLuhan once said. Not only is clothing considered high art in the form of haute couture, but it is also a very integral part of our everyday lives. While one might not be aware of the many ways fashion touches our lives, one of the characters in *The Devil Wears Prada* points out its importance. In a long monologue, she emphasizes that any fashion choice, including buying something at the discount bin at a local department store, has been programmed and market-tested by the fashion industry not only in high fashion but in the clothes that everyone wears.

The fashion industry has potential as a pulpit, for it is effective at reaching a significant portion of the population, circulating the message and creating a forum for discussion. Its deficiency lies in the trickle-down effect, in the process of reaching a larger demographic of people; at every step the message gets watered down and perhaps at the end of the line it gets washed away completely.

Both Galliano and Meisel have been accused by the media of fetishizing and glamorizing torture and suffering in order to sell clothing, by capitalizing on the well-known slogan that sex sells. It can be argued that the fashion world is not the right place for this type of message because it is far too wrapped up in frivolity and superficiality to be taken seriously. Some say that stripped down on its most basic level, the images in "State of Emergency" and on John Galliano's runway are essentially just a type of violent porn. The fashion industry is just that, an industry, where profit is the bottom line, and underneath the guise of the designers' creative expression it is all simply a marketing tool in order to sell a product. The important question, according to Joanna Bourke, the author of *Rape: A History* is "what these images are doing and to whom?"[49]

What designers do not take into account perhaps is the number of people their statement will touch. They see their market as those select few, the sophisticated and the wealthy, those who would attend their runway shows and who are accustomed to their form of high culture. These images are most dangerous not to the first hand observer but to the second hand consumer, who will receive the watered down version, free of the antiwar message and only with the sexualized aspects. "Abu Graib was not about sex, they were about people torturing people, (Meisel's) photographs are very beautiful, beautiful from a torture perspective and what concerns me is we are quite literally buying into the war on terror," Bourke concludes.[50]

Another possibility, in the view of clinical psychologist and blogger Michael Evans, is that the sexuality and glamour is part of the message. The use of perfect blank-faced, highly sexualized models "is a luscious lampoon of the America terror state—a situation that has gone so far, it can only be treated as burlesque." It uses the fantastical elements that fashion shoots are known for—the absurd vanity and superficiality—in order to "throw Abu Graib back in America's face as terror for its own sake."[51] In this instance, the frivolity and silliness of fashion only aids in highlighting the surrealism of a situation like Abu Graib. "Fashion is always selling sex, selling power and right now this kind of fashion is commenting on what is powerful and what is titillating today," argues Karen Von Hann, fashion columnist for Toronto's *Globe and Mail*. In echoing the events and images of Abu Graib and parodying them, these artists must evoke the same horrible and disturbing feelings in a way that will captivate an audience. "There is another element besides the mere selling of sex, self expression," she says, and these images express a very clear antiwar sentiment.[52]

Defenders of this politicization of fashion and visual presentation would argue that the disturbingly graphic nature of both the runway show and the photo essay serve to shock us into action. Their intent is to make us uncomfortable in order for the message to stick in our minds and to force us to investigate what is really happening in the world. Abu Graib and other prisons and the U.S. War on Terror are so brutal in themselves and the suffering of the victims is so abhorrent that the violence that the fashion statements display is necessary. Karen Von Hann contends that "[c]ontemporary culture has upped the ante. The video games kids play, the nature of reality TV, and the nature of contemporary culture are brutal to the extreme, they are nihilist, we have upped the ante."[53] Therefore fashion must also up the ante in order for its message to be noticed.

However, one must ask where we draw the line from realistic representation to exploitation of the suffering of real people. Joanna Bourke notes that "It's very easy to be blasé about these images, than to realize these are deeply offensive to people around the world."[54] There has been no public backlash from the Muslim community over this collection or these images, though it might be the case that fashion and the haute couture world in general doesn't have very much influence on the popular culture of that group. It can be argued that the fashion moguls are capitalizing on and making a profit from torture and are therefore benefiting from the incidents at Abu Graib—the very thing their message speaks against. They are unwillingly contributing to a normalization of torture imagery, by exposing us to the taboo in a sexualized way. They are "turning us on" with violence and desensitizing us at the same time. Through these beautiful and sexual images, are they making us oblivious to the notion of terror and torture or worse making it exciting and romantic? Besides making us question our role in the War on Terror, do they also make us feel less empowered and more complacent, that there is nothing we can do, or that this type of thing is just in our nature?

A final way of looking at this is that a link between creative fashion and the issues of the day is inevitable, because at some level fashion design is an art. "In the perspective of costume history, it is plain that the dress of any given period is exactly suited to the actual climate of the time," argues English costume historian James Laver.[55] Perhaps the most important role that fashion as art can play in our lives and on the political landscape is to force us to investigate further what is going on in the world around us. Clothing has always been and always will be political, whether we notice it or not, it is an integral part of our role in society related to class, race, and gender and it is our most noticeable form of self expression.

Throughout history, clothing has been at the center of every political revolution. Kathleen McDermott explains that even as early as the Bolshevik period in Russia, there were

> revolutionary artists who were very interested in casting off what they thought were idle aesthetic types of forms and designs. And they used abstraction and geometry to create what they called political clothing and clothing that could be used and efficiently created in the first worker factories. And so these were artists as political revolutionaries trying to create clothing that had a message both built into it and visually apparent.[56]

While the designers and the fashion houses are often given credit for their revolutionary collections or creations, their ideas come from the street. A classic example comes from the antiwar protesters in the 1960s and 1970s, who took the military uniform and adorned it or painted it with flowers and messages of peace, who grew their hair longer than the acceptable norm thus using their clothing as a part of their protest. Another example is "punk fashion" in 1970s London. What started out as worn-out clothes being held together by safety pins, because of the relative poverty of the wearers, became upscale fashion wear with safety pins playing only a purely symbolic role. Being aware of what our clothing is saying, and using knowledge of fashion and world history to express our beliefs or to challenge others, is one of the most effective ways of rebelling against the culture industry and its political agendas.

Daily Acts of Militaristic Patriotism

As we have said earlier, the U.S. republic was founded upon certain ideas, such as the liberty of the common person, guarantees that government would be divided and weak, and a significant separation between society and the state. This model was only an idea and was not well implemented, but reminding ourselves what the model was can help us put contemporary developments into perspective. One of the themes of this chapter, and this section, is that people in the United States are living within horizons which have been defined both by state and nonstate actors. In fact, one of the insights of Gramscian analysis is that often social institutions work hand-in-glove with the state to impose and conserve a hegemonic system, one that seems natural. One way to do this is for the militaristic version of patriotism to permeate all aspects of life. We say "militaristic version" because there is not just one version. Our dominant version of patriotism is militaristic and to be patriotic means to support foreign wars, no matter how destructive, ill-conceived, or immoral. It is this form of patriotism that puts a yellow "support our troops" ribbon on the SUV, almost as an obligation, and sneers with the words "cut and run" when someone dares to call for bringing the military home. But there is another form of patriotism, one that respects the U.S. Constitution and values the republican form of government as the best means to protect genuine liberty. That latter version of patriotism will be illustrated in chapters 7 and 8. In this section we will discuss some aspects of everyday life that promote militarism and the militaristic version of patriotism as natural and normal.

One way this is done is for signs of patriotism to permeate the society. This is evidenced through the ubiquity of flags, flown every day of the year, but it can also be seen by making patriotic symbols much more common than they have been in the past. In a realm more permanent than fleeting, reports noted the rise of patriotic tattoos in the year after 9/11, depicting the Twin Towers, firefighters, eagles, NYPD and NYFD logos, and many other images.[57] Much of the patriotic in daily life takes the form of kitsch. Derived from the German word *verkitschen*, "to cheapen," Marita Sturken argues that it "conveys a kind of deliberate and highly constructed innocence, one that dictates particular kinds of sentimental responses and emotional registers."[58] One of the best examples, combining both sentimentality and gullibility, is the silver collector coin, made with silver "from the vaults of the World Trade Center site," with the "sculpture" of the Twin Towers that rises on hinges.[59]

The patriotic kitsch of the warrior nation is also illustrated by the new enthusiasm for homemaking, in which patriotic themes are belabored. It is remarkable, for example, how many different ways Martha Stewart can express patriotism through food and crafts. On her website she has designs for patriotic-themed paper ice-cream cone wrappers, napkin rings, fans, drink parasols, bunting, doormats, napkins, cupcakes with sparklers, door medallions, garland, as well as flag-oriented cupcakes and cookies, flag sheet cakes, and red, white, and blue desserts. There are also patriotic votives, candles inside glass jars with red, white, and blue designs.

In her magazine she also has features on flag lapel pins, which we're told became popular during World War II. Because of rationing, pins were a way of freshening up an outfit and were worn as well to boost morale.[60] (As President Obama found out in 2007, wearing one is now obligatory for anyone in public life in a militaristic age.[61]) There have also been features on the different designs of the national flag over the decades and centuries. Elsewhere, there have been quilt shows in which quilters have been able to reflect on the events of 9/11.[62] This may be seen as innocent and trivial, but it does normalize the ubiquity and pervasiveness of militaristic and patriotic symbols.

This everyday militarism is manifested in other ways as well. For years now, an organization in Tennessee, Georgia, and Florida, called Hugs for Our Soldier, organizes the sending of greeting cards, Christmas packages, and Girl Scout Cookies to military personnel overseas, and an adopt-a-soldier program in which participants can provide one-on-one material and moral support for personnel serving overseas.[63] These are now ongoing and annual events and have become a normal part of charitable activity, facilitating the stationing of forces overseas and humanizing the experience for service people. A Milwaukee television station recently reported that two local girls were raising money to send 1,275 boxes of Girl Scout Cookies as treats overseas. "The girls also included a letter inside of the boxes, thanking the troops for their service in the war against terror," the report went on to say.[64] In this case, however innocently, the girls or the media outlet use this as an opportunity to reinforce the neoconservative viewpoint, that this is a "war on terror" rather than the result of eagerness for power and treasure. Henry Giroux notes that "The militarizing of public space at home contributes to the narrowing of community and an escalating concentration of unaccountable political power that threatens the very foundation of democracy in the United States. Militarization is no longer simply the driving force of foreign policy, it has become a defining principle for social changes at home."[65]

Conclusion

This chapter has been about a struggle, but one that few people are really aware of. This is because the subject matter of this chapter was about the deepest, everyday manifestations of militarism and patriotism in daily life. People are most aware of the impact of culture when there are explicit attempts to use culture to promote militarism, particularly when it is connected to pressure to begin a particular war. The longer-term and more subtle issue, however, is when we find that militarism, including the militaristic version of patriotism, intrudes more and more into everyday culture. Over a period longer than just advocating any particular war, the effort to create a warrior nation through everyday culture will rely on the seemingly mundane. This includes the consequences of military recruitment advertising, which may create more positive views toward the military; subtle shifts in fashion and architecture, which normalize the privileging of security over other values, including democracy; fear- and comfort-oriented consumption, such as SUVs and survivalist merchandise; and literature for both children and adults that will often present conservative views in the guise of fiction.

Notes

1. Daniel Ellsberg, *Secrets: A Memoir of Vietnam and the Pentagon Papers* (New York: Penguin Books, 2002), chap. 14.

2. More Gooder, "The Role of Advertising in the U.S. Army Recruiting Process Before and After 9/11," The "Original Stop Loss Blog," November 5, 2008, http://13stoploss.blogspot.com/2008/11/role-of-advertising-in-us-army.html (accessed April 17, 2009).

3. "How Does the Army Advertise to People of Color?" United for Peace & Justice, www.unitedforpeace.org/article.php?id=3444 (accessed April 17, 2009).

4. Carl Chery, "U.S. Army Targets Back Hip-Hop Fans," *The Wire/Daily Hip-Hop News*, October 21, 2003, www.sohh.com/article_print.php?content_ID=5162.

5. Joe Garofoli, "Military Recruiting and Ads Zero in on Mom, Dad: Parents, Many of Whom Never Served, Are Told of Benefits," *San Francisco Chronicle*, October 18, 2005, www.sfgate.com/cgi-bin/article.cgi?file=/c/a/2005/10/18/MNGD9FA4TG1.DTL (accessed April 16, 2009).

6. Mike Doughtry, "Adventures in Military Advertising," *Huffington Post*, October 27, 2008, www.huffingtonpost.com/mike-doughty/adventures-in-military-ad_b_138235.html (accessed April 16, 2009).

7. Gooder, "The Role of Advertising."

8. The Merrow Report, "High School Recruiting: A Look Inside the Army's Recruiting Efforts on High School Campuses," *PBS*, December 13, 2004, www.pbs.org/merrow/tv/newshour/recruit.html (accessed July 9, 2009).

9. U.S. Department of Defense, "DoD Announces Recruiting and Retention Numbers for May 2009," news release, www.defenselink.mil/releases/release.aspx?releaseid=12737 (accessed July 7, 2009).

10. George Nunberg, quoted in Norman Solomon, "Branding New and Improved Wars," *Media Beat, FAIR*, October 29, 2002, www.globalissues.org/article/383/branding -new-and-improved-wars (accessed April 17, 2009).

11. Victoria De Grazia, "Bush Team Enlists Madison Avenue in War on Terror," *International Herald Tribune*, August 6, 2002, www.globalissues.org/article/365/bush -team-enlists-madison-avenue-in-war-on-terror (accessed April 17, 2009).

12. Quoted in Laura Miller, "War Is Sell," *PR Watch* 9, no. 4 (2002), www.prwatch .org/prwissues/2002Q4/war.html (accessed July 7, 2009).

13. Steve Watson, "Pro War Ads Falsely Link 9/11 to Iraq," Alex Jones' Infowars .net, August 23, 2007, www.infowars.net/articles/august2007/230807ads.htm (accessed July 7, 2009).

14. Sheldon Rampton and John Stauber, "Trading on Fear," *Guardian*, July 12, 2003, www.commondreams.org/views03/0712-01.htm (accessed April 15, 2009).

15. Marita Sturken, *Tourists of History: Memory, Kitsch, and Consumerism from Oklahoma City to Ground Zero* (Durham, NC, and London: Duke University Press, 2007), 36–37.

16. See Conelrad website, www.conelrad.com/nuclearfamilies/ (accessed July 7, 2009).

17. Urban Survival Tools, Deluxe Office Survival Kits, www.urbansurvivaltools .com/home.php?cat=251 (accessed April 17, 2009).

18. Get Ready Gear, Emergency Preparedness Kit in Case of Terrorist Acts, www .getreadygear.com/index.asp?PageAction=Custom&ID=17 (accessed April 18, 2009).

19. Joe Lockard, "Social Fear and the *Terrorism Survival Guide*," in *The Selling of 9/11: How a National Tragedy Became a Commodity*, ed. Dana Heller (New York: Palgrave Macmillan, 2005), 226–27.

20. Julia Reed, "Soldiers of Fashion," *Uncle Sam's Army Navy Outfitters*, July 16, 2009, www.armynavydealsblog.com/2009/07/soldiers-of-fashion.html (accessed August 8, 2009).

21. Jeremy W. Peters, "How to Market Hummers to the Masses," *New York Times*, June 28, 2005, http://query.nytimes.com/gst/fullpage.html?res=9A04EEDF1731F93B A15755C0A9639C8B63&sec=&spon=&pagewanted=all (accessed April 16, 2009).

22. Rampton and Stauber, "Trading on Fear."

23. Sturken, *Tourists of History*, 87.

24. Henry A. Giroux, "The Emerging Authoritarianism in the United States: Political Culture under the Bush/Cheney Administration," *symploke* 14, nos. 1–2 (2006): 98–151.

25. Tom Krisher and Bree Fowler, "GM Moves Ahead with Hummer, Saturn, Saab Sales," *Associated Press*, June 2, 2009, www.wheels.ca/article/616377 (accessed July 7, 2009).

26. "Dell Goes 'Ballistic' with Design for New Latitude E6400 XFR Rugged Laptop," Dell, March 10, 2009, www1.ca.dell.com/content/topics/topic.aspx/ca/corporate/ pressoffice/en/2009/2009_03_10_tor_000?c=ca&l=en&s=corp (accessed April 8, 2009).

27. Ian Austen, "How Tough Is Your Laptop? For Off-Road Typing, and a Rugged Look, Computers Built Like Tanks," *New York Times*, May 20, 1999, www.nytimes

.com/1999/05/20/technology/tough-your-laptop-for-off-road-typing-rugged-look
-computers-built-like-tanks.html?sec=technology (accessed April 16, 2009).

28. Nick Turse, *The Complex: How the Military Invades Our Everyday Lives* (New York: Henry Holt and Company / Metropolitan Books, 2008), 68.

29. Nicolai Ouroussoff, "Medieval Modern: Design Strikes a Defensive Posture," *New York Times*, March 4, 2007, www.nytimes.com/2007/03/04/weekinreview/04ouroussoff.html?_r=1 (accessed July 7, 2009).

30. AO, "Infrastructure as Art," Odlanscape Blog, September 8, 2008, http://od landscape.blogspot.com/2008/09/infrastructure-as-art.html (accessed July 9, 2009).

31. Robert Stahl, *Militainment, Inc: War, Media and Popular Culture* (New York: Routledge, 2009), 1–2.

32. Andy Fillmore, "A Good Day for a Battle: Airsoft Contests Stress Realism and Military Tactics," Ocala, January 23, 2010, www.ocala.com/article/20100123/AR-TICLES/1231020/1001/NEWS01?p=1&tc=pg (accessed February 14, 2010).

33. Giroux, "The Emerging Authoritarianism in the United States," 125.

34. Ruth Rosen, "Politics of Fear," *San Francisco Chronicle*, December 30, 2003, www.commondreams.org/views02/1230-02.htm (accessed August 16, 2009).

35. Amazon.com, product description for *Daddy's in Iraq, but I Want Him Back*, www.amazon.com/Daddys-Iraq-but-Want-Back/dp/1412060427/ (accessed May 29, 2008).

36. Robin Hoecker, "Sesame Street Military Tour to Continue, Expand," *Stars and Stripes*, October 15, 2008, www.stripes.com/article.asp?section=104&article=58182 (accessed July 20, 2009); "Homeland Security, Sesame Style," *Washington Examiner*, September 18, 2008, www.washingtonexaminer.com/opinion/blogs/YeasandNays/Homeland_Security_Sesame_Style.html (accessed July 20, 2009).

37. "Patriotism Gap: Kids Facing a Crisis," *New York Post*, March 18, 2007, www.nypost.com/seven/03182007/postopinion/postopbooks/patriotism_gap_post opbooks_.htm (accessed July 9, 2009).

38. Eerie, "The Perverse Fascination Continues: Sheikh-Themed Romance Novels," August 13, 2005, www.aquol.com/archives/2005/08/the_perverse_fa.php (accessed May 29, 2008).

39. "About the Site," Sheikhs and Desert Love, www.sheikhs-and-desert-love.com/faqs.html (accessed July 8, 2009).

40. Jane Adams, "*The Cutout*: Editorial Reviews, Amazon.com," Amazon, 2008, www.amazon.com/Cutout-Francine-Mathews/dp/0553581503 (accessed May 29, 2008).

41. *Fashion Resistance to Militarism*, DVD, produced by Women of Color Resource Center (2006). Part of the Runway Peace Project.

42. M. J. Stephey, "A Brief History of Camouflage," *Time*, June 22, 2009.

43. Michael Quintanilla, "Get on Board," *Los Angeles Times*, September 10, 1997.

44. The video of "Hard" can be difficult to find but as of this writing it is available here: http://justjared.buzznet.com/2009/12/17/rihanna-world-premiere-of-hard
-video/ (accessed February 16, 2010). See also "Rihanna Is Armed and Scandalous in New 'Hard' Video," *Rock and Roll Daily*, December 17, 2009, www.rollingstone.com/

rockdaily/index.php/2009/12/17/rihanna-is-armed-and-scandalous-in-new-hard
-video/ (accessed February 16, 2010).

45. "Women2Day—Fashion: Military Mania," *Chester Chronicle*, November 8 2009, www.chesterchronicle.co.uk/entertainment-chester/chester-cheshire-women/chester-fashion/fashion-news/2009/11/08/women2day-fashion-military-mania -59067-25119117/ (accessed February 16, 2010).

46. "Enchanted Soldier: From Sgt. Pepper Jackets to Liberty Florals Topped with Trenches, Spring's Military-Inspired Looks Are Anything but Uniform," *Teen Vogue*, www.teenvogue.com/style/market/feature/2009/03/military-inspired-spring -style#slide=1 (accessed February 16, 2010).

47. Cathy Horyn, "Macho America Storms Europe's Runways," *New York Times*, July 3, 2003, A1.

48. Richard Goldstein, "War Horny: Victory Is the Ultimate Viagra," *Village Voice*, April 15, 2003, www.villagevoice.com/2003-04-15/news/war-horny/1#Comments (accessed July 21, 2009).

49. Joanna Bourke in "Terror Chic," *Q: The Podcast*, March 11, 2008, www.cbc.ca/podcasting/index.html?arts#qpodcast.

50. Bourke, "Terror Chic."

51. Michael Evans, "Fashion of the Times," BagNews Notes, September 18, 2009, http://bagnewsnotes.typepad.com/bagnews/2006/09/fashion_of_the_.html (accessed July 8, 2009).

52. Karen Von Hann in "Terror Chic," *Q: The Podcast*, March 11, 2008, www.cbc.ca/podcasting/index.html?arts#qpodcast.

53. Von Hann in "Terror Chic."

54. Bourke in "Terror Chic."

55. James Laver, quoted in "What Is Fashion," *Public Broadcasting System* (n.d.), www.pbs.org/newshour/infocus/fashion/whatisfashion.html (accessed July 8, 2009).

56. Kathleen McDermott, quoted in Mark Willis, "From Fashionista Street to Abu Ghraib," A Blind Flaneur Blog, February 12, 2008, http://blindflaneur.com/?p=249 (accessed July 8, 2009).

57. Petula Dvorak, "Far More Than Skin Deep," *Washington Post*, October 24, 2002.

58. Marita Sturken, *Tourists of History: Memory, Kitsch, and Consumerism from Oklahoma City to Ground Zero* (Durham, NC, and London: Duke University Press, 2007), 21.

59. Steve Burgess, "Terror Schlock: Making a Mint on 9/11," *The Tyee*, September 15, 2007, www.alternet.org/story/62514/terror_schlock:_making_a_mint_on_9_11/ (accessed July 21, 2009). For a graphic presentation of the kitsch, see Ed Strong, "Get Your Kitsch 9/11 Memorabilia Here (9/11 Has Made Us Stupid)," Ed Strong Blog, http://edstrong.blog-city.com/get_your_kitsch_911_memorabilia_here_911_has_made_us_stup.htm (accessed July 21, 2009).

60. This paragraph relies largely on materials on Martha Stewart's website. See the search results for "patriotic" at www.marthastewart.com/portal/site/mslo/menuitem .e28a2ad6d3341f8836eb9e2bd373a0a0?vgnextoid=42cacf380e1dd010VgnVCM10000

05b09a00aRCRD&rsc=search_header&autonomy_kw=patriotic&x=0&y=0 (accessed July 8, 2009).

61. David Wright and Sunlen Miller, "Obama Stops Wearing Flag Pin, Says He'll Show Patriotism through Ideas," *ABC News*, October 4, 2007, http://abcnews.go.com/Politics/story?id=3690000&page=1 (accessed July 8, 2009).

62. "Two Quilt Shows Open at the Hudson River Museum September 28: One Tells of Times Yesterday, the Other Times Today," press release, Hudson River Museum, www.hrm.org/pressbox/Quiltshow.html (accessed July 13, 2009). To view quilts with these themes, see Karey Bresenhan, *America from the Heart: Quilters Remember September 11, 2001* (Lafayette, CA: C&T Publishing, 2002), available online at http://books.google.ca/books?id=w4aiVOhzkeoC&pg=PA76&lpg=PA76&dq=9-11+crafts+quilts+%22america+from+the+heart%27&source=bl&ots=47w_i5WPs8&sig=av8ztj3z6Ti7nCxASqOf-QeLQIg&hl=en&ei=PL1QSvfjAZPKtgfYwPFm&sa=X&oi=book_result&ct=result&resnum=6 (accessed July 13, 2009).

63. See Hugs for Our Soldiers, www.hugsforoursoldiers.org/node/1 (accessed July 13, 2009).

64. Gary Reistad, "Girls Send Girl Scout Cookies to Soldiers in Iraq," TMJ 4, May 21, 2009, www.todaystmj4.com/features/positivelymilwaukee/45746442.html (accessed July 13, 2009).

65. Giroux, "The Emerging Authoritarianism in the United States," 122.

7

"We Support Your War of Terror"

Resisting Militarism through Satire

WASHINGTON—In a slight shift from his campaign trail promise, President Obama announced Monday that his administration's message of "Change" has been modified to the somewhat more restrained slogan "Relatively Minor Readjustments in Certain Favorable Policy Areas." "Today, Americans face a great many challenges, and I hear your desperate calls for barely measurable and largely symbolic improvements in the status quo," said Obama, who vowed never to waver in his fight for every last infinitesimal nudge forward on the controversial issues of torture and the military ban on homosexuals. "Remember: Yes we can, if by that you mean tiptoeing around potentially unpopular decisions that could alienate a large segment of the populace." Washington insiders said that, while the new mottos are certainly in keeping with Obama's pledge of government transparency, they are significantly less catchy.[1]

THIS FAKE NEWS STORY FROM THE SATIRICAL PUBLICATION the *Onion* is a humorous expression of some of the ambiguity regarding the potential for meaningful change under the Obama administration. The first reaction of some activists to the 2008 election was euphoria, based on the idea that the ascension of Obama and a stronger Democratic majority would usher in a new age. Ani DiFranco, singer-songwriter, pioneer of independent musical production, and a strong and long-time advocate for peace and justice, used her song "November 4th, 2008" to declare victory, maybe before seeing evidence of the extent of the victory. In the song she says that with the election of Obama the U.S. voter did better than she expected, and that she'll be proud to show her U.S. passport again.[2] While many hope that their faith will be

rewarded, prominent critics and satirists of the Bush era are not entirely convinced that we have in fact entered a new era of peace. Chalmers Johnson, for
example, suggests that militarism may be irreversible, because it would take "a
revolution" to bring the Pentagon back under the control of the people, or to
close down the CIA, for that matter.[3] In contrast, there is reason to be hopeful
because of all the energy in contemporary life that is challenging militarism
and imperialism in the United States. The phrase "pessimism of the intellect
and optimism of the will," attributed alternatively to Romain Rolland or
Antonio Gramsci, calls on people to take off rose-colored glasses and see the
truth while still accepting the call to action.

Pop Culture as a Site of Resistance

Popular culture has the potential to be the medium by which a warrior culture can be effectively resisted.[4] Stuart Hall argues that popular culture exists
on a continuum at the intersection of resistance to and containment by the
dominant groups. He suggests that popular culture might ultimately be read
as an "arena of consent and resistance . . . where hegemony arises, and where
it is secured . . . one of the places where socialism might be constituted. That
is why 'popular culture' matters."[5] Despite the efforts of the culture industry,
we do not live with a single "mass culture," shared by both elite and masses,
that only constructs a militaristic or patriotic culture that has been successfully imposed without difficulty.[6] Increasingly, analysts are recognizing that
popular culture is a major way in which politics is discussed.[7]

I Ain't Marching Any More

Music was a major part of the social movements in the 1950s and 1960s in the
United States, particularly the civil rights movement, the movement against
the U.S. war in Vietnam, and the women's movement of the late 1960s and
early 1970s. Songs by many singers in the gospel, folk, and popular traditions,
such as Nina Simone, Pete Seeger, Bob Dylan, Joan Baez, Phil Ochs, Tom
Paxton, Marvin Gaye, John Lennon, Cat Stevens, and later Helen Reddy,
as well as many others, made music a significant part of those movements.
People often sang at marches, and concerts were an integral part of the appeal
of protests. Songs like "Billy, Don't Be a Hero," "Dear Uncle Sam," "The Draft
Dodger Rag," "I Feel-Like-I'm-Fixin'-To-Die Rag," and "Where Have All
the Flowers Gone?" featured lyrics often satirical or mournful. Death on the
battlefield, the horrors of war, and war profiteering were featured in "Battle

Hymn of LL Galley" and "The Unknown Soldier." "War" and "Won't Get Fooled Again" revealed that this generation could also be angry and cynical, or at least recognize the cynicism of the rulers. Many songs of peace emerged from the movement, focusing on pacifism rather than "the complexities of negotiated settlements, national goals, disputed boundaries, and political objectives."[8] Examples of this type of song include "Give Peace a Chance," "Imagine," "Stop the War Now," and "We've Got to Have Peace." Lee Cooper notes that "Song lyrics perpetuated the debate about the validity of war as a means of achieving political, economic, or any idealistic ends. It wasn't that America was being torn apart by unpatriotic malcontents who happened to be musicians. The public simply continued to resonate to the issues being discussed in vinyl grooves, on cassette tapes, and on compact discs."[9]

What role does music play in the 2000s, and has this role declined relative to the past, and if so, why? Stephen Walt, a Realist skeptic about some of the recent wars, asks this very question, pointing out that only a small number of songs come to mind as we think about the contemporary antiwar movement. His answer to the question about why no "anthem" has emerged is quite simple—the absence of the draft. Implicitly, he is arguing that since it is an all-voluntary military people are less intensely opposed to the war, because the large majority can choose not to be directly affected.[10] In his answer to a similar question, Joseph Schumacher sees both an "insidious depoliticizing of popular culture," forced largely by the play-it-safe culture industry, and the fact that unlike the 1950s and 1960s, music today is more of a reflection of, rather than a challenge to, the mainstream culture. "The current crop of stars grew up grooving to the self glorifying excesses of the 70s and 80s, listening to Madonna sing 'I am a material girl' and the 'fun first' funk of disco, stadium rock and the personal angst of grunge." In the British context academic Janice McNair has said that there have recently been marches without music because the movements are so large and diverse that no single song or group of songs has a sufficient following.[11]

However, because the movement and era are different it may be that music itself plays a different and less obvious, and possibly lesser, role. We now live in highly wired world, in which people can inform, or misinform, themselves without ever buying a newspaper or watching broadcast television or listening to the radio. This presents certain challenges, in that individuals at home sitting in front of their televisions and computers may be more difficult to get out to protest marches or events. Unlike the contents of the *The Ed Sullivan Show* in the late 1960s, there are few broadly shared experiences today—the immediate fallout from 9/11 is an exception—but this also means that the age of the monopolistic gatekeeper is over. To the extent that leaders are concerned with public opinion polls, the attitudes of these dissenting couch potatoes must be taken into account—and may well have been the undoing of a militaristic leader such as George W. Bush.

While conservative militarists have promoted pro-war music, lyrics and performers, they have not been able to prevent an outpouring of antimilitarist creativity. Perhaps because there are so many different musicians and genres, and no truly mass support has coalesced around any, it seems like music isn't making an impact. It is a segmented industry so mass phenomena like the Beatles and Michael Jackson are rare or nonexistent. But there is still an outpouring of antimilitarist music. Tori Amos, in "Yo George" and "Dark Side of the Sun" (2007) from *American Doll Posse*, questions the direction of her country and also asks whether this direction can just be attributed to a President who is acting like a king. Her antiwar anthem "Dark Side of the Sun" expresses regret that some young men, on both sides, are willing to lay down their lives for religion. Michael Franti, hip hop/folk/reggae artist and ex-lead singer of Disposable Heroes of Hiphoprisy, wrote "Bomb the World" soon after 9/11, and it has become an anthem in the protest communities, advancing the sentiment that bombing won't lead to a durable peace.

To the extent that the music of dissent has a focus in a contemporary genre, it is a major force in rap and hip hop. This should be no surprise. Pioneered on the streets over the last twenty years predominantly by African Americans, it has had a long history of suspicion toward the White establishment, in the forms of government, police, military, intelligence agencies, and private corporations. As Jeffrey Melnick says in his fascinating discussion of "9/11 culture," rap and hip hop were both infused with the post-9/11 cultural mood, and also frequently performed explicit critiques of the pressure for "national unity" and for support for overseas military attacks. African Americans and others who embraced the hip hop sensibility refused to forget, all of a sudden, police shootings and racial profiling of people of color, especially in New York City, and refused to drop their suspicion of a larger society that had decimated their neighborhoods through economic collapse, guns, gangs, and drugs. Many rappers and hip hoppers were openly resistant to accepting the forced, post-9/11 unity of the American people. This is the radical critique of U.S. foreign policy in recitation and song. Nas, with his song "What Goes Around," released in December 2001, asserts that a superpower like the United States cannot stay on top forever, and when a bad thing happens it is a response to past actions of the U.S. government. Boston rapper Mr. Lif, in "Home of the Brave" (2002), provides a "blowback" analysis in which, because the United States supported the Taliban against the Soviet Union, the radical Islamists were strengthened all over the region and 9/11 represented their effort to attack the world's other great secular power, the United States. Of course, there are also plans for a pipeline, the song says.

Feeling and expressing a disconnect with the American victims of terrorism on 9/11 and other days, Dead Prez rapped, in their 2002 song "Know Your Enemy," that this conflict really doesn't involve him, because the 9/11 attackers don't have any disagreement with him or people in his neighborhood. Capital D, in "Start the Revolution" (2004), comments that all the leaders (Blair, Bush, and bin Laden) are rich and they are sending the poor to die.

In "World Wide Suicide" (2006) from Pearl Jam (which reached #1 on Billboard), band leader Eddie Vedder reflects on the death of Pat Tillman. John Mayer, in "Waiting on the World to Change" (2006), from *Continuum*, expresses feelings of powerlessness because even as part of a movement he cannot ensure that no one misses Christmas at home. Perhaps in answer to Stephen Walt's question about why more people aren't on the streets, Mayer sings that people don't believe they can have an impact, and are just left waiting for social change to happen.

One artist making the transition through numerous eras of activism is Neil Young, who started with Buffalo Springfield in the 1960s, and in 2006 released *Living with War* (2006).[12] Recorded in just six days, as Chris Hedges says, Young charges Bush and his administration with, among other things, "lying, spying, waging war with no right or reason and dereliction of duty to the nation's founding ideals. He then calls for the most extreme judgment available to the American people in 'Let's Impeach the President', with rusty-fuzz guitar, the righteous muscle of a hundred-strong choir, a trumpet playing 'Taps' and the self-incriminating voice of Bush himself."[13]

There's also room for surprises. Who would have thought that self-styled conservative Merle Haggard, the man who sang "Okie from Muskogee" as a critique of the 1960s counter-culture, would make it to the antiwar list? In "That's the News" (2005), on his CD *Chicago Wind*, he criticizes the decision to attack Iraq. In "Rebuild America First," his view is that the Iraq War is reducing freedom at home and depriving the United States of the resources to provide for its own needs.

Green Day, by now veteran critics of the establishment, weigh in with title track "American Idiot" (2004), no doubt referring to the president of the day. The Black-Eyed Peas produced the memorable "Where Is the Love?" (2003), from *Elephunk*, with composing help from Justin Timberlake. Backed by a very melodic tune, they point out the irony that the United States is fighting terrorists overseas while terrorists are tolerated at home, such as in the Klu Klux Klan, within the CIA, and urban street gangs. A focus on your own race, your own nation, just leads to discrimination, they conclude. Singer-songwriter Jim Page, in *Collateral Damage* (2002), wrote a whole batch of post-9/11 songs "prophetic, political, personal and even beautiful" for peace and against war. Michael Moore directed a video for System of a Down

("Boom!"), from their CD *Steal This Album!* (2002). Some of the reflections ruminate on the present in light of the past, like Misanthropes "Tranchées 1914" (2000), from *Misanthrope Immortel*. As Chris Hedges describes it, war is always presented as heroic, but in the end it is always about death, terror, horror, and nightmares.[14] In late 2008, Sheryl Crow weighed in with a new CD with her own antiwar contributions. In "God Bless This Mess," about 9/11 and its aftermath, like so many others she says that the president offered condolences to the country but then used the grief to start an aggressive war in Iraq. A later song, "Now That You're Gone," she says is dedicated to Karl Rove, Bush's senior advisor and strategist.[15]

Another musical activist who deserves mention is British ex-punk and current folk-oriented singer Billy Bragg. Bragg has made his name breathing new life into democratic, seventeenth-century ideas of the English Civil War, and he has also released two CDs of Woody Guthrie songs. He is a fixture at pro-Labour and peace rallies and he actively supports progressive political candidates. He has written a number of entertaining songs that compete as contemporary antiwar anthems, such as "The Price of Oil," "Bush War Blues," and "There Is Power in a Union." In "The Price of Oil," Bragg attributes the wars in Afghanistan and Iraq to unspoken motives. He also goes further and reminds listeners that deception on the part of the governors has become so common, whether we think of U.S. support for Hussein, Pinochet, and bin Laden, or the inability to run an honest election, such as in Florida in the year 2000.

"Bush War Blues" is a new set of lyrics set to Leadbelly's classic tune "Bourgeois Blues," and it is both entertaining and topical. Bragg sings about this war making the world safe for Haliburton rather than democracy, about the problem of Christian extremism in U.S. politics, and about the need to fight poverty at home.[16] Finally, even when his songs are on other topics his opposition to war is not far away. In his labor anthem, "There Is Power in a Union," Bragg also brings up the tendency to send the ordinary worker to kill and be killed in war.[17]

Music can also be a way of addressing the pain of the disillusioned. With ideas of vengeance, Tomas Young joined the army in a "knee-jerk reaction to 9/11," on September 13, 2001. But soon he realized that rather than being shipped to Afghanistan to fight the War on Terror, as Bush had been touting, Young was being sent to Iraq, which he considered the wrong battlefield.[18] Young sought out protest music, allowing him to deal with the betrayal he was feeling as well as helping him to cope, when he was shot and paralyzed four days after arriving in Iraq. Young is now a spokesperson for Iraq Veterans Against the War, and has headed the release of the CD *Body of War: Songs That Inspired an Iraq War Veteran*.[19] This album, a thirty-track double CD, includes songs such as Rage against the Machine's "Guerilla Radio," which discusses the corrupt nature of the government in the United States; Bright Eyes' "When the President Talks to God," the lyrics of which mock Bush's claim that "God told me to" when making important decisions as president; Talib Kweli and Cornell West's "Bushonomics" looks at another negative side of George W. Bush; Eddie Vedder of Pearl Jam and Ben Harper's version of the previously unreleased Vedder song "No More," which is a simple plea to bring an end to the war. The album also includes classic antiwar activists and singer-songwriters such as John Lennon, Tom Waits, and Neil Young.[20] While Tomas Young recognizes that these songs may be preaching to the choir, he and others involved remain optimistic that this album will extend the dialogue on the War in Iraq.[21] As should be clear from this section, there is no shortage of antiwar and antimilitarist music, though it is diffused across multiple genres and reflects the fracturing of contemporary culture.

Movie Makers Fight Back

As we saw in chapter 4, films have acted as agents of militarization but they have also been sites for resistance, both in the past and the present. Indeed, as articulated by the organization Culture of Resistance, "film has been and continues to be a powerful tool for opposing war, promoting peace with justice, and building international understanding."[22] Like mainstream Hollywood films, the tradition of antiwar films is also rooted in World War I, when pro-neutrality films like "Intolerance and Civilization" were popular prior to U.S. engagement in the war.[23] Since their emergence, antiwar films have had important impacts on American popular culture, but they were often marginalized by militaristic films during wartime.[24] However, in the 1960s and 1970s, films began to raise significant "questions, in the wake of Vietnam and Watergate, about the military, the intelligence community, and many basic assumptions of American civilization."[25] *M*A*S*H* (1970), *The Deer Hunter* (1978), *Apocalypse Now* (1979), *Platoon* (1986), and *Full Metal Jacket* (1987) are but a few of these cinematic sites of resistance. All of these movies were released after the war that they addressed; in the case of *M*A*S*H*, it may really have been about Vietnam, but it was set in Korea. As Lenny Bruce, the controversial American stand-up comedian of the 1950s and 1960s, noted, "Satire is tragedy plus time. You give it enough time, the public, the reviewers will allow you to satirize it. Which is rather ridiculous, when you think about it."

Thanks at least in part to increased war coverage, as well as decreasing costs and increasing availability of digital technology, cinema critical of the War on Terror has responded much faster than in previous wars. Mainstream

Hollywood films have been produced, including *Syriana* (2005), which shows how the internal politics of oil-producing, Middle East allies of the West have been shaped to suit the West. In *Stop-Loss*, a young American soldier is ordered to return to the front lines. After serving his tour of duty in Iraq, as part of the military's controversial stop-loss policy, he opts instead to go AWOL in a thought-provoking military drama directed by Kimberly Peirce. Paul Haggis directed *In the Valley of Elah*, which looks at the way the war in Iraq brutalizes the young American soldiers who serve there. Other examples include *Rendition* (2007), in which an Egyptian-American is subject to torture and captivity under the U.S. "extraordinary rendition" program, and *Lions for Lambs* (2007), which portrays the national debate over Iraq and Afghanistan, with a star-studded cast including Tom Cruise, Meryl Streep, and Robert Redford.[26] *War, Inc.* (2008), a box office disappointment, was a potent satire starring John Cusack, focusing on a mythical Middle-Eastern country, privately owned and run by a U.S. corporation. Many antiwar and antimilitarist films are U.S. coproductions or are foreign films, many of which do not garner a very large U.S. audience.[27]

Kathryn Bigelow's *The Hurt Locker* (2009), winner of the Director's Guild of America's 2009 Best Director and nominated for numerous Oscars, is a contested film—is it "apolitical," "antimilitarist," or "pro-American"—and there is no consensus regarding which is the correct answer. This is a movie about an explosive ordinance disposal (OED) team in Iraq that mainstream critics have raved about and award juries have favored. Some liberals see it as antiwar and antimilitarist because it does portray a coldness toward Iraqis by some U.S. soldiers, and its portrayals of U.S. military officers is unflattering. For these reasons, it is disliked by some conservatives, including conservative bloggers, one of whom ("Greg Scott") says, un-self-consciously, that "Where our soldiers are concerned Hollywood must learn to portray them as they had during WW2."[28] Interestingly, it is a conservative movie reviewer, John Nolte, who has captured some of the issues.[29] He calls the movie "masterful," but it also offers "a troubling depiction of our troops and an even worse portrayal of the Iraqi people." On the latter point, he notes that:

> The women are portrayed as either cannon fodder or screaming like savages, and other than a short, strange encounter with a man who wonders if James is CIA, the men are alternately terrorists, a menacing presence, victims, the butt of jokes or utterly clueless. The only Iraqi with a hint of personality is Beckam, but he's never given a dimension beyond that of a hustler poisoned by our crass American consumer culture.

But even if this is an antiwar or antimilitarist film, as many conservatives think, it is still plagued by the hidden assumptions that Boggs and Pollard identify and which were raised in chapter 4. Specifically, like so many before, this movie focuses on the American experience rather than the Iraqi one; there is an assumption of American innocence, at least of the ordinary soldier; the Iraqis are either one-dimensional, invisible, or treated as inferior; and the film provides no historical context or explanation for how and why the United States is fighting this war in someone else's country.

When a commercial antiwar or antimilitarist film does make a break-through, it is often one that addresses a parallel situation, either future or past. *V for Vendetta* (2005), directed by James McTeigue, is one such movie, both a commercial hit but also one that pulls no punches. Set in the United Kingdom in the future, the country is ruled by an authoritarian, theocratic elite that engages in foreign wars, tortures people—including its own dissenters—and benefits from an allied class of propagandists in civil society. The hero is a futuristic Guy Fawkes who wants to blow up the British Parliament, spark a revolution, and bring down the state, which he does. As critic Justin Raimondo says:

> The right wing hates this movie, and it isn't hard to see why: it explodes all their pretensions about being the party of "freedom," and it pretty clearly parallels the hypocritical cant of the War Party as it pretends to battle "terrorism" while engaging in a campaign of state terrorism that far surpasses anything a small band of amateurs could possibly hope to dish out. They must find particularly galling a subplot in which evidence emerges that a deadly series of biowarfare attacks attributed to "religious fanatics" (and we don't mean George W. Bush and Jerry Falwell) turn out to be the work of a sinister cabal inside the government—the perfect excuse for a crackdown.[30]

Another example of this is James Cameron's smash hit *Avatar* (2009), the largest earning film of all time, which was nominated for a 2009 Best Picture Oscar. It provides a thinly veiled critique of the U.S.-centered private military corporation trying to take over a planet in the year 2154 for its resources, only to find the indigenous Navi people successfully oust them with the help of a small band of humans and their own ecology. The departure of the defeated-but-spared "military contractors" at gunpoint reminds the viewers of countless previous scenes of imperialists or aggressors departing a land against their will.

However, although films have a long history as a site of resistance, many of these dissident films don't break through to popular acceptance, as evidenced by some antiwar films' poor box office performances: *Rendition* barely grossed $10 million[31] and 80 percent of *Lions for Lambs'* $63 million gross revenue came from overseas.[32] It may be that the U.S. audience isn't ready for critically oriented films while the wars are still going on and casualty reports continue to roll in.[33] Because of this marginalization, many critical directors are co-opted by mainstream Hollywood. Oliver Stone, director of antiwar Vietnam films like *Platoon* and *Born on the Fourth of July*, faced so much criticism that he created the patriotic *World Trade Center* (2006) "to show that he can be a good, solid mainstream filmmaker, and he's not a wacko, as a lot of people thought." Even those who resist co-optation can still unwittingly perpetuate militarism in popular culture because, as articulated by Boggs, "when you make a war movie, especially a high-tech spectacle, even if it's anti-war, it still comes across in a sense as kind of glorifying the episodes, the weaponry, the technology." Ultimately, although film has played a significant role as a site of resistance to militarism, particularly since 9/11, "[dissent films] are a subordinate tendency, not a dominant tendency. . . . The dominant tendency is still Hollywood."[34]

The legacy of the 1970s would lead us to expect that fictional portrayals would be the leading and most popular medium of skepticism about war, but in the last ten years the documentary film has exploded both in critical and box office impact. For us documentary films, like news media, are not a central focus in this work on "popular culture," but documentaries have risen in popularity and we should take notice. Among the many resistance documentaries are Eugene Jarecki's work *Why We Fight* (2005), a critical study of the American military-industrial complex, *My Country, My Country* (2006), an "intimate journey into the heart of war-ravaged Iraq,"[35] and *Iranian Films for Peace: A Series of Shorts produced by Bahman Ghobadi* (2008), a compilation of short videos on war and peace by up-and-coming Iranian filmmakers.[36] Michael Moore's *Fahrenheit 9/11* (2004) won numerous awards and all told grossed hundreds of millions of dollars once video sales are included. Robert Greenwald has directed and produced numerous critically oriented documentaries that have garnered widespread attention, including *Iraq For Sale: The War Profiteers*, *Outfoxed: Rupert Murdoch's War on Journalism*, *Unconstitutional: The War on Our Civil Liberties*, and *Uncovered: The War on Iraq*. The era of digital technology and commercialization incentives have meant that documentaries, such as PBS's *Bill Moyers Reports* or *Frontlines* contributions ("The Trial of Saddam Hussein," 2008) are not fleeting one-hour broadcasts but live on in personal and library collections as widely marketed DVDs.

Fools Are My Theme, Let Satire Be My Song[37]

First released in 1973, "Tie a Yellow Ribbon" by Tony Orlando and Dawn has become an iconic song and has given rise to one of America's great patriotic symbols. The yellow ribbons depicted in the song began to take on political overtones during the 444-day Iranian Hostage Crisis, in which 53 Americans were held hostage in the U.S. embassy in Tehran from 1979 through early 1981. It is about the return home of an ex-convict, who tells his wife to tie a yellow ribbon round the old oak tree if he is welcome. It has since become of sign of hope for the missing and solidarity with troops in war. But in the hands of the musical comedy group the Asylum Street Spankers, this becomes a song of critique of U.S. foreign policy and the folks back home. As a song-and-dance number, it is sung from the perspective of a resentful soldier, who is disappointed that he has been sent to Iraq with inadequate armor on his humvee. He doesn't think people putting magnetized yellow ribbons on SUVs is really sufficient support, considering that the gas-guzzlers they are driving are the reason for the war in the first place. The Spankers' version of the song is notable for not only its antiwar message, but also for its satirical style in delivering said message. Like much opposition to and criticism of the American-led War on Terrorism, satire and comedy are used as the media through which antiwar messages are channeled. It will be clear in the remainder of this chapter that satire, especially on cable television, is the leading form of cultural opposition to militarism in the contemporary period.

The most successful film critiques of the War on Terror, in terms of audience attendance and impact, are found among the satires and comedies, led by *Borat*. Known formally as *Borat: Cultural Learnings of America for Make Benefit Glorious Nation of Kazakhstan*, it was a 2006 mockumentary featuring British comedian and actor Sacha Baron Cohen. He first came to attention playing the fictional Kazakh reporter on HBO's *Da Ali G Show*, and in this film he plays Borat Sagdiyev, a fictional journalist assigned by the Kazakhstan Ministry of Information to make a documentary about the United States. Much of the film is composed of Borat interacting with Americans of all walks of life who don't realize that they are part of a mockumentary. The ordinary folks, like the country's foreign policy, don't always come off so well. A line in the film is the inspiration for this chapter's title. At one point, Borat appears at a Western rodeo where he tells the cheering crowd that his people support the United States and that they want the United States to kill every terrorist, drink the blood of every Iraqi, and blight their country for a thousand years. In a famous slip of the tongue, he also refers to it as a war of terror.

Borat is also a strong example of the risks and difficulties of satire. By any standard this is a crude film, which contains sexist, homophobic, and anti-Semitic elements, along with titillating sexual content. Joe Quinlan writing in the *Manchester Guardian*, calls the film "contemptible" and calls U.S. film critics who liked it "nincompoops."[38] While it is also a biting satire that makes some insightful observations about American militarism, it is always hard to know how the audience will respond to the humor. Mark Kermode argues in his British radio review of the film that the comedy in *Borat* may come from a certain British "smugness," "contempt," and position of "superiority." He notes that it makes fun of too many easy "soft targets," especially "Southern American hicks" who are easy to mock but who aren't doing too much harm and don't always deserve it. Politicized comedy always runs the risk of just reinforcing people's existing opinions, as illustrated by the various reactions toward the Archie Bunker character in *All in the Family* in the 1970s. Kermode says that some of the laughter on viewing *Borat* is coming from those who support the sexism, homophobia, anti-Semitism, and racism, and not just those laughing *at* it.[39]

Satire of the War on Terror can be found in the most unlikely of places. The sequel to the movie *Harold and Kumar Go to White Castle* is called *Harold and Kumar Escape from Guantanamo Bay*, and follows the story of two friends who are shipped to the Guantánamo Bay prison after a misunderstanding on an airplane headed for Amsterdam. The movie lampoons the climate of paranoid suspicion that has permeated America since 9/11, highlights injustices in Guantánamo Bay, and portrays President Bush as someone whose sole interests are doing drugs and playing video games, not fighting an international war on terrorism.[40]

Perhaps because of the corporate sensitivities of the major television networks, today antimilitarism is present on television *only* in the form of satire and comedy and almost exclusively on specialty channels such as Comedy Central, HBO, and others. There is a long history of making political statements via television comedy, and in the 1960s and 1970s it was on the major networks. Though *The Smothers Brothers Comedy Hour* in the late 1960s was highly politicized and had trouble with the network censor, and with staying on the air, it *was* on broadcast television. *All in the Family* (1971–1989) was centered on bigot Archie Bunker's (played by Carroll O'Connor) arguments with his grad student son-in-law Mike Stivic (played by Rob Reiner), his African American neighbors the Jeffersons (Sherman Hemsley and Isabel Sanford), and his liberal cousin Maude (Bea Arthur), and his belittling of wife, Edith (Jean Stapleton), and daughter Gloria (Sally Struthers). The program may or may not have changed many minds, but it was a smash hit for many years and gave voice to debates happening at dinner tables all over the country. Another show was only broadcast late Saturday evenings, but *Saturday Night Live* (1975–) did not shy away from political topics, including militarism, and was the launching pad for numerous high-profile performers, such as Steve Martin, Chevy Chase, Dan Ackroyd, John Belushi, Jane Curtin, and Gilda Radner. (Before the 2008 elections, Tina Fey's mocking portrayal of McCain running mate Sarah Palin on *SNL* was memorable and made it hard for the candidate to be taken seriously outside her base of core supporters.)

What gives comedy and satire their bite, their power? For us, it is first of all the tool of those out of power, which usually means dissenters against militarism, the "liberals and the political left." But it is not only that, for in 2009 and 2010 we have not seen an explosion of right-wing stand-up comedy or satire, cheered by large audiences. There is very little of this type of comedy, let alone an explosion, for comedy is a *popular* medium, one where a large audience laughs. The other factor is that laughter is so effective because of the strategy of our current leaders. So much emphasis is placed on building up the mediocre leader's image, or building up the "brand," in a marketing sense, that the person behind it, or the image, cannot but become pompous and pretentious. An idea is not just an idea but a "product to be launched," with charts and graphics, and the more dubious the idea, the more that it needs to be inflated by artificial means. This building up of the idea, of the leader, is like filling the balloon with air. The greater the volume of air, the tauter the balloon, and the easier for comedy or satire, the pin, to prick it and watch it fly around the room.

In the Danish fairy tale by Hans Christian Andersen, "The Emperor's New Clothes," it takes a boy at the end of the story to say the truth of the matter, that the Emperor is not wearing any clothes at all. The satirists are like the boy, saying through comedic means what the political class and punditry dare not say. This environment is very fertile for satirical comedy. As comedian Robin Williams quipped, "People say satire is dead. It's not dead; it's alive and living in the White House."

News Satire You Can Trust

Fake news is a very popular form of contemporary satire. Also known as parody news, mock news, or faux news, it makes fun of network television newscasts and exploits the absurd in current events for humorous intent rather than being concerned with providing complete and well-balanced information. While some fake news formats do manufacture news stories, the Urban Dictionary notes that fake news is somewhat of a misnomer because it often covers actual public figures when they are caught making comments that reveal their utter stupidity and/or hypocrisy. The *New York Times* noted that "most satirists say the popularity of fake news reflects a polarized electorate that suspects the media of doing the other side's bidding, coupled with recent high-profile journalistic scandals such as reporters having been fired from the *New York Times* and *USA Today* for plagiarism."[41] The *Onion* is famous for its "fake news" featuring satirical articles on current events, both real and imagined. It parodies traditional newspaper features, such as editorials, man-on-the-street interviews, as well as traditional newspaper layout and AP-style voice. Between the print and Web editions, it reaches 3 million people worldwide.[42] Many of their headlines, both in the Bush and post-Bush era, provide an insightful analysis of militarism and its effects while still offering a good laugh: "Terror Experts Warn Next 9/11 Could Fall on Different Date"; "Unmanned Military Drone Briefly Grasps Senselessness of War"; "U.S. to Fight Terror with Terror"; "Military Promises 'Huge Numbers' for Gulf War II: The Vengeance"; "U.S. Vows to Defeat Whoever It Is We're at War With"; "U.S. Continues Quagmire-Building Effort in Afghanistan"; "Obama Tells Nation He's Going Out for Cigarettes: 'I'll Be Right Back' Claims Commander in Chief"; "Heroin Addicts Pressure President to Stay Course in Afghanistan"; "Karzai Vows to Crack Down on Self."[43] On several occasions the *Onion*'s satirical news stories have been taken as fact and reproduced by the mainstream news media at home and abroad.[44]

Former *Onion* employees have gone on to help develop other comedy vehicles with this format, including *The Daily Show* and *The Colbert Report*. Megan Boler, a professor of media studies and philosophy of education at the Ontario Institute for Studies in Education (OISE) at the University of Toronto, notes that "Part of the pleasure of watching [fake news] is that it's making fun of news formats. . . . It's doing that by pretending to be news and it's doing it by using clips from actual news and then making a joke about how straight news is doing its job. And it's urging you to ask questions about the role of media in a democracy."[45] Theodore Hamm, in his pioneering book on the role of comedy in contemporary political affairs, *The New Blue Media: How Michael Moore, MoveOn.org, Jon Stewart and Company Are Transforming Progressive Politics*, notes that the *Onion* frequently pointed out how the war enabled Bush to shift the nation's attention from other problems. In "Bush on Economy: 'Saddam Must Be Overthrown,'" for example, the war solved problems ranging from a weak manufacturing sector to the ongoing corporate scandals, which at the time involved WorldCom and Enron.[46]

Two of the most notable comedians to use satire in order to criticize the War on Terror are Jon Stewart and Steven Colbert. Jon Stewart, on his program *The Daily Show*, offers up a satirical take on modern news media through self-referential "fake" news. To mark the fifth anniversary of the invasion of Iraq in March 2008, *The Daily Show* aired a satirical advertisement for an "Iraq Fifth Anniversary Pendant" that mirrored the De Beers commercials in which two figures appear in silhouette, one receiving the gift of diamonds. The commercial ends with the voice over, "Tell her you'd invade, all over again." The satirical advertisement also makes reference to the lack of planning and justification for the invasion, the Abu Ghraib torture scandal, and the sacrifice of civil liberties in the name of the War on Terror, all in a space of forty seconds.[47]

Since the swearing in of Barack Obama, Stewart has continued his attacks on conservatives, but he has not let the new president totally off the hook. In general, Stewart takes a "plague-on-both-your-houses" approach, when it comes to the Democrats and Republicans. As he said on February 3, 2009, "Can Barack Obama bring hope that Republican and Democratic crooks can work together in a bipartisan criminal enterprise?"[48] In a continuation of his "Mess O'Potamia" series, on March 3, 2009, he had fun with Obama by playing excerpts of his speech to marines at Camp Lejeune, on the future of U.S. forces in Iraq. Stewart celebrates, including with music and streamers, when Obama announces all forces will be leaving Iraq by August 2010, and then raises an eyebrow, in his own distinctive way, when he plays a clip of Obama saying that 35,000 to 50,000 troops will remain in the country as a "transitional force." He then gets good laughs from his audience when he juxtaposes Obama's speech with President Bush's speech of September 13, 2007, in which Bush also talks about a "transitional force," and then Stewart uses a mock side-by-side computer analysis to show the similarities in the two leaders' language.[49]

Jon Stewart and Jon Oliver, in mocking Obama's propensity to rename things, say that the people must be "confused into reassurance."[50] In response to Obama's announcement that Camp X-Ray at Guantánamo Bay would be closed in a year, Stewart said, "A year? How long can it take, a few mattresses, a few Korans. Moishe's [moving company] could do it in an afternoon."[51] In January 2009 Stewart revived his "Gitmo's World" feature, starring "Gitmo," a rip-off of *Sesame Street*'s Elmo puppet character. Gitmo tells Jon that he doesn't believe that he will be released, that it is a trick, and in any event, he's crazy now.[52] In May 2009 Stewart skewers House Speaker Nancy Pelosi for her equivocation on whether she was briefed as House minority leader on "aggressive interrogation techniques."[53]

In criticizing Obama's decision not to release torture photos, Stewart notes that the U.S. government has crossed a lot of lines in the War on Terror, and "the only line we won't cross" is allowing gay Arabic translators to stay in the military—fifty-four have been discharged since the invasion of Iraq. On the same episode Jon Stewart and his correspondent Jon Oliver have fun with the specific dismissal of West Point graduate Lt. Dan Choi, on Obama's watch, for admitting he's gay, based on the "Don't Ask, Don't Tell" policy, which the Obama administration has continued. Of course, Stewart plays campaign clips showing Obama criticize the policy.[54] In the same month Stewart again notes that Obama seemed to lift a foreign policy speech from a past Bush speech—"Cowboy words in a lawyer's voice," he says.[55]

Stewart hasn't let up on Obama or the Democrats as the months have passed. In October 2009, after President Obama was announced as the winner of the

Nobel Peace Prize, Stewart raised an eyebrow and noted that "90 minutes after [the president] heard he had been awarded the Nobel Peace prize, NASA literally bombed the moon." In October 27, 2009, in an "Eff'dghanistan" segment, Stewart covered Senator John Kerry's marathon meeting with Afghan president Hamid Karzai, and referred to Kerry as "slow tongue McWindsurfington," and accused him of bringing Karzai around by "waterboring" him. In reporting on Obama's acceptance speech on the occasion of the awarding of the Nobel Peace Prize, Stewart said on December 10, 2009, "Let's see how Mr. Europe balances overseeing one war while escalating another," and then he plays some clips of the speech. With reference to the wars, and channeling Al Pacino's Michael Corleone in *The Godfather (Part III)*, Stewart says "Every time we think we're out, he pulls us back in."

As 2009 turned into 2010, Stewart felt compelled to comment on the Christmas Day passenger jet bombing attempt and the new identification of Yemen as a terror hot spot. Stewart often does things like this by twisting familiar, everyday expressions. His first segment on Yemen (January 4, 2010) was entitled "Terror 2.0," presumably referring to Yemen as the new version of the War on Terror. Television watchers are probably familiar with advertisements of Speedstick antiperspirant. So in Stewart's hands, his segment becomes "Terror 2.0 . . . by Yemen," with male voices that sing "by Yemen" instead of "by Mennen," the brand for which Speedstick is a product. Stewart comments on the failure to identify the alleged perpetrator, saying, "Hey intelligence community, I know you're busy. Three hundred million Americans can't wiretap themselves, but c'mon!" Two days later, after playing a clip making reference to the difficulty of traveling within Yemen, Stewart asks "Can't we get in a war with a paved country?" But this is not all he has to say about Yemen. His guest that evening was Adm. Mike Mullen, Obama's chairman of the Joint Chiefs of Staff, and most of the interview was played straight, talking about issues like the all-volunteer U.S. military. But he does ask Mullen, "When are we going to bomb Yemen? I have things in storage there." Doing his best not to say the wrong thing, Mullen replies "Not any time soon."[56]

On Steven Colbert's television program *The Colbert Report*, a satirical version of "talking head" punditry shows such as Bill O'Reilly's *The O'Reilly Factor*, Colbert assumes the role of an ultra-conservative, Christian political analyst. His trademarks are his narcissism, his extreme statements, and running around his studio drinking in the worship of the audience. The extremism of his statements is chiefly a means of undermining neoconservatism, by taking it to its logical conclusion. As a cheerleader for the War on Terror, Colbert's alter-ego succeeded, during the Bush era, in revealing to his audience both the humor and the weakness associated with such a strategy. In one segment in

2008, Colbert concludes that the United States did not actually invade Iraq. According to Sherlock Holmes, if all possible explanations for a phenomenon have been exhausted, then whatever remains must be true, no matter how improbable. Colbert reasons that if all the given reasons for invading Iraq have been proven false, then the United States did not invade Iraq at all, since it is the only remaining explanation.[57]

Like Stewart, Colbert has also not left President Obama and the Democrats untouched since the inauguration. His digs at Obama take the form of plaudits from his conservative alter-ego on the centrism or even conservatism of some of Obama's early policy positions. On his April 15, 2009, program, Colbert "praises" President Obama for appealing the judicial ruling that detainees at Bagram air base in Afghanistan have the right to challenge their detention based on the principle of habeas corpus.[58] On May 18, 2009, Colbert congratulated President Obama for deciding that he won't release detainee photos and will reinstate military tribunals at Guantánamo. Colbert could be described as pleasantly surprised that instead of transforming the country, Barack Obama has transformed himself—into George Bush. Showing clips from various right-wing pundits, Colbert, self-identifying as a "conservative," welcomed the president to the real world, even if the real world for conservatives was composed of gated communities.[59] On December 10, 2009, reflecting on President Obama receiving the Nobel Peace Prize, Colbert made fun of Obama's plan to win in Afghanistan, comparing it to similar but mock versions of Soviet and British plans from the 1980s and 1920s. He also introduced his audience to a new board game, "Afghandyland," in which most of the game roles are opium growers, and all the game cards say "go back to start" or "go back 600 years." In another segment, Colbert responds to Fox News personality Glenn Beck, who chastised President Obama for apparently not listening to his battlefield commander, Gen. Stanley McChrystal. Seemingly agreeing with Beck, Colbert suggested to the president that he should take orders from the general rather than give them.[60]

As much as Stewart and Colbert are satirical and comedic responses to the "real" news, the role of their programs in not only entertaining but educating their audience has become notable. A 2008 telephone survey by the Pew Research Center determined that 30 percent of The Daily Show viewers and 34 percent of The Colbert Report viewers correctly identified Secretary of State Condoleezza Rice, British prime minister Gordon Brown, and the majority party in the House of Representatives, compared to a national average of only 18 percent.[61] In 2004, a study by the Annenburg Public Policy Center of the University of Pennsylvania determined that Daily Show audiences knew more about presidential candidates and election issues than those who regularly read the newspaper or watched television news programs.[62] Satire and comedy can be used to critique and entertain, but also to inform.

Late Night Stands Up against War

Bill Maher, the current host of HBO's *Real Time with Bill Maher*, made no secret that he was in opposition to the Bush administration and its War on Terror, both before and after he was fired from his previous program in 2002. His approach is less as a satirist and more as a wry, cynical truth-teller. His ideology is more ambiguous than some of the others—more libertarian or populist than liberal—but he represents another important strand. In a discussion on his program about the War on Terror, Maher accused the Republicans of being simplistic, of being obsessed with them-as-evil and us-as-good, and of using the army in an old-fashioned war against a people that don't have one. As for the Democrats, he chastised them for not pointing out the idiocy of the Republican strategy.

In September 2009, having seen enough, Bill Maher called on President Obama to ignore the 30 percent of the population that is crazy, instead of bending over backwards to try to satisfy opponents who will never support him. On September 19, 2009, speaking with a panel on the Obama administration's decision to change U.S. policy on the "missile-defense shield" in Central Europe, Maher captured the frustration of many in his audience, and asked the question, "Why do we have troops in Japan? That war ended 60 years ago. We have troops in South Korea and Germany. Can America ever leave anywhere?"[63] As for the Afghanistan surge of 2009, Maher told Jay Leno that "I thought the whole cowboy-liberator dreamworld was over, but this is more sameness I can believe in."[64]

David Letterman has also targeted Iraq and the War on Terror on *The Late Show with David Letterman*. In one of his famous "Top Ten" routines, Letterman ranked the top ten fictional "new strategies for victory in Iraq," as outlined by President Bush, including making an even bigger "Mission Accomplished" sign, new slogans for the war, and putting Saddam Hussein back in power and leaving. In 2007, the comedy show *MadTV* aired a sketch mocking both Apple and the Iraq war. The sketch consists of Apple founder Steve Jobs unveiling the newest piece of Apple technology—the "iRack." During the course of the routine, the iRack is described negatively by the audience members, who don't want anything to do with it. When Jobs proceeds to place multiple Apple items into the iRack, an audience member tells him not to put them in there. Jobs defends the iRack, but as the audience gets irate he tells them he wants them to look at a new product, the iRan.

The Simpsons and *South Park* Make Fun of the War

Animated television shows have also tried their hand at satire and comedy regarding the War on Terror, quite successfully. *The Simpsons* have set the standard for animated comedy, and its creator has also approached the War on Terror from a satirical standpoint. Created by cartoonist Matt Groening, *The Simpsons* has been on the air as a half-hour program since 1990, after a stint on *The Tracey Ullman Show*. It focuses on a family of five in Springfield, and is an antidote to the idealized portrayal of the American family on television that was dominant from the 1950s through the present. The family consists of a dopey father, "Homer"; a devoted mother, "Marge"; a trouble-making, rebellious ten-year-old, and star, "Bart"; the brilliant little sister, "Lisa"; and the baby, "Maggie"; along with a variety of memorable supporting characters. Occasionally, the program delves into politics. At the conclusion of the annual Halloween special in 2006, the audience is shown the crumbling ruins of Springfield three years after an invasion by hostile aliens. Two aliens are arguing. One says that the Earthlings are continuing to resent their presence as part of Operation: Enduring Occupation, while the other holds up a human heart and brain and says that the invaders have won human hearts and minds. The alien leader, Kodos, also says that they had to invade because the Earthlings were working on weapons of mass disintegration, which the subordinate doubts.

In "G.I. (Annoyed Grunt)," aired a week later, on November 12, 2006, Bart pre-enlists for the military and Homer ends up taking his place. Marge and Grandpa also join up, based on what the viewer would understand as questionable recruitment tactics. Having survived basic training, the whole group participates in a military exercise to test new computer equipment, and Homer beats the computer. The whole gang then escapes to Springfield for fast food, and then are mistaken for terrorists.[65] Like in these other programs, Matt Groening hasn't stopped just because a different party controls the federal government. In the November 30, 2008, episode, Homer makes a fool of himself by breaking in to a Moslem family's home "a la Jack Bauer" because he thinks they are terrorists.[66] In the May 19, 2009, episode, "Coming to Homerica," the show mocks the America-first nativism of people like Lou Dobbs of CNN. In this episode, unemployment in the nearby town of Ogdenville leads people to rush into Springfield, so Mayor Quimby closes the border of the town, calls for volunteers to do guard duty, and Homer starts a border patrol unit, with predictable results.[67]

The program *South Park* was started in 1997 by Matt Stone and Trey Parker, and nothing is off limits. This animated show is based on the adventures of four grade four boys (Stan Marsh, Kyle Broflovski, Eric Cartman, and Kenny

McCormick) in a fictional small town in Colorado called South Park. The program is aimed at adults, and it is firmly within the Borat school, in that the main characters use a lot of foul language and most people would regard much of what goes on as vulgar and disgusting but nonetheless humorous. However, everything is subject to mockery and the creators certainly inject their own analysis of the world they live in.

Daniel Kurtzman has written that the United States lost its sense of humor after 9/11, but less than two months after the event, Stone and Parker were among the first to tackle the issues. *South Park*'s famous "Osama Bin Laden Has Farty Pants" episode, which aired on November 7, 2001, addressed the U.S. invasion of Afghanistan. The creators give the prevailing mood of patriotism and fear a satirical spin as the residents of South Park display the American flag at every opportunity but are also glued to the television news in expectation of another attack. As the episode title suggests, Osama bin Laden is portrayed as a comedic buffoon, eventually being killed by an American soldier (with the help of one of the main characters, Cartman). However, the show attempts to give a voice to Afghans in the form of four children meant to mirror the show's four American protagonists. Despite hating America, the four Afghan children come to the rescue of their American counterparts with the reasoning that if they do not help protect the innocent, then they are no better than the America they hate.[68] In confirmation of Kurtzman's viewpoint, however, this episode exemplified more muted comedy than most of *South Park*'s material, a reflection of the sober times.[69] The episode was nominated for an Emmy award.

Stone and Parker have returned to mock militarism and the United States on numerous occasions. In their November 6, 2002, episode, entitled "A Ladder to Heaven," Cartman and the boys decide to build a ladder to heaven because their dead friend Kenny has a ticket stub that entitled them to win a shopping spree at the local candy store. The military gets wind of this effort, and takes over the project on the grounds that Saddam Hussein is building WMDs in heaven. The community and military abandons the effort, however, when the boys find the ticket, get the candy, and then come clean on their real motivations. The episode ends with Saddam Hussein really building WMDs up in the clouds.[70] On December 11, 2002, in "Red Sleigh Down," in order to get the Christmas present he wants Cartman has to do something really great, so he decides to bring the joy of Christmas to Iraq. He and his friends enlist Santa, who is shot down over Baghdad, unfortunately, by an Iraqi with a surface to air rocket. Santa is captured and tortured with electroshock treatment. The boys then decide that only Jesus can save Santa, so they find him and he agrees to help. To everyone's surprise Jesus opens the church's weapons locker and everyone arms themselves. Jesus and the boys go to Iraq, kill the

Iraqis and rescue Santa, but then Jesus is killed in the escape attempt. Santa appears at the South Park tree lighting ceremony and puts a new spin on the saying that Jesus saves, and that he died for us. One of the boys says, correctly as it turns out, that the Iraqis killed Jesus.

In the April 9, 2003, episode, just after the beginning of the Iraq war, *South Park* produced its most critical and cynical program yet. In this one, entitled "I'm a Little Bit Country," Cartman and the boys participate in a peace march, as a way of getting out of school, but when they don't know anything about the issues, their teacher assigns them a presentation on what the Founding Fathers thought about protest. Cartman tries various tricks to have a flashback to 1776; this eventually works and he witnesses the debates in Philadelphia. But what he sees looks suspiciously like the radical critique of contemporary U.S. political life, with a cynical twist, of course.

Cartman returns to the present and makes his presentation in front of the whole town. He advocates that the United States should go to war but that at the same time a portion of the population should protest it. This rings true for community members, who say that the government can attack whoever they want if they can give the impression that the U.S. public doesn't support it. One of the pro-war citizens tells the crowd that this will ensure that foreigners will hate the U.S. government but not the American people. The militarists need the peace movement so that the world will think the United States is a liberal democracy, while the peace movement needs the militarists so that the country won't be a pushover if it is attacked, the program audience is told.[71]

Like Jon Stewart, Stone and Parker are not partisans and will take their laughs where they can get them. Their 2008 election episode presented Barack Obama and John McCain in cahoots to use the victory of one of them to allow their joint crime ring to use the White House tunnels to steal the Hope diamond, worth over $200 million.[72] A story of symbolic importance, no doubt.

Conclusion

The U.S. empire and militarism are vulnerable for a number of reasons. Empire is not paying at the moment for the United States, and the United States is financially and economically dependent on other states that may decide that U.S. policies are no longer in their interests. In the period 2006 to 2008, the domestic U.S. majority went part of the way in understanding the truth, rather than the fantasies peddled by the Bush administration in the first part of this decade. In this period, popular culture, created by large organizations such as cable television, movies, and the recording industry, has been used to expose, mock, satirize, and criticize U.S. militarism and imperial tendencies. It seems to be the nature of contemporary leadership that it cannot survive the pin-pricks of satire. We have seen that antiwar movies have been coming to the screen, though the feature-length documentaries have sometimes made commercial breakthroughs in the 2000s. While the audience for popular music is highly segmented between different genres, there has been an outpouring of creative music in opposition to U.S. militarism. Efforts to mock and lampoon U.S. foreign and defense policy on television and through animation has boomed in the Bush and early Obama eras. Since many people, especially young people, get much of their information from this type of programming, it is no exaggeration to state that it is of importance in shaping their opinions and in activating them, and others, politically.

Notes

1. "Obama Revises Campaign Promise," *Onion*, May 29, 2009, www.theonion.com/content/news_briefs/obama_revises_campaign (accessed August 5, 2009).

2. Ani DiFranco's performance of the song "November 4th, 2008," is available at www.youtube.com.

3. Chalmers Johnson, *The Sorrows of Empire: Militarism, Secrecy and the End of the Republic* (New York: Metropolitan Books / Henry Holt and Company, 2004), 12.

4. Gordon Lynch, *Understanding Theology and Popular Culture* (Malden, MA: Blackwell, 2005), 11–13.

5. Stuart Hall, "Notes on Deconstructing 'The Popular,'" in *People's History and Socialist Theory*, ed. Raphael Samuel (London: Routledge and Kegan Paul, 1981), 230–31, 239.

6. Lynch, *Understanding Theology and Popular Culture*, 11–13.

7. Timothy Dale, "Political Discourse in Popular Culture: Expanding a View of the Public Sphere" (paper presented at the annual meeting of the Midwest Political Science Association 67th Annual National Conference, The Palmer House Hilton, Chicago, IL), www.allacademic.com/meta/p361202_index.html (accessed July 28, 2009).

8. B. Lee Cooper, "Rumours of War: Lyrical Continuities," in *Continuities in Popular Culture: The Present in the Past & the Past in the Present and Future*, ed. Ray Broadus Browne and Ronald J. Ambrosetti (Bowling Green, OH: Bowling Green State University Popular Press, 1993), 132.

9. Cooper, "Rumours of War," 132.

10. Stephen M. Walt, "'Where Have All the Political Songs Gone?' (with apologies to Pete Seeger)," *Foreign Policy*, March 6, 2009, http://walt.foreignpolicy.com/posts/2009/03/06/where_have_all_the_political_songs_gone_with_apologies_to_pete_seeger (accessed July 28, 2009).

11. Joseph Schumacher, "Is Protest Music as Dead as Disco?" *Peace and Conflict Monitor*, University of Peace, May 12, 2003, www.monitor.upeace.org/archive.cfm?id_article=5 (accessed August 2, 2009).

12. Many other veteran activists, such as Pete Seeger and Barbara Dane, are also still active, often at concerts with multigenerations. See "Protest Music for a New Generation: Vietnam-Era Musicians Lead Chorus of Voices against War," NPR, March 29, 2003, www.npr.org/templates/story/story.php?storyId=1212060 (accessed August 2, 2009).

13. The quote and the content of the preceding two paragraphs are excerpted from Chris Hedges, "War and Popular Culture," *War Is a Force That Gives Us Meaning,* www.firstyearbook.umd.edu/warisaforce/popculture.html (accessed July 29, 2009).

14. Hedges, "War and Popular Culture."

15. "In the Studio: Sheryl Crow Dials Up Old Friends, Protests War on Upcoming Album," *Rolling Stone,* January 11, 2008, www.rollingstone.com/rockdaily/index .php/2008/01/11/rewind-the-week-in-rock-daily-26/ (accessed August 5, 2009).

16. "Lyrics to Billy Bragg's 'Bush War Blues'?" Yahoo!Answers, http://answers .yahoo.com/question/index?qid=20090317085619AAjP5b0 (accessed August 5, 2009). Numerous performances are available at www.youtube.com.

17. Billy Bragg, "There Is Power in a Union," Rhapsody, www.rhapsody.com/ billy-bragg/must-i-paint-you-a-picture-the-essential-billy-bragg/there-is-power-in -a-union/lyrics.html (accessed August 5, 2009).

18. Edna Gundersen, "Paralyzed Iraq Veteran Transforms Pain into Protest Music," *USA Today,* April 7, 2008, www.usatoday.com/life/music/news/2008-04-06 -body-of-war_N.htm.

19. Gundersen, "Paralyzed Iraq Veteran Transforms Pain into Protest Music."

20. Gundersen, "Paralyzed Iraq Veteran Transforms Pain into Protest Music."

21. Gundersen, "Paralyzed Iraq Veteran Transforms Pain into Protest Music."

22. "Films to Change the World," Cultures of Resistance, May 12, 2008, www .culturesofresistance.org/make-films-not-war/resources/films-to-change-the-world (accessed February 22, 2009).

23. Andrew Kelly, *Cinema and the Great War* (New York: Routledge, 1997), 19.

24. Nick Turse, "The Golden Age of the Military-Entertainment Complex: Six Degrees of Kevin Bacon, Pentagon Style," *TomDispatch,* March 20, 2008, www.tom dispatch.com/post/174908 (accessed February 21, 2009).

25. Christopher Sharrett, "Hollywood and the New Militarism—Reed World," *USA Today,* May 2002, http://findarticles.com/p/articles/mi_m1272/is_2684_130/ ai_86062113 (accessed February 21, 2009).

26. Ewen MacAskill, "Hollywood Tears Up Script to Make Anti-war Films While Conflicts Rage," *Guardian,* August 14, 2007, www.guardian.co.uk/world/2007/ aug/14/iraq.film (accessed February 22, 2009).

27. For lists and descriptions, see "Films to Change the World," *Culture of Resistance,* May 12, 2008, www.culturesofresistance.org/make-films-not-war/resources/ films-to-change-the-world (accessed August 2, 2009).

28. See his posting, at Big Hollywood Blog, http://bighollywood.breitbart.com/ jjmnolte/2009/07/02/review-the-hurt-locker-2/ (accessed February 6, 2010).

29. John Nolte, "Review: 'The Hurt Locker,'" Big Hollywood Blog, http://bigholly wood.breitbart.com/jjmnolte/2009/07/02/review-the-hurt-locker-2/ (accessed February 6, 2010).

30. Justin Raimondo, "Go See *V for Vendetta*: Culture and Resistance to Imperialism," Antiwar, April 5, 2006, www.antiwar.com/justin/?articleid=8809 (accessed August 2, 2009).

31. "*Rendition* (2007)," Box Office Mojo, www.boxofficemojo.com/movies/?id=Rendition.htm (accessed July 29, 2009).

32. "*Lions for Lambs*," The Numbers, www.the-numbers.com/movies/2007/LNLMB.php (accessed July 29, 2009).

33. "Anti-war Movies Faltering at the Box Office," *National Public Radio*, November 16, 2007, www.npr.org/templates/story/story.php?storyId=16349134 (accessed August 2, 2009).

34. Jonathan Kiefer, "Hollywood War Machine," *Sacramento News and Review*, August 31, 2006, www.newsreview.com/sacramento/Content?oid=169049 (accessed February 22, 2009).

35. "Films to Change the World," Cultures of Resistance.

36. "Conflict Zone Film Fund," Cultures of Resistance, www.culturesofresistance.org/make-films-not-war/conflictzonefilmfund (accessed February 22, 2009).

37. The quote is by George Gordon (Lord Byron), in *English Bards and Scotch Reviewers: A Satire* (New York: Charles B. Richardson Pubs, 1865), 31.

38. Joe Queenan, "The Honeymoon Is Over," *Guardian*, November 24, 2006, www.guardian.co.uk/world/2006/nov/24/usa.film (accessed August 4, 2009).

39. Mark Kermode, "Review of Borat," *BBC Five Live*, November 2006, www.bbc.co.uk/fivelive/entertainment/kermode_archive_b.shtml (accessed August 4, 2009).

40. Eileen Jones, "Gitmo Injustices Get Satirical Treatment from Harold & Kumar," *AlterNet*, April 26, 2008, www.alternet.org/movies/83578/gitmo_injustices_get_satirical_treatment_from_harold_&_kumar_/ (accessed July 29, 2009); Alonso Duralde, "Harold and Kumar: Dopey, Smart, Timely Satire," *MSNBC*, April 24, 2008, www.msnbc.msn.com/id/24298068/ (accessed July 29, 2009).

41. Warren St. John, "The Power of Fake News," *New York Times*, November 15, 2004.

42. Wells Tower, "*Onion* Nation," *Washington Post*, November 16, 2008.

43. These headlines come from various dates through early January 2010 and can be accessed at www.theonion.com, accessed January 21, 2010.

44. Daniel Terdiman, "*Onion* Taken Seriously, Film at 11," *Wired*, April 14, 2004, www.wired.com/culture/lifestyle/news/2004/04/63048 (accessed August 5, 2009).

45. Megan Boler cited in Andrea Janus, "Is 'Fake News' Informative? Study Tests Fun vs Facts," *CTV News*, September 15, 2008, www.ctv.ca/servlet/ArticleNews/story/CTVNews/20080912/news_feature_080912/20080914?hub=TopStories (accessed August 5, 2009).

46. Theodore Hamm, *The New Blue Media: How Michael Moore, MoveOn.org, Jon Stewart and Company Are Transforming Progressive Politics* (New York: New Press, 2008).

47. Jon Stewart, "Iraq—an Occupation Is Forever," *The Daily Show*, 2008, www.youtube.com/watch?v=F5UFq09j-N4 (accessed July 29, 2009).

48. Jon Stewart, "Big 'Bama's House," *The Daily Show*, February 3, 2009, www.thedailyshow.com/videos (accessed August 3, 2009).

49. Jon Stewart, "The Iraq War Is Over," *The Daily Show*, March 3, 2009, www .thedailyshow.com/videos (accessed August 3, 2009).

50. Jon Stewart, "New Euphemisms," *The Daily Show*, March 31, 2009, www.the dailyshow.com/videos (accessed August 3, 2009).

51. Jon Stewart, "Obama Closing Gitmo," *The Daily Show*, January 22, 2009, www .thedailyshow.com/videos (accessed August 3, 2009).

52. "Gitmo's World—Death to America," *The Daily Show*, January 22, 2009, www .thedailyshow.com/videos (accessed August 3, 2009).

53. Jon Stewart, "Waffle House," *The Daily Show*, May 12, 2009, www.thedaily show.com/videos (accessed August 3, 2009).

54. Jon Stewart, "Moral Kombat," *The Daily Show*, May 14, 2009, www.thedaily show.com/videos (accessed August 3, 2009).

55. Jon Stewart, "American Idealogues," *The Daily Show*, May 19, 2009, www .thedailyshow.com/videos (accessed August 3, 2009).

56. Material in the last two paragraphs comes from various episodes of *The Daily Show*, www.thedailyshow.com/videos (accessed January 17, 2010).

57. Stephen Colbert, "The Word—Sherlock," *The Colbert Report*, October 18, 2006, www.colbertnation.com/home (accessed August 3, 2009).

58. Stephen Colbert, "Obama Denies Habeas Corpus," *The Colbert Report*, April 15, 2009, www.colbertnation.com/home (accessed August 3, 2009).

59. Stephen Colbert, "Welcome to the Real World," *The Colbert Report*, May 18, 2009, www.colbertnation.com/home (accessed August 3, 2009).

60. Stephen Colbert, "Afghandyland" and "U.S. Army Chain of Command," *The Colbert Report*, December 10, 2009, www.colbertnation.com/home (accessed January 21, 2010).

61. "Key News Audiences Now Blend Online and Traditional Sources," Pew Research Center for the People & the Press, August 17, 2008, http://people-press.org/ report/?pageid=1356 (accessed July 29, 2009).

62. Bryan Long, "Daily Show Viewers Ace Political Quiz," *CNN*, September 29, 2004, www.cnn.com/2004/SHOWBIZ/TV/09/28/comedy.politics/index.html (accessed July 29, 2009).

63. See these excerpts at www.huffingtonpost.com/2009/09/12/bill-maher-chal lenges-oba_n_284314.html and www.youtube.com/watch?v=XuWHO6d8tkE (accessed January 22, 2010).

64. "Bill Maher Talks Afghanistan, Banking Rates, and Tiger Woods," *Huffington Post*, December 1, 2009, http://www.huffingtonpost.com/2009/12/01/bill-maher-talks-afghanis_n_375472.html (accessed January 22, 2010).

65. "G.I. (Annoyed Grunt)," *The Simpsons*, November 12, 2006, www.thesimp sons.com/episode_guide/1805.htm (accessed August 4, 2009).

66. "Mypods and Boomsticks," *The Simpsons*, November 30, 2008, www.thesimp sons.com/recaps/season20/ (accessed August 4, 2009).

67. "Coming to Homerica," *The Simpsons*, May 19, 2009, www.thesimpsons.com/ recaps/season20/ (accessed August 4, 2009).

68. "Osama Bin Laden Has Farty Pants," *South Park*, November 7, 2001, www .southparkstudios.com/ (accessed July 29, 2009).

69. Daniel Kurtzman, "The Return of Irony," *AlterNet*, September 10, 2002, www .alternet.org/911oneyearlater/14068/the_return_of_irony/ (accessed August 3, 2009).

70. "A Ladder to Heaven," *South Park*, November 6, 2002, www.southparkstudios .com/ (accessed August 3, 2009).

71. "I'm a Little Bit Country," *South Park*, April 9, 2003, www.southparkstudios .com/ (accessed August 3, 2009).

72. "About Last Night," *South Park*, November 5, 2008, www.southparkstudios .com/ (accessed August 3, 2009).

8

Waging Peace

Culture Jammers Take Resistance to the Streets

XCUSE ME—IS THAT BLOOD IN YOUR GAS TANK?" reads the tag line on an anti-
ad featuring a glossy image of a bright red Hummer. Cleverly commenting on the oil agenda behind the ongoing bloodshed in Iraq, Dave Ward, a
professional photographer, designed this antiwar spoof ad that was virally
distributed on the Internet.[1] Arianna Huffington notes that "the symbolism
of these impractical machines' military roots is too delicious to ignore. We go
to war to protect our supply of cheap oil in vehicles that would be prohibi-
tively expensive to operate without it."[2] In this chapter we profile the creative
people, activists, performers and entertainers, and sports celebrities who
are using innovative ways to expose and criticize U.S. militarism. As we will
see, to make their point, anti-militarist activists engage in culture jamming,
postering, crafts, fine art, both street and staged theater, use of entertainer
and athletic status, video gaming, comics and graphic novels, fashion, and
transforming war toys into peace art.

Culture Jamming

Culture jamming seeks to interrupt an intrusive corporate culture "whose
operant mode is the manufacture of consent through the manipulation of
symbols."[3] The term "cultural jamming" was first used by the sound-collage
band *Negativland* to describe billboard alteration and other forms of media
sabotage. On Jamcon '84, a mock-serious band member observes, "As awareness of how the media environment we occupy affects and directs our inner

life grows, some resist. . . . The skillfully reworked billboard . . . directs the public viewer to a consideration of the original corporate strategy. The studio for the cultural jammer is the world at large."[4] Kalle Lasn, one of the founders of the Vancouver-based Adbusters Media Foundation, is famous for his use of "subvertising" as a means of critiquing and attacking the messages of consumer capitalism.[5] Well-made subvertisments need to efficiently "mimic the look and feel of the targeted ad, promoting the classic 'double-take' as viewers suddenly realize they have been duped."[6] Lasn argues that the radicalism of un-commercials or anti-ads lies not so much in the ad's content, but in Marshall McLuhan's notion that "the medium is the message." Lasn notes, "We are actually digging around with the actual tone and the feeling of television. We are saying that this aesthetic which we have come up with on commercial television, that this is a mind-fuck aesthetic. And to change it we have to start putting in all kinds of strange, weirdo messages that change the whole feeling."[7] Sut Jhally, a professor of communication at the University of Massachusetts at Amherst and executive director of the Media Education Foundation, states that "The only language that operates in the modern world is the language of advertising culture. And if you want to fight, you've got to use that language. You've got to turn the power of your opponent back on itself."[8] Culture jammers, like visual and other artists, would probably agree with the sentiment attributed to Toronto video artist Colin Campbell: "Culture is what they do to us, and art is what we do to them."[9]

Creative spoofs of advertisements have been developed to convey antiwar messages on billboards and in print and electronic media. In "What Goes Around Comes Around. Stop the Iraq War," New York–based agency Big Ant International won a Gold Pencil for Design at the One Show Design Awards with their work for Global Coalition for Peace. A brilliant use of media and message, four posters were designed to wrap around utility poles, campaigning for an end to the war in Iraq. Grenades, rifles, missiles, and tank guns come round the pole to catch up with the aggressor in each poster in order to illustrate that "what goes around comes around."[10]

Attacking the establishment has its price, as students learned in Australia in 2003 when Australia's Department of Defense withdrew advertising from all student media across the country in response to a controversial full-page parody of military recruitment advertising published in *Vertigo*, a student newspaper at the University of Technology, Sydney. The spoof ad satirically portrayed the Australian Department of Defense as "a political tool of an Australian government intent on participating in an unsanctioned invasion of Iraq" and was followed up and reprinted by other student publications.[11] Project Billboard, a group of San Francisco Bay–area women, found their efforts thwarted by the dominant interests that govern the mainstream media and public spaces. The group purchased space on the Marriott Marquis Hotel on Broadway, proposing an illustration of a star-spangled bomb accompanied by the words "Democracy is best taught by example, not by war."[12] Clear Channel's Spectacolor division, which rents the Marriott space, rejected Project Billboard's message because of the bomb illustration. When it was changed to an image of a dove, Clear Channel declared that they also disliked the phrase "not by war," and that proposals would not be accepted that were "unsuitable for children" or that could be considered "personally offensive."[13] AntiWar Video Fund and Not in Our Name created TV spots questioning the War on Terror that were also rejected, by Comcast's CNN and MTV respectively. Comcast stated that they could not run the antiwar advertisement because it contained "unsubstantiated claims," which Scott Lynch, communications director at Peace Action, said was "ironic" because "the President's case for war on Iraq rests largely on the same."[14] Lynch protests these restrictions, arguing that "by not running the ads Comcast is stifling the most important American debate in a generation."[15] Nonetheless, some resistance groups have managed to use advertising strategies and media to their advantage. One common strategy is the purchasing of time on local channels, as a few minutes of commercial time are generally reserved hourly for local affiliates and cable operators. Furthermore, advocacy groups often gain media coverage by holding news conferences to denounce their advertisements' rejections.[16]

Counter-Propaganda

Historically, posters were a powerful means of communication used by the U.S. government during the world wars for propaganda purposes, to recruit and influence soldiers and civilians alike. In the last ten years, postering has been revived by antiwar activists like artist Micah Wright, who have taken wartime propaganda posters and given them a contemporary twist. A World War II–era poster picturing a Japanese soldier peeking over a barrier, with the original caption "He's Watching You," has been revised to say that (then attorney general) "John Ashcroft's Watching You," with a Christian cross in the background. In another revised poster, the American air force pilot declares "You Back the Attack, We'll Bomb Who We Want."[17] These posters have been featured in art shows such as at the Chisholm Gallery in New York, and are widely available for downloading on the Web. Many variations have also been done on James Montgomery Flagg's iconic 1917 recruiting poster picturing Uncle Sam, including "I want you to resist tyranny," "I want you to kill for that oil," and "I want you to kill all who oppose."[18]

A classic form of culture jamming is the art of graffiti. In New York City an unknown artist decorated public sites with a stencil with the caption "Made in America," picturing the Statue of Liberty with a machine gun held high instead of the torch. Stickers with captions like "American Fascism Top Quality" have been put high on traffic control devices, where they cannot be easily removed or defaced. Paul Notzhold projected a soldier's silhouette and an empty thought bubble, with a caption that reads "Who are you afraid of," with a phone number for answers via text message. He then projected viewers' responses in the thought bubbles. People have made stencils of the Statue of Liberty with captions such as "Lost Liberty," and have spray-painted falling bombs with Bush's head in them. There are also "Bush" stickers that have been put beneath the "Stop" on stop signs, and an "h" has been added after the "s" to signs that otherwise say "Bus Stop." A stencil with a TV and the word "lies" has been sprayed on top of the U.S. flag. Jammers have also linked Bush to the Nazis, by superimposing Bush's face within the swastika, with the swastika on his forehead, and by substituting the swastika for the "s" in his last name. There is also a stencil for spray painting purposes that has Hitler's head on the left, a recycle sign in the middle, and Bush's head on the right. (While the comparison between Bush and the Nazi Germany may be extreme, it is based in part on the basic reality that both leaders "waged aggressive wars," a violation of international law.)

A particularly creative sticker in Britain (which is easily transferable to other countries) asks the question, "Is the UK Government doing a good job?" and has "No" on the left and "Yes" in the center, with a hole underneath both answers. But this was designed for, and was pasted to, a pedestrian traffic control device for requesting a "walk light," and the only pushable button goes through the "yes" hole. This plays on a general recognition that voters, and those being surveyed, don't really have a meaningful choice when it comes to conventional politics. Another great example of culture jamming is the army recruiting billboard that says "Ever Thought of Joining? Talk to Someone Who Has"; but the words "Lost a Son in Iraq" are added as the third and concluding line, in a similar font. Another striking poster, made by Roufixte Designers Productions, presents, in green, the outline of the iconic robed and hooded detainee figure from Abu Ghraib, standing on a cardboard box in a stress position, except hung with red Christmas ornaments. The caption at the top reads "Amerrycan Christmas."[19]

Culture jammers taking on the Obama administration have creatively reworked the now-iconic red, white, and blue Obama HOPE campaign poster designed by street artist Shepard Fairey. In the altered versions activist artists express their doubts about the integrity of the new administration by featuring

Obama in military gear with a button labeled Afghanistan. In others the word hope under the image of Obama is replaced with "Obey," and with "Hopium."

The Urban Dictionary site defines "Hopium" as "A substance that the media and press abuse, it makes them mesmerized by Barack Obama."[20] Commercial websites sell antiwar designs and slogans on a multitude of consumer items from buttons and bumper stickers to T-shirts and coffee mugs. These include "How did our oil get under their sand?" "Not Bitter? Not Paying Attention," and "United We Bomb."

In another creative outburst, Kathy Eder, a California high school teacher, made up her own deck of cards in response to the Iraqi deck of cards distributed to U.S. soldiers. "My taxes paid for this war. I have an obligation to do something," she said. In 2003 the U.S. military developed a set of playing cards known as *Most-Wanted Iraqi Playing Cards* to help troops identify members of President Saddam Hussein's government. In the spoof pack, President George Bush, labeled the "Dictator of the World," is the Ace of Spades, while Donald Rumsfeld is the Ace of Clubs. The cards, packaged under the title "Operation Hidden Agenda," also feature prominently the famous 1983 photo of Donald Rumsfeld visiting Saddam Hussein, at the behest of President Ronald Reagan. She has sold thousands of copies, and shares the profits with a number of veterans groups.[21]

Crafting Resistance

War art has a long history going back to the ancient world. In the twentieth century some war art was government-sponsored, particularly in the two world wars, in order to document the wars from an artistic perspective.[22] Since World War II, artists have predominantly played their role as canaries in the coal mine of society; the more dubious the war, the earlier that artists have recognized this and the more vociferous their expressions of dissent. Certainly, a great deal of art has been produced in the 2000s in response to the "War on Terror," and we can only scratch the surface here. An art show held at the Hyde Park Art Center in Chicago in November 2007 illustrates how clever and brilliant war art (and generally, antiwar art) can be. In an installation entitled "All of it/Everything" from 2006, Mary Brogger has presented a partial car chassis undercarriage strapped on top of oil drums, which are lined up on their side to provide the sense of wheels. This evokes the idea of a diving dock or raft, with the possibility that the derelict lower chassis is being rescued.[23] Conversely, given the theme of the show, could the oil drums and chassis symbolize an eight-wheel light armored vehicle, in which the oil drums and car chassis, in whatever decayed state, represent the purpose of the vehicle, the purpose of contemporary war?[24]

In an antiwar art show in Istanbul, Turkey, there was a showing of Armenian-Canadian Atom Egoyan's film *Ararat* on the Armenian genocide, an act which itself is controversial in that country. Chinese artist Huang Yong Ping posed a sculpted minaret tower at a forty-five-degree angle, shielded largely by a cloth fence, calling forth the image of an antiaircraft gun. Turkish artist Banu Cennetoglu presented a series of mundane state "surveillance photos" of Turkish men on the street. Britain's Jonathan Barnbrook designed posters, one of which in particular is quite striking. With a pinwheel design, he depicts a cycle of violence in which a symbolic Moslem is aiming and shooting a handgun at a symbolic Jew, who is aiming and shooting a symbolic Moslem and so forth around in a circle. A Star of David and Crescent and Star are where the heads should be, to signal the figures' state/religious affiliation, and the viewer is given the impression of the motion of the pinwheel and eternal recurrence. Finally, in another clever presentation, "RGB's War," Thai artist Porntaweesak Rimsakul set up several, small remote-controlled vehicles with army helmets on them. As performance art, they ran in a large sandbox-type surface, with sufficiently high sides to contain them, and they collided with each other and also with tiny houses filled with liquid paint in primary colors. The tires of the vehicles, soaked with the paint, then produced a work of "abstract expressionism."[25]

Crafting is far more widespread than the "fine arts," and there are many examples of crafters making peace-oriented products. Videos and instructions are widely available to make peace-themed objects and ornaments, Japanese origami peace cranes, peace lanterns, peace poles, and peace jewelry.[26] A growing movement is "Peace Tree Day," based on Mitra Sen's award-winning film *The Peace Tree*. An official day in a growing number of Canadian cities and elsewhere in the world, the goal is to encourage children and families to gather together and make peace symbols from their various ethnic, religious, and linguistic traditions. The symbols are then hung on a tree to commemorate the show of unity.[27]

Peace Artists

Some poets and critics, like Sean Arthur Joyce, criticize contemporary poets for not being sufficiently engaged with the world and not addressing the permanent war footing of the United States and the Western world more generally. They note that Lawrence Ferlinghetti (U.S.), George Orwell (UK), and Pablo Neruda (Chile) all wrote such poetry in the mid-twentieth century.[28]

But this is not to say that poets have made no contribution in the 2000s. February 12, 2003, was "Poetry Against the War" day, which included readings at the White House gates, in addition to over 160 public readings in many different countries and almost all fifty states. In the run-up to the war Nation Books published a volume of over 130 poems submitted to the website of Poets Against the War.[29] This international association, founded by Sam Hamill, counts nine thousand members and "continues the tradition of socially engaged poetry by creating venues for poetry as a voice against war, tyranny and oppression."[30] Another organization, the Artists and Writers' against War on Iraq, organized a petition that circulated early after the U.S. invasion of Iraq. Author Ursula Le Guin presented the petition to the White House on March 18, 2003, the document asserting the important moral obligation artists have to spread truth through their art.[31] British Nobel literature laureate Harold Pinter has also attacked the decision of both the United States and Great Britain to invade Iraq, stating "We have brought torture, cluster bombs, depleted uranium, innumerable acts of random murder, misery, degradation and death to the Iraqi people and call it 'bringing freedom and democracy to the Middle East.'"[32]

Split This Rock, a national organization of socially engaged poets, continues to hold a poetry festival in Washington every two years. The 2010 edition was called Split This Rock Poetry Festival: Poems of Provocation & Witness, on March 10–13 in Washington, DC, and examples of antiwar poetry are available on the Web to encourage activists to organize their own festivals around the country.[33]

Taking It to the Streets

Theatre, both formal and informal, has been another venue used to satirize the War on Terror. In June 2007 a platoon-size group of U.S. soldiers, clad in desert combat uniforms, descended on Times Square in New York City as the first move in Operation First Casualty, activities that would take them through the streets of New York from Times Square to Union Square. They proceeded cautiously in the area, eyes focused upward looking for snipers, arresting suspects, putting hoods over their heads and tying their hands behind their backs with flex ties. They evacuated their own wounded as a result of enemy fire. They confronted a local protest, and as an outnumbered force, they took care to identify and arrest the protest leaders while not further inflaming the large crowd. Afterwards, they held a press conference and answered media questions. Of course, this was street or guerilla theater, organized by Iraq Veterans Against the War (IVAW). The purpose

of these actions is to bring home to U.S. citizens "the truth and the brutality of the U.S. invasion and occupation of Iraq," said Paul Abernathy,[34] who
served in Iraq with the U.S. Army's 3rd Infantry Division. The video of the
event—which documents the first of numerous of these events in U.S. cities—shows citizens who as spectators are getting a taste of what it's like to
live with the disruption of an occupying army. The IVAW credits the support of local activists, who act as confederates for the action, playing the
roles of detainees and protestors confronting the U.S. forces.[35] In an action
fit only for an authoritarian state, IVAW cochair Adam Kokesh received a
"general discharge under honorable conditions" (a notch below "honorable
discharge") from the Marine Reserves in June 2007 for participating in a
IVAW action, even though he was not on active duty and he said that he had
stripped insignia off his fatigues.[36]

The IVAW undertakes many other activities as well, both creative and
conventional. On August 18, 2007, a group of IVAW members, dressed in
black T-shirts printed with the organization's name, appeared at a military recruitment booth at a job fair and, in military call-and-response style, chanted
repeatedly, "War is not a game." At St. Lawrence University in Canton, New
York, in November 2007, IVAW members also did a public performance piece
in which they cut their combat uniforms off their bodies. They then turned
the cloth into paper, and then used it to make prints and produce books. Eli
Wright said it is "powerful to me to take that uniform and make something
positive out of it." IVAW members have participated in Winter Soldier hearings, in which they testify regarding the things they did and witnessed in Iraq,
and they have also appeared on television. One member, Casey Porter, was
called back to service during his four-year individual-ready-reserve period, an
example of the "stop-loss" policy to keep people in the military longer than
they expected or were told by recruiters. He was interviewed on the U.S. media
while on active service in Iraq, at considerable risk to his own liberty.[37]

Elements of the theatrical have been incorporated into the venerable demonstration. On December 14, 2008, Iraqi journalist Muntadhar al-Zeidi threw
a shoe at President Bush at a Baghdad press conference.[38] Nine days later, a
demonstration outside the White House was organized to place pairs of shoes
for killed Iraqi civilians, and protestors also hurled shoes at a demonstrator
wearing prison stripes and a giant likeness of George W. Bush's head.[39] The
"die-in," a variation of the "sit-in" pioneered in the mid- to late twentieth
century, enjoyed a revival in 2002 and 2003 as people wanted to protest the
U.S. rush to war in Iraq. In these events, dozens to hundreds of individuals
simulate dead people in order to bring home the human costs of war. However, "The drawback to staging a 'die-in', Sachin Anand discovered this winter, is that when people shout 'Communist!' at you, you can't answer back,"

wrote Joanna Weiss in the *Boston Globe*.[40] One of the biggest die-ins in recent years was held at the Capitol building in Washington on September 15, 2007, as part of ongoing opposition to the U.S. war in Iraq.[41] Vigils and singing for peace have long been favored techniques, but a group of women during the run-up to the Iraq war held nude protests in the San Francisco Bay Area, in which they used their bodies to spell out antiwar slogans.[42]

Staging Resistance

Of course U.S. militarism has not escaped the attention of the "high culture" form of theater. Before the launch of the invasion of Iraq, a play entitled *The Madness of George Dubya* was a hit on the London theater scene. Actor Nicholas Burns, who plays Tony Blair, noted in early February 2003 that "as war comes closer, the mood among the audience has changed. The audience is actually laughing more but the tension behind their laughs has grown. People are scared."[43] Tim Robbins's satirical play *Embedded* targets neoconservative policy makers and the journalistic practice of "embedded reporting," in which journalists embed themselves within military units in order to report on their activities. Robbins has long been subject to attacks from militarists for using his status as a famous actor to speak out on overtly political subjects such as the Iraq war. VJ Foster, who starred in Robbins's play, explained that the motivation for such a play is not anti-Americanism: "In America, if you go against the administration, then they say you must not be patriotic and that you must not love your country. But we love our country, we just think it's going in the wrong direction."[44]

Readings of the classical antiwar play *Lysistrata* was another way in which the arts were used to oppose the war in Iraq. The *Yale Daily News* reports that before the U.S. war on Iraq in 2003, there were three readings of the play in New Haven, Connecticut, alone, and over a thousand in fifty-nine countries around in the world. The play, written by Aristophanes, is an account of the women in two warring city-states, who decide to withhold sex in order to end the fighting, a tactic that is ultimately successful. Christopher Arnott of New Haven wrote a quick, one-page version of the play for presentation at antiwar rallies, and also commented that it is "a timeless satire about how people re-think their values in wartime. It's a chance to have an amusing rally for the cause, we should try to make it funny." The play has been performed by regular people as well as celebrities, including Julie Christie, Kevin Bacon, and Eric Stoltz. "Our purpose is to make it very clear that President Bush does not speak for all Americans. Our message is simple: If you oppose this war, then speak up!" said New York actor Sharron Bower.[45]

A play entitled *Jihad: The Musical*, billed as "a madcap gallop through the wacky world of international terrorism," also stirred up controversy in the United Kingdom. The satire follows an Afghan poppy farmer as he attempts to make money selling poppy flowers to Westerners. He becomes involved in a terrorist cell and must decide where his loyalties lie. A petition against the show began, with opponents saying, "The idea of making light of Muslim extremism is extremely offensive, most especially for its victims." The creators of *Jihad* insist that their show is a satirical effort to laugh in the face of terrorism.

Star Power

People pay attention to celebrities and historically they have had a variety of opinions, like other Americans. During the Vietnam War, actor John Wayne was a conservative and enthusiastic supporter of U.S. militarism, while Jane Fonda was an advocate of social justice. Like the Dixie Chicks, Fonda stuck to her beliefs and was proven correct in the end, but was a victim of collateral damage in the process. In 1972 Jane Fonda traveled to North Vietnam to see the war conditions for herself, and made public statements that led militarists to accuse her of giving "succor to the enemy" and "treason."[46] Conservatives labeled her "Hanoi Jane" and sought to make her name synonymous with dilettantism, liberalism, weakness, and other such traits. Republican Mitt Romney, primary candidate in 2008, was quoted as saying that Obama went "from Jane Fonda to Dr. Strangelove" in a matter of weeks, knowing that for Republicans reference to "Hanoi Jane" is the greatest insult.[47] Of course, as Robert Freeman argues, had it not been for Jane Fonda and other antiwar protestors, both prominent and ordinary, the pointless U.S. war in Vietnam might well have gone on much longer and killed a far greater number of both Americans and Vietnamese.[48]

Despite the abuse heaped on antimilitaristic celebrities, it is remarkable how often their views are borne out in the end. In the case of the Iraq War in 2003, it also puts to a lie the claim that "everyone thought there was WMDs in Iraq." In Washington, actress Susan Sarandon, who supports numerous liberal causes, accused Bush of having "hijacked our losses and our fears." Sarandon said terrorism could not be fought with violence and that most Americans did not want a conflict. "Let us resist this war," she told the cheering crowd. "Let us hate war in all its forms, whether the weapon used is a missile or an airplane." Demonstrators of all ages, many religions, and many nationalities gathered at the Vietnam Veterans Memorial before marching to the White House. President Bush, however, was in Mexico for a summit of Pacific Rim leaders. On CBS TV's *The Early Show* on February 14, 2003, Sarandon, appearing with Phyllis Bennis of United for Peace and Justice, expressed doubts about whether Iraq had WMDs, about whether there was a connection between Iraq and "terrorism," about whether Iraq was an imminent threat, and about whether the United States had an adequate plan to run and leave the country after the invasion. She also noted that a U.S. invasion would undermine global order, alienate allies, and create a humanitarian disaster.[49] Pretty good for a celebrity!

Like in other militaristic eras, the media did not pay much attention to dissenters until well after the beginning of the Iraq War, but as the crisis there worsened and manufactured public support transformed into active opposition, the media started to allow debate and controversy. One of the most notable of these was the widely viewed and discussed debate between Rosie O'Donnell and Elisabeth Hasselbeck on ABC's *The View*. As blogger Stuart Heritage notes, "no disagreements on *The View* were ever like the splitscreen battle royale between Rosie O'Donnell and Elisabeth Hasselbeck back in May [2008]." This was a fierce debate between Hasselbeck, a committed neoconservative and Bush supporter, and O'Donnell, the committed liberal and opponent of the Republicans. Viewers unaccustomed to seeing genuine disagreements, outside of "reality television" and staged wrestling matches, blasted the women for their views: Blogger SM called Hasselbeck a "rightwing lunatic" and O'Donnell a "paranoid conspiracy theorist."[50]

But O'Donnell's views have also been largely vindicated. In a February 24, 2003, interview with Phil Donahue, she said that the plan to attack Iraq didn't square with American values and she argued in favor of following UN protocols prior to launching an invasion of Iraq. On April 30, 2005, she told Geraldo Rivera: "This President invaded a sovereign nation in defiance of the UN. He is basically a war criminal. Honestly. He should be tried at The Hague. This man lied to the American public about the reasons for invading a nation that had nothing to do with 9/11."[51] Other antimilitarism celebrities, like George Clooney, Richard Gere, Sean Penn, and Martin Sheen, also are frequently attacked by militarists, regardless of the strength of their positions.[52]

Tackling Militarism

Athletes have a reputation for being more conservative than other celebrities, but it is certainly the case that not all professional athletes endorse militarism and war. Despite all of the multifaceted connections between sport and war, there is also a long history of athletes struggling for peace. One of the greatest heavyweight boxers, Mohammed Ali (born Cassius Clay), went to jail for resisting the draft during the Vietnam War and was stripped for a time of his championship. At the 1968 Mexico City summer Olympics, two African American athletes, Tommie Smith and John Carlos, won gold and bronze medals in the two-hundred-meter sprint and stood on the podium during the playing of the U.S. national anthem with their heads bowed and a black-gloved hand raised, black-power style, as a protest against racism at home.[53] They were expelled from the Olympic Village and the International Olympic Committee stripped them of their medals.

In the 2000s, among the most outspoken athletes against war and militarism are cyclist Lance Armstrong,[54] major league baseball (MLB) player Carlos Delgado,[55] boxer Anthony Mundine,[56] NFL linebacker Adalius Thomas, tennis player Martina Navratilova, Ultimate Fighting champion Jeff Monson, and NBA players Steve Nash[57] and Adonal Foyle.[58] These athletes have faced considerable public criticism for their political stances. Carlos Delgado, who refused to stand for "God Bless America" played at every Sunday MLB game, faced taunts and boos during games at Yankee Stadium.[59] During Super Bowl week 2010, sports author David Zirin pointed out that Scott Fujita, who was raised by Japanese American parents and whose adoptive father was born in an internment camp, has been a long-time critic of secret American incarceration and was finally getting broader exposure playing on a Super Bowl winning team. As an antidote to the militarism of major sports events including the Super Bowl, Zirin also reported that he was teaming up with Iraq Veterans Against the War (IVAW) to hold an antimilitarist Super Bowl party at the IVAW house in Washington, DC. "[W]e're going to watch the game, without question, but we're also going to speak about de-linking the fun of football with the reality of war," he said.[60]

Canadian-raised NBA star Steve Nash appeared at a 2003 NBA All-Star event wearing a T-shirt reading "No War. Shoot for Peace," and was told that "maybe [he] should be in a different country" by U.S. Navy Academy graduate and San Antonio Spurs player David Robinson.[61] Further, despite his apologies and attempts at clarification, Australian Aboriginal and Muslim boxer Anthony Mundine was indefinitely stripped of his twenty-sixth-place world ranking, after stating that he did not support Australia's involvement in the War on Terror and that "America's brought it upon themselves in what they've done in the history of time."[62] Sports broadcaster Howard Cosell once stated that "Rule Number One of the 'Jockocracy' is that pro-athletes and politics should never mix."[63] However, militaristic politics and professional athletes have long mixed. It seems that it is only the politics of these marginalized, antiwar athletes that are unwelcome, since no athlete has ever been disciplined for making pro-war statements.

There are also sports-oriented organizations dedicated to peace. For example, University of Tennessee doctoral students Sarah Hillyer and Ashleigh Huffman founded Sport 4 Peace, an organization with the goal of "empower[ing] girls and women in countries where cultural, political, and religious obstacles may exist for them." Through this organization, Hillyer has coached softball in Iran and basketball in Iraq.[64] UK-based Football 4 Peace also emphasizes the relationship between sport and peace, and it is a "sport-based co-existence project for Jewish and Arab children" that has been operating since 2001 in northern Israel.[65]

Furthermore, sport has been recognized as an effective development tool, used by international humanitarian organizations like Right to Play, which "uses sport and play programs to improve health, develop life skills, and foster peace for children and communities in some of the most disadvantaged areas of the world."[66] The United Nations also acknowledges the development potential of sport—a 2003 report from the UN Inter-Agency Task Force on Sport for Development and Peace describes how sport can positively impact community health, conflict resolution, education, and sustainable development.[67] Clearly, despite the fact that dominant social forces employ sport for propagandistic militarism, it also has great promise as a mechanism for peace.

Joystick Resistors

Earlier in this book we showed the ways in which video games have been and are being used to promote militarism and recruit military personnel. Every coin has two sides, so in a society with so many creative, dissenting people it should be no surprise that activists are subverting militaristic efforts. Sometimes this is done through the creation of alternative games. The game *September 12* takes realism to a new level; players who respond to a terrorist attack by destroying buildings in an Arab town, face realistic consequences as a result, as "women weep over their dead children and new enemies are created as civilians grab guns to defend their homes."[68] Some gamers subvert militaristic games to raise questions about war, like artist Joseph DeLappe, who in 2006 began playing *America's Army* online with the username "dead-in-iraq." He uses the game's messaging system to manually type the name, age, service branch, and date of death of each service person who has died in Iraq. Lappe says that he is a character in the game but that he drops his rifle and uses the text message system until his character is killed. Other players can see his messages and can respond, some supportive and some negative. He describes his work as "a fleeting, online memorial to those military personnel who have been killed in this ongoing conflict."[69] *Velvet-Strike*, initiated by Anne-Marie Schleiner and Joan Leandre, utilizes a collection of virtual spray paints in the counterterrorism game *Counter-Strike*. Schleiner and Leandre designed the graffiti tags, with messages like "We Are All Iraqis Now,"[70] to be applied to the walls, ceilings, and floors that players encounter in the team-based online game. The designers used the tradition of player protest modification to make the point that "there is no difference between entertainment and propaganda."[71]

It is possible to design video games that provoke us to ask questions and undermine militarism. A British game development firm has a project in development called *Gitmo: Rendition*. The game has been set in the future, after the United States no longer uses its internment facilities at Guantánamo Bay. In this scenario, private mercenaries kidnap people and hold them for ransom or engage in human trafficking and sell them to people for scientific experimentation. For enhanced realism, the game is being developed with the assistance of Moazzam Begg, a British Muslim who was held at Gitmo for three years and then released back to the United Kingdom without charge.[72] Clearly, although video games and the gaming industry are being used as agents of militarization, this medium can also be utilized to question that very militarism.

Comic Relief

The contents of comics have always been socially contested, in that for decades comic artists and illustrators have attempted to push the boundaries of the acceptable and have struggled with the authorities. In an earlier chapter we saw the role that some comics played in beating the drums of war. But as Henry Jenkins notes, most comic book creators, even those working for DC and Marvel (the dominant forces in the market), were much more thoughtful and critically minded about the events that began with the attacks on 9/11. In other words, to say that George W. Bush had a "comic-book view of the world" is an insult to comic books. As Jenkins says, "September 11 represented a brief opening for a new way of thinking about America's place in the world, for a response not so much 'anti-American', as conservative critics might claim, but global."[73] He quotes Dennis O'Neil of DC, who refers to the comic and graphic novel industry as "the R&D division" of the entertainment industry, one that can pilot ideas and creativity at relatively low cost, some of which are then picked up for television series or movies requiring major financial investments.[74]

The history of antiwar illustrations and cartoons goes back a long way, and they have often been produced by high-profile artists. The seventeenth-century etchings of François Callot on the destruction wrought by the Thirty Years' War (1618–1648) were hardly precedented and still have a chilling effect on the viewer.[75] Francisco de Goya drew antiwar graphics during the Napoleonic Wars (1810), and George Grosz did the same in World War I (1918).[76] In the 1960s Neal Adam and Denny O'Neil's Green Lantern/Green Arrow series provided a thorough critique of American culture in the midst of the Vietnam War and antiwar sentiments were a staple of the underground comics which had split from the mainstream precisely so that they could be more outspoken in their critique of American society.[77]

As we have seen, after 9/11 some comic creators used their medium to promote militaristic patriotism. Alternative Comics publisher Jeff Mason remarked, "I am really shocked and dismayed by some of the rhetoric and behavior I've seen from some in the guise of patriotism and I think that a book that promotes an alternative to xenophobia and antagonism would be a good thing."[78] As if in answer to this call, Marvel responded to the horrors of 9/11 with a new version of Captain America that was markedly different from the patriotic jingoism of the early wartime Cap. In *Captain America: The New Deal* (vol. 4, no. 11, 2003), the archetypal superhero sees shades of grey where he once saw black and white. The mood can be described as nostalgia for an era when those who believed the country was correct were themselves likely to be correct, and despite 9/11 the current cause is less noble than the grand one of World War II.

To refer to just a sample of what's available, several comic series and graphic novels deal with the War on Terror in innovative ways, including *Army@Love* by Rick Veitch; *Shooting War* by Lappe and Goldman; *Greendale*, a graphic novel by Neil Young and Joshua Dysart; *Pride of Baghdad* by Vaughan and Henrichon; *Iraq: Operation Corporate Takeover* by Wilson and O'Connor; *DMZ* by Brian Wood; *To Afghanistan and Back* by Ted Rall; and *The War Within* by Garry Trudeau.

Set in a futuristic civil war, *DMZ* tells the story of a photojournalist reporting from the demilitarized zone of Manhattan which has been taken over by Middle America's antiestablishment militias. Launched in 2005, the antiwar comic by Brian Wood features many elements that parallel the War on Terror including deceptive leadership, profiteering contractors, and savage mercenaries. Wood states that "Real-world politics are a big factor in this book, in a very direct but limited way. . . . Typically I'll find myself inspired by a certain bit of real-world events, such as military contracting or kidnapped journalists. I'll then apply that to the DMZ scenario and see where it takes me."[79]

Pride of Baghdad is a political allegory that explores the experiences of a pride of lions that escaped from the Baghdad Zoo during an American bombing raid in Iraq. In documenting the plight of the lions, *Pride of Baghdad* "raises questions about the true meaning of liberation—can it be given, or is it earned only through self-determination and sacrifice? And in the end, is it truly better to die free than to live life in captivity?"[80] Written by Brian K. Vaughan and illustrated by Niko Henrichon, it won the Imagine Games Network (IGN) Award for best original graphic novel in 2006. Vaughn explains his choice of nonhuman protagonists:

> With fiction, audiences can watch endless horrors inflicted on human beings, even children, but put a dog in danger, and watch people walk out in droves. Similarly, I think it's hard for even the most sympathetic person to truly feel for the civilian victims of foreign wars we see on TV, but strangely, many of us can somehow bridge that emotional gap when it comes to seeing innocent animals suffer. I wanted to write about war from the perspective of noncombatants, and because animals transcend race or creed or nationality, having them be our sole protagonists hopefully allowed us to tell a story that's universally relatable.[81]

Set in 2011, *Shooting War* depicts a dark future, with the continuing war in Iraq, oil crisis, and corporate greed. The protagonist is an anticorporate video-blogger who finds himself working for a Fox News–type network ("Your home for 24-hour terror coverage"). The *Village Voice*'s Julian Dibbell writes, "The searing political satire of *Shooting War* is taking the Sunday comic strip places it could never have gone before."[82]

Some critically oriented observers also used the comic format to get their message across. Perhaps the most impressive work in this genre is *Addicted to War: Why the U.S. Can't Kick Militarism*, an "illustrated exposé" by Joel Andreas. Running seventy-seven pages, this is an accessible distillation of critically oriented research on the history of the United States and the real motivations for its historical, outward expansion both on the North American continent and around the world. It provides a full treatment of subjects such as the Spanish-American War, World War I and II, Korea, Vietnam, 1980s counterinsurgency, the first Gulf War and the NATO War in Kosovo in the 1990s, and 9/11 and the wars in Afghanistan and Iraq in the 2000s. The book's point of departure is a family's realization that while they're told there's no money for schools, there seems to be no end of money for the military, roughly half of the U.S. federal spending. One panel features Major General Smedley Butler, who at the time of his death was the most decorated marine in U.S. history. After he retired in 1931, he said "I spent 33 years and four months in active military service and during that period I spent most of my time as a high class muscle man for Big Business, for Wall Street and the bankers. In short, I was a racketeer, a gangster for capitalism."[83] Humorous and well documented, Andreas shows how people in the past have resisted militarism, often with some success, and what they can and must do to resist it now.[84]

Writing in strip format, Stephanie McMillan's *Minimum Security* is concerned with "some of the most pressing issues of our time: the global environmental crisis, rampant consumerism, U.S. imperialism and institutionalized gender and class inequality."[85] She is also among the critically oriented who are raising doubts about the lack of results so far in the Obama era. In her July 3, 2009, strip, entitled "Unruined Faith," she uses one her major characters, "Bunnista," a talking bunny, to express the optimism of those who think that President Obama will free the Guantánamo prisoners. Bunnista's friend then intimates that this won't happen, only leading Bunnista to say that her disillusion is on the level of learning the truth about the Great Pumpkin. Befitting the Independence Day strip, Bunnista then wishes that a freedom fairy will come and bring her a new revolution.[86] Henry Jenkins argues that comics do important cultural work:

> Popular culture is not univocal; that it remains a space of contestation and debate; that it often expresses messages which run counter to dominant sentiment within the culture; and that it often opens up space for imagining alternatives to the prevailing political realities. It is also worth remembering that people working within the cultural industries exert an active agency in shaping the ideas which circulate within popular culture and that on occasion, they may act out of political ideals rather than economic agendas.[87]

War Is Out of Style

The connection between war, militarism, and fashion is not a new one. Zoot suits were first popularized in the late 1930s and 1940s among marginalized youth, including Filipino Americans, Mexican Americans, African Americans, and Italian Americans. The zoot suits were elaborate men's suits that featured padded shoulders, wide lapels, and wide-legged cuffed pants. Stuart Cosgrove notes that, "The zoot-suit was more than the drape-shape of 1940s fashion, more than a colorful stage-prop hanging from the shoulders of Cab Calloway, it was, in the most direct and obvious ways, an emblem of ethnicity and a way of negotiating an identity. The zoot-suit was a refusal: a subcultural gesture that refused to concede to the manners of subservience."[88] During World War II American authorities targeted racialized groups by outlawing these suits and characterized them as unpatriotic because they used too much fabric during war-time rationing. In

June of 1943, American servicemen in Los Angeles were lauded as heroes and supported by the police when they attacked zoot suiters, beating them, stripping them, urinating on and burning their clothes. The Zoot-Suit Riots spread throughout California to cities in Texas and Arizona as well as Detroit, New York, and Philadelphia. Following the riots, an un-American activities investigation was ordered "to determine whether the present Zoot-Suit Riots were sponsored by Nazi agencies attempting to spread disunity between the United States and Latin-American countries." California State Senator Jack Tenney, a member of the un-American Activities committee for Los Angeles County, claimed he had evidence that the Zoot-Suit Riots were "axis-sponsored" but the evidence was never presented.[89] Many postwar activists were inspired by the zoot-suit disturbances and the zoot-suit became a symbol of Black America's cultural resistance. In other words, clothes matter.

In an earlier chapter we showed how mainstream fashion designers are taking inspiration from military designs and integrating them into everyday life. In response to this, activist groups are raising questions about militarism by mounting explicitly antimilitarist fashion shows. Artists and activist designers create fashions for three themed runway presentations: "Camo nation" highlights how militarism seeps into our everyday lives; "modeling war" shows how contemporary fashions are inspired by and legitimize militarism; and "fashion resistance" presents outfits that actively challenge militarism in fashion. In the 2009 Washington show, Christine Ahn designed an outfit which symbolizes current federal government spending, including the huge sums devoted to militarism. She created a camouflage jacket to symbolize military spending, and a skirt based on a bar chart with different colors for different spending categories, such as health, energy, transportation, and international affairs. She writes: "Tucked between the pleats of the skirt is more camouflage, representing more military spending: the Veterans Administration sneaks into the health budget, Homeland Security creeps into transportation, NASA and nuclear weapons research is buried in energy, and international affairs money trains foreign troops." The model wears a top emblazoned with the corporate logos of the largest Pentagon contractors, such as Boeing, Lockheed Martin, and Northrop Grumman. Finally, the model wears an Uncle Sam hat, though inside the hat there is a Chinese cap because these contemporary wars are being prosecuted based on money borrowed from China. She comments that next time, "this outfit will need some alteration, as Obama announced to a recent joint session of Congress that he'll include these wars in the military budget."[90]

With an outfit entitled the "People's Budget," Gwen Kirk envisions a much better world. She features camo pants with money in the pockets for veterans, retraining for soldiers, conversion of military bases for civilian use, and clean up of the toxic mess made by the military and warfare. The artist describes her project, saying,

> The pants, shirt, and vest have deep pockets, inside pockets, and pockets within pockets. A roomy padded Social Security pouch is zipped up tight and padlocked. Sandra throws out a stack of dollar-bill leaflets showing that there's plenty of money—for education, for health care for everyone, money for drug treatment, AIDs research, renewable energy, good public transit, affordable homes, parks and gardens, filling in potholes, cleaning up trash, mending everything that's broken, and bringing good food to poor neighborhoods.[91]

Another outfit, based on the theme "war is not sexy," is designed to symbolize the false promises of military recruitment and was produced as a group effort by the Portland, Oregon, chapter of the American Friends Service Committee. The model, Genevie Gold, wears fabric based on the army dress uniform, and wears jewelry where the medals are pinned, to symbolize the obsession with medals for military achievement, and gold bling, to symbolize the promise of money for college or military pensions. But she also wears a black cape, which she reveals has skull designs, to symbolize the long-term damage in death and injury inflicted by militarism.

Attention was also paid to the particular ways in which militarists count on, and deploy, gender. This included narration and outfits showing "Rosie the Riveter," "a woman in bikini," "Military Bride," "Patriotic Woman," and "Power Suit." The woman in the "power suit" wore "a deceptively simple cotton army drab tee-shirt and pants ensemble, with combat boots, dog leash, cigarette, smirk, and 'thumbs up' gesture." This was inspired by U.S. soldier Lynndie England, a guard at Abu Ghraib military prison near Baghdad. She was a

> symbol of a terrible new twist on sexualized military violence, usually perpetrated by men against women. Lynndie's gender was deployed in the sexualized humiliation and oppression of male prisoners—a kinder, gentler torturer? Her race and nation placed her in the dominator role, with Arab men in the victimized "female" role.[92]

Designers have also paraded men and women in outfits inspired by Guantánamo guards and orange-jump-suited detainees. The Women of Color Resource Center, based in Oakland, California, has established the Runway Peace Project (RPP) and provides activists with a kit to organize their own antimilitarist fashion show. They report that hundreds of these fashion shows have been organized.[93]

From War Toys to Peace Art

Concern about war toys has a long history, sometimes addressed seriously as an important policy and lifestyle issue, and sometimes through performance and even humor. In a well-known sketch from the 1977 season of *Saturday Night Live*, Dan Aykroyd plays a fly-by-night toy manufacturer in plaid sports coat and sunglasses, while Jane Curtin, as the "straight person," is the interviewer. The characters Irwin Mainway and Joan Face discuss combat Halloween costumes in a daring fashion for 1970s-era comedy. The upshot is that Aykroyd's character, looking shifty, in dark sunglasses and a polyester suit, defends militarized Halloween costumes for kids, including a working M-1 rifle, helmet, field glasses, and military uniform. Ammunition is not provided, the audience is assured, but the costume is still said to be particularly popular in Texas and Detroit.

There are numerous community-based groups that focus on challenging the militarized toys marketed to children in the United States. One such group, CodePink: Women for Peace, employs a variety of means of resistance to put an end to the focus on war toys for children. They advocate for education and communication between adults and children, supplying children with a context for war toys and as an opportunity to promote peace and anti-violence. They offer advice for buying toys at Christmas:

> Every holiday season manufacturers prey on our children with pro-war propaganda disguised as innocent toys. Don't let your child be a victim of G.I. Joe! As you're out buying holiday gifts, make a point this year to show little ones that war is not a game. Set an example for the children in your life and use the opportunity to teach them non-violence.[94]

Under the title "Hope for the Holidays," in 2009 CodePink recommended dressing up in pink camo and handing out pamphlets outside stores that sell war toys; stickering with downloadable art from the website; purchasing toys and then forming long line-ups to return them on the grounds that they are dangerous, for the benefit of the media; and lobbying retailers and organizing consumer boycotts unless the store managers stop selling war toys.[95]

Christian Peacemaker Teams, the international conflict transformation organization, made its presence felt at a Chicago-based Toys 'R' Us in the 2007 Christmas season to protest the dissemination of war toys as presents for children. They staged a Nativity scene inside the store complete with a full Christmas choir, acting out a dramatic take on the Christmas play and inserting scenes of war violence: "The scene inside the store began with traditional Magi presenting the Holy Family with life-giving gifts. But soon, military recruiters and vengeful video game characters intruded, offering blood, gore and violence to the newborn babe."[96]

On December 5, 2009, a group called the Granny Peace Brigade descended on the Toys 'R' Us flagship store in New York's Times Square. They paid for admission to the indoor ferris wheel, and they then unfurled banners that read "No More War Toys" and "War Is Not A Game!" They also sang John Lennon's "Give Peace a Chance" and a revised version of a famous Christmas carol, "Joy to the World," in which they called for an end to the wars in Iraq and Afghanistan, no more war toys, and an effort to build peace on earth.

After twenty minutes they were asked politely to leave the ferris wheel, and the group expressed amazement that they were refunded their money! They then sang for an hour outside the store. "The grandmothers think their campaign is particularly timely coming on the heels, as it did, of the President's disappointing announcement of more troops being sent to Afghanistan." In the words of the oldest participant, Lillian Pollak, ninety-four, "We won't be here forever, and if we can't stop these deplorable wars in Iraq and Afghanistan in our lifetime, we must at least do all within our power to teach our grandchildren while we are still here that war and violence are not the answer."[97]

Many nonprofit organizations have recognized the need to advocate for the responsible purchasing of appropriate toys for children, urging parents to avoid war toys. For example, over the July 4 weekend in 2004, "antiwar protestors demanded that the Minnesota Twins baseball team cancel a promotional giveaway of 'G.I. Joe' action figures" which they had planned to give away to the children in attendance at the game. The national group Veterans for Peace organized the protest, and as president John Varone said "For gosh sakes, the last place we need to promote war is at our national pastime."[98] The Coalition for Peace Action likewise advocates for an abolition of war toys. On one of their fact sheets at their website, they state:

> Some toys help children play together. Other toys teach them new things. But some toys are for fighting. Such toys teach children to accept a militarized world. They teach children that people who look or think differently should be defeated and that war and killing are acceptable ways of dealing with conflict. They create the impression that might is right, and in doing so, denigrate kindness, conciliation, cooperation, skill, and thoughtfulness toward others. The topic of war toys and games is a family concern. This pamphlet has been created in an effort to assist parents and children in working together to discover alternatives to war toys.[99]

They advocate education, believing that children should recognize and understand social context and history, and that ignorance does not beget good choices. The Coalition's activities open up lines of communication to discuss war and the implication of toys in society.

In the Canadian province of British Columbia, teachers decided to explore the problem of child soldiers, social responsibility, and art, by addressing the question of war toys in their classrooms. In the lead-up to the 2006 World Peace Forum in Vancouver, Sam Fillipoff and Susan Ruzic, teachers in Coquitlam, BC, had their students bring in guns and war toys in order to create art and develop alternative uses. (Fillipoff commented that he was inspired by his Doukhobor ancestors, a pacifist minority living in the Russian Empire who, in 1895, burned their weapons and renounced service in the czar's military, only to find themselves persecuted and forced to flee to North America.) Weapons were "decommissioned" and then used in peace-sign designs and other peace-oriented sculptures. In some cases, military items and vehicles were altered for humanitarian and civilian uses, such as rescue vehicles, delivery trucks, and ambulances. The students held a show at an art gallery to display their work, and toy stores even provided "goody bags" in exchange for the toys. The British Columbia Teachers Federation has since produced a manual to help teachers implement this curriculum.[100] In fall 2009, in the nearby community of Anmore, British Columbia, staff and students undertook a similar peace project and decorated a large drawing of a hummingbird with war toys, and had an assembly to hear speakers and sing songs. As one of the speakers told the students, "When you choose to talk, rather than hit, speak rather than yell, create rather than destroy, include rather than exclude you make a difference. Our War Toy Artwork represents this daily commitment to peace."[101]

Another example of protest against war toys was developed by a Chicago resident, Sallie Gratch. Profiled on National Public Radio, Gratch "is protesting the Iraq War by leaving green plastic toy soldiers around town with antiwar messages on them. [She] asks people to contact her when they find the soldiers, and then to leave them someplace else themselves."[102] Her actions are a reminder that the U.S. government is pursuing war on multiple fronts, and it is an attempt to educate and inform U.S. citizens about the dangers of normalizing militarism for children.

Conclusion

After the terrorist attacks on 9/11 there was a great deal of pressure on American citizens to conform to social pressure and support the U.S. state's decision to invade Afghanistan, an attack that in general terms had been planned for months and was now justified by the need to root out al-Qaeda training camps and capture Osama bin Laden. In the run-up to the U.S. invasion of Iraq in 2003, the patriotism of anyone who opposed the war was challenged. A false sense of unanimity pervaded the media and most of popular culture. What this chapter has shown is an increasing number of brave and creative people engaged in all kinds of activities in opposition to U.S. militarism. Many of these activities we described as culture jamming, such as undermining Internet-based video games from within, using comics as a medium to present a different interpretation of reality, undermining militarism and pro-militaristic trends in fashion through alternative fashion, interrogating and altering violent and war-oriented toys, commissioning advertising that undermines militarism, and intervening in public advertising, such as billboards, to point out the unspoken counterarguments. In conventional high-culture theater, poetry, and art, we have witnessed an outpouring of creativity that questions the values of a militaristic world. But ordinary people, including military veterans and school teachers, have also felt empowered to "take it to the streets," to ensure that people are aware of what being a militaristic, imperial state means to the world. Finally, in this chapter we have noted the significant number of entertainers and athletes who, with no fancy PhDs or access to inside information, were able to see through the lies. They got it right, whereas a shocking number of "experts"— at least those who were recruited as state policy advisors and media talking heads—got it wrong. In this chapter we have only scratched the surface of the quantity of independent, anti-militaristic activity that is going on in the country and the world.

The courage of all those featured in this chapter is a testament that claims of the unanimity behind militarism were false, and the importance of dissent to the political health of the republic. It is also worth noting that "your silence will not save you." The most vocal opponents of militarism, whether the Dixie Chicks or Jane Fonda or Susan Sarandon, and other prominent people, have done all right in the end. Their careers have not been ruined, and having been seen as correct, their reputations are stronger now than they were in the 2002–2003 period. Their public prominence led to attacks on them, but maybe also to supporters watching out for them. They were not arrested and they have not been blacklisted. The light of day has prevented it.

Notes

1. "Two-Edged Media Sword: 10 Examples of Counteradvertising, Commerce Jamming and Propaganda Remixes," *CultCase*, January 4, 2008, www.cultcase.com/2008/01/two-edged-media-sword-10-examples-of.html (accessed August 13, 2009).

2. Arianna Huffington, "Why Oil Sheiks Love a Good Hummer," *Common Dreams,* November 25, 2002, www.commondreams.org/views02/1125-08.htm (accessed August 13, 2009).

3. Mark Dery, *Culture Jamming: Hacking, Slashing and Sniping in the Empire of Signs* (New York: Grove Press, 1999).

4. Dery, *Culture Jamming.*

5. "Kalle Lasn: Clearing the Mindscape," *Adbusters,* March 4, 2009.

6. "Two-Edged Media Sword," *CultCase.*

7. "Kalle Lasn: Clearing the Mindscape," *Adbusters.*

8. G. Beato, "Does It Pay to Subvertise?" *Mother Jones,* May/June 1999.

9. For information on this artist, see his website at www.colincampbellvideoartist .com/ (accessed February 16, 2010).

10. See the Big Ant International website for the posters, http://bigantinternational .com/main/WORKS.asp?A_idx=2.

11. "Two-Edged Media Sword," *CultCase.*

12. Scott Lynch, "Anti-war Ads Pulled by Comcast," *Action Alert Network,* January 29, 2003, www.peace-action.org/pub/releases/rel012903.html (accessed April 10, 2009).

13. Demian Bulwa and Leah Garchick, "Bay Area Group in Flap over Anti-war Billboard: Clear Channel Kills Nonprofit's Ad for N.Y.'s Times Square," *San Francisco Chronicle,* July 12, 2004, www.commondreams.org/headlines04/0712-01.htm (accessed April 18, 2008).

14. Lynch, "Anti-war Ads Pulled by Comcast."

15. Lynch, "Anti-war Ads Pulled by Comcast."

16. Nat Ives, "MTV Refuses Antiwar Commercial," *New York Times,* March 13, 2003, www.nytimes.com/2003/03/13/business/media/13ADCO.html (accessed April 11, 2009).

17. Micah Ian Wright, *You Back the Attack! We'll Bomb Who We Want! Remixed War Propaganda* (New York: Seven Stories Press, 2003).

18. Stacey Vanek Smith, "Propaganda Artists Give Uncle Sam a Makeover," *Christian Science Monitor,* April 4, 2003, www.csmonitor.com/2003/0404/p18s01-alar.html (accessed August 7, 2009).

19. The examples from the last two paragraphs come from Eleanor Mathieson, *Street Art and the War on Terror: How the World's Best Artists Said NO to the Iraq War* (London: Rebellion Books, 2007).

20. See "Hopium," Urban Dictionary, www.urbandictionary.com/define.php ?term=hopium.

21. Kim Curtis, "Teacher's Anti-war Playing Cards Flying Off Bookstore Shelves," *Associated Press,* July 15, 2003, www.mombu.com/culture/iraq/t-anti-war-playing -cards-2790069.html (accessed August 7, 2009).

22. Laura Brandon, *Art and War* (London and New York: I. B. Taurus, 2007).

23. Michael Lithgow, "Consuming War: How Consumer Culture and Media Have Influenced the American Perception of War," *Art Threat,* November 3, 2007, http:// artthreat.net/2007/11/consuming-war-how-consumer-culture-and-media-have -influenced-the-american-perception-of-war/ (accessed August 11, 2009).

24. For an image, see www.au.af.mil/au/awc/systems/dvic371.jpg (accessed August 11, 2009).

25. John Feffer, "The Art of Anti-war," *Foreign Policy in Focus*, September 21, 2007, www.fpif.org/fpiftxt/4568 (accessed August 11, 2009).

26. "Holiday Peace Craft for Children," Squidoo, www.squidoo.com/peace-crafts#module13517834 (accessed August 11, 2009).

27. "Peace Tree Day, June 1st," Peace Tree Day, www.peacetreeday.com/peacetreedaykit.htm (accessed August 11, 2009).

28. Sean Arthur Joyce, "The Silence That Says Nothing: The Poetics of Dissent," ChameleonFire: The Work of Sean Arthur Joyce, www.chameleonfire.ca/PDFs/Essays_Poetics_of_Dissent.pdf (accessed August 11, 2009).

29. See Amazon.com's listing for *Poets Against the War*, www.amazon.com/Poets-Against-War-Sam-Hamill/dp/1560255390 (accessed August 11, 2009).

30. "Mission," Poets Against the War, 2008, www.poetsagainstthewar.org (accessed June 1, 2008).

31. Douglas Lain, "Artists and Writers against War on Iraq" and "The Petition," Douglaslain.com, www.douglaslain.com/aawii (accessed May 28, 2008).

32. "UK Nobel Literature Laureate Brands Iraq War a 'U.S. Crime,'" *People's Daily Online*, December 9, 2005, http://english.people.com.cn/200512/09/eng20051209_226825.html (accessed May 29, 2008).

33. Split This Rock, "Poets for Peace," ed. Sarah Browning, *Foreign Policy in Focus*, December 14, 2009, www.fpif.org/articles/poets_for_peace (accessed February 18, 2010).

34. For information on this spokesperson, see his biography on Iraq Veterans Against the War, www.ivaw.org/member/paul-abernathy (accessed August 7, 2009).

35. Meerkat Media Collective, "IVAW Takes Manhattan: Operation First Casualty," http://justtv.wordpress.com/2007/06/04/anti-war-guerrilla-performance/ (accessed August 7, 2009).

36. Susanna Schrobsdorff, "Vocal Minority: Adam Kokesh Has Become a Charismatic Spokesman for a Small but Growing Number of Iraq Veterans Who Now Oppose the War," *Newsweek Web Exclusive*, September 14, 2007, www.newsweek.com/id/40939/output/print (accessed August 7, 2009).

37. Numerous short videos are available on Meerkat Media Collective, "IVAW Takes Manhattan."

38. "Iraq Shoe Thrower Sentenced to 3 Years," *CBS News*, March 12, 2009, www.cbsnews.com/stories/2009/04/07/iraq/main4925167.shtml (accessed August 7, 2009).

39. To see the video, go to http://atlantis2.cbsnews.com/video/watch/?id=4674873n%3Fsource=search_video (accessed August 7, 2009).

40. Joanna Weiss, "For Protesters, Silent 'Die-Ins' Deliver a Loud Message against War," *Boston Globe*, March 22, 2003, www.commondreams.org/headlines03/0322-06.htm (accessed August 11, 2009).

41. M. Boorstein, D. Haynes, and A. Klein, "Dueling Demonstrations: As Thousands March to Capitol to Protest Iraq Conflict, 189 Arrested," *Washington Post*, September 16, 2007, A08, www.washingtonpost.com/wp-dyn/content/article/2007/09/15/AR2007091500826.html (accessed on August 12, 2009).

42. Joe Garofoli, "A Cheeky Protest: Bay Area Anti-war Activists Go Nude in Surge of Creative Vigils," *San Francisco Chronicle*, January 12, 2003, www.commondreams .org/headlines03/0112-09.htm (accessed August 11, 2009).

43. "Bush Satire Is a Hit," *BBC News*, February 6, 2003, http://news.bbc.co.uk/2/hi/ entertainment/2731981.stm (accessed July 29, 2009).

44. Louise Jury. "Act of War: Robbins' Anti-Bush Satire Takes to the Stage in London," *Independent*, August 28, 2004, www.independent.co.uk/arts-entertainment/ theatre/news/act-of-war-robbinss-antibush-satire-takes-to-the-stage-in-london -558027.html (accessed July 29, 2009).

45. Erin Donar, "Worldwide 'Lysistrata' Readings Protest War," *Yale Daily News*, March 3, 2003, www.yaledailynews.com/articles/view/7211?badlink=1 (accessed August 10, 2009).

46. For a current example of this, see www.1stcavmedic.com/jane_fonda.htm (accessed August 10, 2009).

47. Nicholas M. Guariglia, "Barack Obama's Silly Month: From Jane Fonda to Dr. Strangelove," *Global Politician*, August 27, 2007, www.globalpolitician.com/23336 -elections-obama (accessed August 10, 2009).

48. Robert Freeman, "Cindy Sheehan: Rosa Parks or Jane Fonda?" *Common Dreams*, August 14, 2005, www.commondreams.org/views05/0814-20.htm (accessed August 12, 2009).

49. Tatiana Morales, "Sarandon to Bush: Get Real on War: Susan Sarandon and Policy Expert Phyllis Bennis Share Their Views," *CBS News*, February 14, 2003, www .cbsnews.com/stories/2003/02/14/earlyshow/living/main540658.shtml (accessed August 10, 2009).

50. Stuart Heritage, "Rosie O'Donnell & Elisabeth Hasselbeck: The War Is Over!" Heckler Spray, January 11, 2008, www.hecklerspray.com/rosie-odonnell-elisabeth -hasselbeck-the-war-is-over/200811790.php (accessed July 31, 2009).

51. Deborah White, "Profile of Rosie O'Donnell, Liberal Activist & Talk Show Host," About.com: U.S. Liberals, http://usliberals.about.com/od/celebrityactivists/p/ RosieProfile.htm (accessed August 10, 2009).

52. Joe Kovacs, "U.S. Citizens Attack Anti-war Celebrities: Fed Up with Opinions of TV, Movie Stars, Ordinary People Go on Massive Offensive," *World Net Daily*, February 27, 2003, www.wnd.com/news/article.asp?ARTICLE_ID=31261 (accessed August 10, 2009).

53. See the photo at http://photosthatchangedtheworld.com/olympics-black -power/ (accessed July 31, 2009).

54. David Zirin, "Live Strong or Live Wrong? Why Lance Must Break with Bush," *Common Dreams*, July 27, 2005, www.commondreams.org/views05/0727-34.htm (accessed January 10, 2009).

55. David Zirin, "Blue Jays Slugger Carlos Delgado Stands Up to War," *Common Dreams*, July 9, 2004, www.commondreams.org/views04/0709-02.htm (accessed January 10, 2009).

56. Mark Falcous and Michael Silk, "Global Regimes, Local Agendas: Sport, Resistance and the Mediation of Dissent," *International Review for the Sociology of Sport* 41 (2006): 318.

57. Vittorio Tafur, "Nash Speaks Mind against War in Iraq," *Oakland Tribune* (California), March 25, 2003, www.commondreams.org/headlines03/0325-09.htm (accessed July 31, 2009).

58. David Zirin. "Organizing the Jocks for Justice," Daily Sports Column, Edge of Sports, November 30, 2006, www.edgeofsports.com/2006-11-30-212/index.html (accessed January 17, 2009).

59. Mike Glover, "Blue Jays' Delgado Protests War in Iraq," *Associated Press*, July 22, 2004, www.commondreams.org/headlines04/0722-04.htm (accessed July 31, 2009).

60. "Dave Zirin on Super Bowl Fever in New Orleans and the Militarization of Sport's Biggest Spectacle," *Democracy Now!*, February 5, 2010, www.democracynow .org/2010/2/5/dave_zirin_on_super_bowl_fever (accessed February 12, 2010).

61. "Nash Defends Anti-war Views," *CBC*, March 21, 2003, www.cbc.ca/sports/ story/2003/03/21/nash030321.html (accessed July 31, 2009).

62. Falcous and Silk, "Global Regimes, Local Agendas," 318.

63. David Zirin, *What's My Name, Fool? Sports and Resistance in the United States* (Chicago: Haymarket Books, 2005), 268.

64. University of Tennessee, "Sport 4 Peace in Iraq," n.d., www.utk.edu/features/ sport4peace2/ (accessed January 14, 2009).

65. University of Brighton and the British Council, "Welcome to Football 4 Peace," Football 4 Peace, www.football4peace.org.uk/ (accessed January 15, 2009).

66. "About Right to Play," Right to Play, n.d., http://rtpca.convio.net/site/PageSer ver?pagename=overview (accessed January 14, 2009).

67. United Nations, "Sport for Development and Peace: Toward Achieving the Millennium Development Goals," United Nations Inter-Agency Task Force on Sport for Development and Peace, 2003, www.unicef.org/sports/reportE.pdf (accessed January 16, 2009).

68. Henry Jenkins, "A War of Words over Iraq Video Games," *Guardian*, November 15, 2003, www.guardian.co.uk/technology/2003/nov/15/games.iraq (accessed January 28, 2009).

69. Joseph DeLappe, "Dead-in-Iraq: Performance/Memorial/Protest," *TDR: The Drama Review* 52, no. 1 (2008): 2.

70. Tilman Baumgartel, "The Lucid Hack: Artistic Explorations of Computer Games," in *Network Art: Practices and Positions*, ed. Tom Corby (New York: Routledge, 2006), 61; Anne-Marie Schleiner, "Sprays," Velvet-Strike, www.opensorcery .net/velvet-strike/sprays.html (accessed January 28, 2009).

71. Anne-Marie Schleiner, "Velvet-Strike: War Times and Reality Games," Velvet-Strike, February 3, 2002, www.opensorcery.net/velvet-strike/about.html (accessed January 28, 2009); Anne-Marie Schleiner, as cited in Jennifer Buckendorff, "The 'Velvet-Strike' Underground," *Salon* 4 (May 2004), http://dir.salon .com/story/tech/feature/2004/05/04/velvet_strike/print.html (accessed January 27, 2009).

72. Ryan Powers, "Guantanamo Bay Video Game in Development?" *Think Progress*, June 1, 2009, www.alternet.org/blogs/media/140397/guantanamo_bay_video_ game_in_development/ (accessed February 18, 2010).

73. Henry Jenkins, "Captain America Sheds His Mighty Tears: Comics and September 11," in *Terror, Culture, Politics: Rethinking 9/11*, ed. D. Sherman and T. Nardin (Bloomington and Indianapolis: Indiana University Press, 2006), 94.

74. Jenkins, "Captain America," 73.

75. See Howard Daniel, ed., *Callot's Etchings: 338 Prints* (New York: Dover Publications, 1974).

76. See Craig Yoe's forthcoming book, *The Great Anti-War Cartoons*; see preview at http://yoe.com/antiwar (accessed August 8, 2009).

77. Henry Jenkins, "Comic Book Foreign Policy? Part One," Confessions of an Aca-Fan: The Official Weblog of Henry Jenkins, July 27, 2006, www.henryjenkins.org/2006/07/comic_book_foreign_policy_part.html (accessed June 17, 2008).

78. Jenkins, "Comic Book Foreign Policy? Part One."

79. Brian Wood interview posted on www.myninjaplease.com/?p=4706 (accessed August 14, 2009).

80. See DC Comics website, www.dccomics.com/vertigo/graphic_novels/?gn=5723 (accessed August 14, 2009).

81. Vaughn quoted in Tim Walker, "Iraq: How a Daring New Generation of Graphic Novelists View the Art of War," *Independent*, June 23, 2008, www.independent.co.uk/news/world/middle-east/iraq-how-a-daring-new-generation-of-graphic-novelists-view-the-art-of-war-852259.html (accessed August 14, 2009).

82. Larry Smith, "Shooting War," *Huffington Post*, July 19, 2006, www.huffingtonpost.com/larry-smith/shooting-war_b_25423.html (accessed August 14, 2009).

83. Joel Andreas, *Addicted to War: Why the U.S. Can't Kick Militarism* (Oakland, CA: AK Press, 2004). The book is available online at www.addictedtowar.com/book.html (accessed August 8, 2009).

84. Andreas, *Addicted to War*.

85. Kyle Boggs, "Cartooning Resistance: An Interview with Stephanie McMillan," *Z Magazine*, March 2009, p. 18.

86. See the *Minimum Security* comic strip at http://minimumsecurity.net/blog/2009/07/ (accessed August 8, 2009). It should be no surprise that "Bunnista" is a large, talking rabbit.

87. Henry Jenkins, "Comic Book Foreign Policy? Part Two," Confessions of an Aca-Fan: The Official Weblog of Henry Jenkins, July 28, 2006, http://henryjenkins.org/2006/07/comic_book_foreign_policy_part_1.html (accessed August 14, 2009).

88. Stuart Cosgrove, "The Zoot-Suit and Style Warfare," *History Workshop Journal* 18 (1984): 77–91.

89. Cosgrove, "The Zoot-Suit and Style Warfare," 77–91.

90. Christine Ahn and Gwyn Kirk, "Fashioning Resistance to Militarism," *Foreign Policy In Focus*, March 9, 2009, www.fpif.org/fpiftxt/5929 (accessed August 7, 2009).

91. Ahn and Kirk, "Fashioning Resistance to Militarism."

92. Ahn and Kirk, "Fashioning Resistance to Militarism." For a brief video on this movement see http://imaginingourselves.imow.org/pb/Story.aspx?id=1266&lang=1 (accessed August 7, 2009).

93. "Bring Runway Peace Project to Your Community!" U.S. Labor Against the War, www.uslaboragainstwar.org/article.php?id=11719 (accessed August 7, 2009).

94. CodePink, "Say No to War Toys," *Code Pink: Women for Peace*, www.code
pink4peace.org/article.php?list=type&type=96 (accessed July 8, 2008).

95. CodePink, "Say No to War Toys."

96. Staff Writers, "Peacemakers Involved in Challenge to Violent Toys," *Ekklesia: A New Way of Thinking*, January 21, 2007, www.ekklesia.co.uk/news/world/
070121toys (accessed July 8, 2008).

97. Joan Wile, "Peace Grannies Tell Toys 'R' Us: 'War Toys 'R' Not Us,'" *OpEdNews*,
December 5, 2009, www.opednews.com/articles/PEACE-GRANNIES-TELL-TOYS
-by-Joan-Wile-091204-700.html (accessed February 18, 2010).

98. William R. Hawkins, "Why GI Joe Riles the Left," *Front Page Magazine*, July
8, 2004, http://frontpagemag.com/articles/Read.aspx?GUID=3C068266-A98C-4857
-9F36-1ED79A57D773 (accessed July 8, 2008).

99. "Toys Are for Fun, Not Fighting," Coalition for Peace Action, www.peace
coalition.org/facts/toys_are_for_fun.html (accessed July 8, 2008).

100. "Acts of Transformation: War Toys to Peace Art," Working TV, August 2007,
www.workingtv.com/wartoys-peaceart.html (accessed August 12, 2009).

101. Anmore Elementary School, "War Toys Project Unveiled at Anmore Elementary," *Anmore Times*, December 21, 2009, www.anmoretimes.com/2009/12/21/war
-toys-project-unveiled-at-anmore-elementary/ (accessed February 18, 2010).

102. Jason DeRose, "A Toy Soldier Protest against Iraq War," *NPR*, November
21, 2005, www.npr.org/templates/story/story.php?storyId=5021524 (accessed July 20,
2008).

Conclusion

I N THIS BOOK WE HAVE DOCUMENTED THE ROLE that popular culture plays in both encouraging and resisting warlike values and behavior. There is potentially a very broad segment of the population that wants to end militarism, and our challenge is to organize it around commonly agreed goals. Stephen Duncombe, in his introduction to *Cultural Resistance Reader*, points out the strength of creating a "liberatory culture," as an alternative, or complement, to conventional protest action. By becoming a Sex Pistols/Ramones style punk as a young man, he learned the value of a more genuine community. He also learned that "the politics of culture is not predetermined. Culture is pliable; it's how it is used that matters."[1] As he shows by the selections in his edited collection, for several centuries people of all walks of life having been working through these problems. As another potential member of the broad coalition, but coming from a very different perspective, William J. Astore's views should be widely read and seriously addressed. As a retired air force lieutenant colonel he knows the military and militarism from the inside. He argues that America needs a seven-step program to wean itself off of militaristic patriotism, and much of what he says has cultural implications. The seven steps include reducing the military budget, ending deference to generals, redefining the meaning of "support the troops," reducing private profit in war to reduce wars, taking care of veterans rather than venerating soldiers, banning aircraft fly-overs at sporting events, and developing genuine inner patriotism rather than insecure, outward flag-waving. He concludes by saying, "It's increasingly clear that our outward swagger conceals an inner desperation. If we're so strong, one might ask, why do we need so much steroidal piety, so many in-your-face patriotic props, and so much parade-ground conformity?"[2]

We live in a highly media-saturated society in which advocates of militarism and war use culture in their effort to "sell the war," resisted at the same time, to the extent that they are allowed by the media, by opponents of militarism. We live in an age of uncertain and fleeting military victories, so over time, when the bubble of their lies and wishful thinking bursts, the militarists lose the upper hand and we see an explosion of cultural creativity that challenges militarism. Even if Iraq becomes "stable," requiring only a small, permanent U.S. garrison, Afghanistan (and other "theaters") presents challenges that may occupy the United States for decades. Media reporting indicate that by the end of the Obama surge in Afghanistan in 2011 the United States will have more forces in that country than the Soviet Union did in the 1980s, and analysts with Obama's ear say that the United States is likely to be in Afghanistan for at least ten and perhaps as many as forty years.[3] That this situation is so often seen as normal, or even desirable, needs to be challenged. The struggle to break free from the grip of militarism is of central importance to the future of the United States as both a republic and a democracy, in any meaningful sense of those words. As Henry Giroux says:

> As a rhetorical ploy to silence dissent, patriotism is used to name as unpatriotic any attempt either to make governmental power and authority responsive to its consequences at home or to question how the appeal to nationalism is being used to legitimate the U.S. government's bad-faith aspirations to empire building overseas. This type of anti-liberal thinking is deeply distrustful of critical inquiry, mistakes dissent for treason, constructs politics on the moral absolutes of "us and them," and views difference and democracy as threats to consensus and national identity. Such patriotic fervor fuels a system of militarized control that not only repudiates the authority of international law but also relies on a notion of preventive war in order to project the fantasies of unbridled American power all over the globe.[4]

This struggle is not just about the use of the U.S. military abroad, but is also about what the country will become in the near future.

At the point where militarism is in crisis, do we have an accurate awareness of the challenges we face, or are challenges looming on the horizon that, if they are not addressed, may perpetuate militarism? What is it that the American people want, and is it focused enough to force the state to develop a different approach to the world? Finally, we have seen that human agency has been activated and harnessed to oust the most extreme of militarists from political power, but can this revived human agency be sustained to force the new leaders to chart a different course? Providing some initial answers to these questions will be the focus of this conclusion.

Challenges on the Horizon

By necessity, our focus, and that of many of the domestic dissenters to militarism over the last number of years, has been ending the wars in Afghanistan and Iraq. But militarism is an iceberg, and the War on Terror is the portion that is visible above the water line. There are many new developments—the rest of the iceberg—just barely discernible or currently out of view. This includes the continuing effort by militarists to contract out the work of the military, with the result that the domestic costs in lives can be reduced, along with domestic opposition. Another is the development of the automated battlefield, where combat for soldiers becomes like playing video games from remote sites. There is also the new frontier of militarism, an arms race in space, based on the U.S. development of anti-satellite weapons. As Chalmers Johnson documents very well, the United States continues to build *permanent* bases in Iraq, Afghanistan, and all over the world, and the Middle East in particular, even as it says it will leave these countries.[5]

There is no ruling out a U.S. and/or Israeli attack on Iran, and a revived system of detention of prisoners is also possible. As *Foreign Policy in Focus* wrote in 2008, the massive U.S. base on the island of Diego Garcia in the Indian Ocean—home only to the base after 2000 indigenous people were relocated by the U.S. military in the early 1970s—has been used as a launching pad for attacks on Iraq and can serve the same purpose with regard to Iran. There has also been a "black site" prison at that location as part of the CIA's "Extraordinary Rendition" program, one that can easily be expanded.[6] Another dark-horse challenge in the near future is the possibility of hitting an ecological tipping-point, in which suddenly, after being in official denial regarding our long-term environmental problems, the U.S. state faces a sudden acceleration of ecological decline. Shortages of fuel, water, or ecological breakdown may be used to rally domestic support for aggression. As Richard Falk pointed out at the beginning of the 2003 War in Iraq, "The U.S. Government is devoting huge resources to the monopolistic militarization of space, the development of more usable nuclear weapons, and the strengthening of its world-girdling ring of military bases and its global navy, as the most tangible way to discourage any strategic challenges to its preeminence."[7] Student of military history Gwynne Dyer has put these issues well:

> Some generation of mankind was eventually bound to face the task of abolishing war, because civilization was bound to endow us sooner or later with the power

to destroy ourselves. We happen to be that generation, though we did not ask for the honor and do not feel ready for it. There is nobody wiser who will take the responsibility and solve this problem for us. We have to do it ourselves.[8]

As bad as things seem in Iraq and Afghanistan, below the surface there are additional developments that will challenge activists in the coming years. As Barbara Ehrenreich has written, "War, at the end of the twentieth century, is a more formidable adversary than it has ever been. It can no longer be localized within a particular elite and hence overthrown in a brilliant act of revolution. . . . This does not mean that social hierarchies cannot be overthrown; only that those who would overthrow them should be aware of their almost lifelike power to persist."[9]

Battle Fatigue

Part of the basis for the breach between public opinion and the Bush-era leadership was the gap on the question of "American Exceptionalism." While a high percentage of Americans love their country and think highly of it, political leaders are much more likely to have an "evangelical" approach to this secular faith—leaders are much more eager to spread the "American way of life" than the ordinary person.[10] In recent years support among U.S. citizens for a clear global leadership role for the United States has declined. In polling in October 2006, only 9 percent of the respondents supported that idea that "As the sole remaining superpower, the United States should continue to be the preeminent world leader in solving international problems." Conversely, 69 percent supported working through multilateral institutions, and a surprisingly high 61 percent agreed that "the United States should be more willing to make decisions within the United Nations, even if this means that the United States will sometimes have to go along with a policy that is not its first choice."[11] Among survey respondents there has been a rise in recent years in what is referred to as "isolationism." Most simply, this is the view that the United States should "mind its own business internationally." In December 2002, after 9/11 but before the Iraq war, 30 percent of respondents supported this, while by 2005 and 2006 this number had grown to 42 percent.[12] With the election of a Democratic Congress and the Obama administration there seems to be increasing disengagement from the realities of the U.S. war in Afghanistan, as if a media weariness has set in. In addition, as the Pew Research Center reported in March 2008, fewer respondents have an accurate idea of U.S. war deaths in Iraq. Only 28 percent of respondents were able to say at that time that approximately four thousand Americans had died in the Iraq War. News coverage about Iraq has declined and so has public interest.[13] Of course, to the "surprise" of all, Iraq can easily flare up in the future and the story of Iraq having been solved can once again lose all credibility. So long as this pattern of public opinion continues, militarism in whatever form is vulnerable to criticism.

What If They Gave a War and Nobody Came?

Growing public distaste for war offers an important opportunity to build on as we move forward. The big challenge is harnessing this obvious skepticism toward a militaristic and imperial foreign policy, transforming deeper patterns and thereby going beyond only changing the party in power. Whatever the establishment might say, there is great truth in the slogan of the World Social Forum, that "a better world is possible." This has been proven many times and will be proven again. As Antonio Gramsci wrote over seventy years ago, "A given socio-historical moment is never homogeneous; on the contrary, it is rich in contradictions."[14] These contradictions, between public opinion versus state policy, between the need for productive investment versus military waste, and ecological sustainability versus the life-draining force of militarism, to name only three, are clearly visible. In the contemporary context of globalization, militarism has become what David Theo Goldberg calls a "new regime of truth," a new epistemology defining what is fact and fiction, right and wrong, just and unjust.[15] The establishment's claim that "there is no alternative," even in a period of seeming stability, was always false; it is only "true" if people believe it.

Before 1999, and the global revolt against globalization from above, the last major global challenge to the political-economic system of power was in 1968. In that year, the Vietnamese launched the Tet offensive against the United States in their country, Czechoslovakia was in revolt against the Soviet Union, and the Rev. Martin Luther King Jr. and Senator Bobby Kennedy gave hope to antipoverty and antiwar progressives in the United States, only to see that optimism dashed by their assassinations only two months apart. Students in the United States, Mexico, and many other countries in the world were in revolt, and in France for a time there was a chance of a coalition between students and the country's often-restive working class. This momentum for change inspired many individuals and organizations who managed to achieve progressive innovations but supporters of the military industrial complex were able to continue their agendas, finding new ways to harness the dynamic of globalization to further extend their power and influence.

The Global Justice Movement, third wave feminism, gay and lesbian rights movements, disability rights campaigners, and environmentalists have not given up in the face of consolidation of corporate power. Their persistence in exposing lies and pursuing human liberation is paralleled in social theory. Social theorists realized that too much attention has been paid to "structures" and not enough to what constitutes structures—that is, human agency. No one did a better job in developing this thought than Anthony Giddens, who would go on to advise Tony Blair in the transition away from the long period of Conservative rule in Britain.[16] The potential for social change is greatly increased when there is widespread recognition that social structures, those patterns of belief, action, and social organization, can only exist if they are reproduced by human agency. Where "structuralists" saw structures as constraining, limiting, or defining human action, new perspectives see structures as both "enabling and constraining." If social institutions such as the military can exist only through reproduction—through public participation, funding, and support—then human action can transform these structures by refraining from this reproduction—withdrawing their tolerance, participation, and support for the military. While it is clear that the agency of people within the ruling class can have a greater impact than those without political and economic power, history is rife with examples of the agency of the ordinary person, especially when they were organized in a mass social movement, to trump the agency of the establishment.

Demanding the Peace Dividend

When the public has rejected imperialist agendas and spoken, and voted, for change, it is important that their will not be subverted. It is a sign of how far we have departed from sanity that another quote from President Eisenhower is in order. As he said those many decades ago, "Every gun that is made, every warship launched, every rocket fired, signifies in the final sense a theft from those who are hungry and are not fed, those who are cold and not clothed." No doubt this is a sentiment the voters had in mind at the polls in 2008. But leaders who feel confident in the unquestioning support of their base can lose sight of their principles they held on election day by falling into the trap of triangulation. Christopher Hitchens characterizes "triangulation" as a form of amoral politics in which the leader calculates what little he must do to retain his own support, and how much he can do to take potent issues away from the opposition party and attract their supporters and campaign dollars. This is similar to what is still referred to as "brokerage politics," where the politician acts not from commitment but rather from the motive of self-perpetuation, by changing their own ideas to meet their perception of "public opinion." But the concept of "triangulation" is a more manipulative one, in which the leader and media and allied social forces manipulate the agenda and debate to advance their shared interests. In the 1990s Hitchens noted that President Bill Clinton consistently made promises to the left, including opponents of militarism, but delivered results for the right.[17] In foreign policy terms the U.S./NATO war in Kosovo was justified as humanitarian intervention, but partisan opposition from congressional Republicans aside, militarists would know that this was a continuation of past policies.

By presenting himself as an antiwar candidate, particularly regarding Iraq, Obama was engaging in triangulation. Obama changed his tune on Iraq after he was elected, by the time he spoke to the marines at Camp Lejeune. By claiming that the United States will leave Iraq he appeals to the antiwar constituency, but by claiming that Afghanistan is the good war and that it is time to escalate the mission there he is "delivering the goods" to the militarist constituency. As blogger Chris Floyd comments, with regard to Iraq:

> The moral depravity of [Obama's] stance is breathtaking. Invade a country for no reason, kill a million of its people, drive four million into exile, destroy its infrastructure, plunge it into civil war, abet its "ethnic cleansing," loot its wealth, put it in the hands of religious extremists, unleash disease, poverty and social breakdown: this is an "extraordinary achievement," says the progressive paladin. And now the Iraqis must "take responsibility" for the hell on earth created by their invaders.[18]

Despite its promises, it is still questionable whether the Obama administration will profoundly alter the "don't ask, don't tell" rules regarding gays in the military, which is important on the issue of militarism because keeping gays out of the military is essential to the socially conservative, masculine, heterosexist self-image of the U.S. armed forces. Though in the spirit of triangulation Obama has granted celebrated gay activists like San Francisco City supervisor Harvey Milk a posthumous Presidential Medal of Freedom, and tennis star Billie Jean King as well, as a cost-free sop to an important Democratic constituency.[19] But the risk is that supporters of social progress and antimilitarism will settle for too little, as they did in the Clinton era.

Opponents of militarism need to press the new leaders to defy those who would claim that the decision not to attack is a sign of weakness. Let us shake off the belief that a leader's virility is connected to the "power of the state," which must somehow be generated by the occasional show of force. It is time to realize that the world's survival requires that we force our leaders to shake off their old ways. These old ways were illustrated by India's Hindu nationalist leader, Balasaheb Thackeray, justifying India's 1998 nuclear weapon tests. He commented that we "had to prove that we are not eunuchs."[20] It helps that we live in times when the momentum of events is our ally, not our adversary.

Peter Beinart, a senior fellow for the mainstream Council on Foreign Relations, argues that the present day is not the early 1950s: the U.S. people are not overly concerned about security right now, and Republican efforts to paint Democrats as "soft on defense" will not gain them inroads in public opinion.[21] (The Democrats should not make the mistake Lyndon Johnson did in 1964 and 1965, when he pursued the Vietnam war based on his memories of the McCarthyite attacks on those Democrats who "lost China" in 1949.) But this moment of popular skepticism regarding militarism may not last, and must be taken advantage of. We need to avoid defending militaristic decisions by Democrats just because of the memory of worse horrors perpetuated in the Bush era. As the late Howard Zinn has written, "Our job is not to give him a blank check or simply be cheerleaders. It was good that we were cheerleaders while he was running for office, but it's not good to be cheerleaders now. Because we want the country to go beyond where it has been in the past."[22]

The need to fight it out, persist, and avoid compromise or expediency are certainly the lessons we should take from the rise of the British Labour Party in the 1940s and the creation of the British welfare state, as well as the success of the U.S. Civil Rights movement in the 1950s and 1960s, and the opposition to the U.S. war in southeast Asia in the 1960s and early 1970s. The reality of the importance of agency led to significant social and cultural change in the 1970s. In the hands of a new generation, it also helped those who traveled to Seattle, Québec City, and Rome and many other protests beginning in 1999, in order to challenge neoliberal globalization-from-above. As Barbara Ehrenreich argues, in this struggle

> We will need all the courage we can muster. What we are called to is, in fact, a kind of war. We will need "armies," or at least networks of committed activists willing to act in concert when necessary, to oppose force with numbers, and passion with forbearance and reason. We will need leaders—not a handful of generals but huge numbers of individuals able to take the initiative to educate, inspire, and rally others. We will need strategies and cunning, ways of assessing the "enemy's" strength and sketching out the way ahead. And even with all that, the struggle will be enormously costly. Those who fight war on this war-ridden planet must prepare themselves to lose battle after battle and still fight on, to lose security, comfort, position, even life.[23]

The struggle of agents against U.S. militarism picked up speed in the 2000s, and by 2006 delivered a major setback to the Bush administration. With the election of 2008 the conservative Republican dream of control for a generation was shattered. This was a significant achievement, but it should be clear that the struggle is not over. Now is not the time to withdraw from public life.

The new rulers must be held to account, just as all rulers, no matter how good their intentions, must be. Let us give the final word to Howard Zinn:

> Where progress has been made, wherever any kind of injustice has been over-turned, it's been because people acted as citizens, and not as politicians. They didn't just moan. They worked, they acted, they organized, they rioted if neces-sary to bring their situation to the attention of people in power. And that's what we have to do today.[24]

Notes

1. Stephen Duncombe, introduction to *Cultural Resistance Reader*, ed. Stephen Duncombe (London and New York: Verso, 2002), 3–5.

2. William Astore, "American Militarism on Steroids: Whatever Happened to Gary Cooper? A Seven-Step Program to Return America to a Quieter, Less Mus-cular, Patriotism," *TomDispatch*, September 4, 2009, www.commondreams.org/view/2009/09/04-0 (accessed February 26, 2010).

3. Lisa Millar, "Troop Boost Tipped to Avoid Afghanistan 'Chaos,'" Austra-lian Broadcasting Corporation, August 10, 2009, www.abc.net.au/news/stories/2009/08/10/2651702.htm?section=world (accessed August 13, 2009); Walter Pincus, "Afghan War Will Exceed Cost of Iraq, Say Experts," *Brisbane Times*, www.brisbane times.com.au/world/afghan-war-will-exceed-cost-of-iraq-say-experts-20090809 -ee60.html (accessed August 13, 2009).

4. Henry A. Giroux, "The Emerging Authoritarianism in the United States: Politi-cal Culture under the Bush/Cheney Administration," *symploke* 14, nos. 1–2 (2006): 98–151.

5. See especially chapter 6, "The Empire of Bases," in Chalmers Johnson, *The Sorrows of Empire: Militarism, Secrecy, and the End of the Republic* (New York: Metro-politan/Henry Holt, 2004).

6. David Vine, "The Other Guantanamo," *Foreign Policy in Focus*, April 3, 2008, www.fpif.org/fpiftxt/5120 (accessed August 13, 2009).

7. Richard Falk, "Will the Empire Be Fascist?" Transnational Foundation for Peace and Future Research, March 24, 2003, www.transnational.org/SAJT/forum/meet/2003/Falk_FascistEmpire.html (accessed August 13, 2009).

8. Gwynne Dyer, *War* (Toronto, ON: Stoddard, 1985), 265.

9. Barbara Ehrenreich, *Blood Rites: Origins and History of the Passions of War* (New York: Metropolitan Books, 1997).

10. Andrew Kohut and Bruce Stokes, "The Problem of American Exceptionalism," Pew Research Center for the People & the Press, May 9, 2006, http://pewresearch.org/pubs/23/the-problem-of-american-exceptionalism (accessed August 13, 2009).

11. Miriam Pemberton, "Poll: Fewer Guns, More Talk," *Foreign Policy in Focus*, October 27, 2006, www.fpif.org/fpiftxt/3649 (accessed August 13, 2009).

12. Andrew Kohut, "Foreign Policy: The Public Sends a Muddled Message," Pew Research Center for the People & the Press, March 8, 2007, http://pewresearch.org/pubs/424/foreign-policy-the-public-sends-a-muddled-message (accessed August 13, 2009).

13. "Awareness of Iraq War Fatalities Plummets," Pew Research Center for the People & the Press, March 12, 2008, http://people-press.org/report/401/awareness-of-iraq-war-fatalities-plummetsl (accessed August 13, 2009).

14. Antonio Gramsci, *Selections from Cultural Writings* (London: Lawrence & Wishart, 1985), 93.

15. Quoted in Giroux, "Emerging Authoritarianism in the United States," 98–151.

16. Anthony Giddens, *The Constitution of Society: Outline of the Theory of Structuration* (Berkeley and Los Angeles: University of California Press, 1984).

17. Christopher Hitchens, *No One Left to Lie To: The Triangulations of William Jefferson Clinton* (London and New York: Verso Books, 1999), chap. 1.

18. Chris Floyd, "Hero Blues: Liberals Line Up with Militarism," *Empire Burlesque*, April 8, 2009, www.chris-floyd.com/component/content/article/1736-hero-blues-liberals-line-up-with-militarism.html (August 14, 2009).

19. Paula Brooks, "Obama Awards Presidential Medal of Freedom to LGBT Icons Milk and King," LezGetReal: A Gay Girl's View on the World, August 12, 2009, http://lezgetreal.com/?p=20473&cpage=1 (accessed August 13, 2009).

20. Ella Page, "Men, Masculinity and Guns: Can We Break the Link?" *International Action Network on Small Arms (IANSA)*, May 2009, www.iansa-women.org/node/157 (accessed August 15, 2009).

21. Peter Beinart, "The Fear Democrats Can Jettison," *Washington Post*, July 6, 2008, www.cfr.org/publication/16724/fear_democrats_can_jettison.html (accessed August 16, 2009).

22. Howard Zinn, "Changing Obama's Military Mindset," *Progressive*, May 15, 2009, www.alternet.org/politics/140035 (accessed August 14, 2009).

23. Ehrenreich, *Blood Rites*, 240.

24. Zinn, "Changing Obama's Military Mindset."

Bibliography

Adair, Gilbert. *Vietnam on Film: From "The Green Berets" to "Apocalypse Now."* New York: Proteus, 1981.

Adema, Pauline. "Betty Crocker." In *American Icons: An Encyclopedia of the People, Places, and Things That Have Shaped Our Culture,* edited by Dennis Hall and Susan Grove Hall, 73–81. Santa Barbara, CA: Greenwood Publishing Group, 2006.

Adorno, Theodor W. "Culture Industry Reconsidered." Translated by Anson G. Rabinbach. *New German Critique* 6 (Fall 1975): 12–19.

Alexander, Matthew, with John R. Bruning. *How to Break a Terrorist: The U.S. Interrogators Who Used Brains, Not Brutality, to Take Down the Deadliest Man in Iraq.* New York: The Free Press, 2009.

Ali, Tariq. "Afghanistan: Mirage of the Good War." *New Left Review* 50 (March–April 2008). www.newleftreview.org/?view=2713 (accessed July 21, 2009).

Andreas, Joel. *Addicted to War: Why the U.S. Can't Kick Militarism.* Oakland, CA: AK Press, 2004.

Augé, Etienne. "Hollywood Movies: Terrorism 101." *Cercles* 5 (2002): 147–63. www.cercles.com/n5/auge.pdf (accessed February 16, 2010).

Barbera, Joseph. *My Life in "Toons": From Flatbush to Bedrock in Under a Century.* Atlanta, GA: Turner Publishing, 1994.

Barry, John M. *Rising Tide: The Great Mississippi Flood of 1927 and How It Changed America.* New York: Simon and Schuster, 1997.

Barry, Ann Marie. *Visual Intelligence: Perception, Image, and Manipulation in Visual Communication.* Albany: State University of New York Press, 1997.

Baumgartel, Tilman. "The Lucid Hack: Artistic Explorations of Computer Games." In *Network Art: Practices and Positions,* edited by Tom Corby, 57–67. New York: Routledge, 2006.

Bell, Wendell. "The American Invasion of Grenada: A Note on False Prophecy." *The Yale Review* 75, no. 4 (1986): 564–86.

Bennett, Andy. *Remembering Woodstock.* Aldershot, UK: Ashgate Publishing, 2004.

Bignell, Jonathan. *Postmodern Media Culture.* Edinburgh: Edinburgh University Press, 2000.

Boggs, Carl. "Pentagon Strategy, Hollywood, and Technowar." *New Politics* 11, no. 1 (2006). www.wpunj.edu/newpol/issue41/Boggs41.htm#r7 (accessed July 21, 2009).

Boggs, Carl, and Tom Pollard. "Hollywood and the Spectacle of Terrorism." *New Political Science* 9 (2006). www.ocnus.net/cgi-bin/exec/view.cgi?archive=103&num =26261 (accessed June 25, 2009).

———. *The Hollywood War Machine: U.S Militarism and Popular Culture.* Boulder, CO, and London: Paradigm Publishers, 2007.

Boje, David M. "Deconstructing Visual Theatric Imagery of the Bush Presidency." Paper presented to August 2003 meeting of the Academy of Management in Seattle, Pre-conference on visual imagery, June 3, 2003. http://peaceaware.com/documents/ Boje_essays/Bush_spectacle/boje_Bush_image_handling.htm (accessed July 18, 2009).

Brandon, Laura. *Art and War.* London and New York: I. B. Taurus, 2007.

Brenner, Robert. *The Economics of Global Turbulence: The Advanced Capitalist Economies from Long Boom to Long Downturn, 1945–2005.* London and New York: Verso, 2006.

Bresenhan, Karey. *America from the Heart.* Lafayette, CA: C&T Publishing, 2002.

Brown, Kenneth Douglas. *The British Toy Business: A History since 1700.* London and Rio Grande: Hambledon Press, 1996.

Burstyn, Varda. *The Rites of Men: Manhood, Politics, and the Culture of Sport.* Toronto, ON: University of Toronto Press, 1999.

Butterworth, Michael L., and Stormi Moskal. "Football, Flags, and Fun: The Bell Helicopter Armed Forces Bowl and the Rhetorical Production of Militarism." *Communication, Culture & Critique* 2, no. 4 (2009): 411–33.

Castonguay, James. "Intermedia and the War on Terror." In *Rethinking Global Security: Media, Popular Culture and the "War on Terror,"* edited by Andrew Martin and Patrice Petro, 151–78. New Brunswick, NJ, and London: Rutgers University Press, 2006.

Clarke, Richard A. *Against All Enemies: Inside America's War on Terror.* New York: The Free Press, 2004.

Cooper, B. Lee. "Rumours of War: Lyrical Continuities." In *Continuities in Popular Culture: The Present in the Past & the Past in the Present and Future,* edited by Ray Broadus Browne and Ronald J. Ambrosetti. Bowling Green, OH: Bowling Green University Popular Press, 1993.

Corkin, Stanley. *Cowboys as Cold Warriors: The Western and U.S. History.* Philadelphia: Temple University Press, 2004.

Cosgrove, Stuart. "The Zoot-Suit and Style Warfare." *History Workshop Journal* 18 (1984): 77–91.

Croft, Stuart. *Culture, Crisis and America's War on Terror.* Cambridge: Cambridge University Press, 2006.

Curry Jansen, Sue. *Critical Communication Theory: Power, Media, Gender, and Technology.* Lanham, MD: Rowman and Littlefield, 2002.

Cusiak, Suzanne G. "Music as Torture/Music as Weapon." *Transcultural Music Review* 10 (2006). www.sibetrans.com/trans/trans10/cusick_eng.htm (accessed July 14, 2009).

Dailly, Christian. "Captain America: The United States versus Itself, Through the Eyes of a Wartime Fictional Hero." *American Studies Today* 16 (September 2007).

Dale, Timothy. "Political Discourse in Popular Culture: Expanding a View of the Public Sphere." Paper presented at the annual meeting of the Midwest Political Science Association 67th Annual National Conference, The Palmer House Hilton, Chicago, IL. www.allacademic.com/meta/p361202_index.html (accessed July 28, 2009).

Daniel, Howard, ed. *Callot's Etchings: 338 Prints.* New York: Dover Publications, 1974.

Davis, Doug. "Future-War Storytelling: National Security and Popular Film." In *Rethinking Global Security: Media, Popular Culture and the "War on Terror,"* edited by Andrew Martin and Patrice Petro, 13–44. New Brunswick, NJ, and London: Rutgers University Press, 2006.

DeLappe, Joseph. "Dead-in-Iraq: Performance/Memorial/Protest." *TDR: The Drama Review* 52, no. 1 (2008).

Dery, Mark. *Culture Jamming: Hacking, Slashing and Sniping in the Empire of Signs.* New York: Grove Press, 1999.

Edge, Marc. *Asper Nation: Canada's Most Dangerous Media Company.* Vancouver, BC: New Star Books, 2007.

Ehrenreich, Barbara. *Blood Rites: Origins and History of the Passions of War.* New York: Metropolitan Books, 1997.

Ellsberg, Daniel. *Secrets: A Memoir of Vietnam and the Pentagon Papers.* New York: Penguin Books, 2002.

Engelhardt, Tom. *The End of Victory Culture: Cold War America and the Disillusioning of a Generation.* Rev. ed. Amherst: University of Massachusetts Press, 2007.

Enloe, Cynthia H. *Does Khaki Become You? The Militarisation of Women's Lives.* Boston: South End Press, 1983.

Falcous, Mark, and Michael Silk. "Global Regimes, Local Agendas: Sport, Resistance and the Mediation of Dissent." *International Review for the Sociology of Sport* 41 (2006): 317–38.

Faludi, Susan. *The Terror Dream: Fear and Fantasy in Post-9/11 America.* New York: Metropolitan Books / Henry Holt and Company, 2007.

Ferguson, Niall. *Colossus: The Price of America's Empire.* New York: Penguin, 2004.

Ferrero, G. *Militarism: A Contribution to the Peace Crusade.* Translated by Anon. Boston: L. C. Page and Company, 1908.

Fiske, John. "The Commodities of Culture." In *The Consumer Society Reader,* edited by Martyn J. Lee. Oxford and Malden, MA: Blackwell, 2000.

Formanek-Brunell, Miriam. *Made to Play House: Dolls and the Commercialization of American Girlhood, 1830–1930.* Baltimore: John Hopkins University Press, 1998.

Fox, Aaron A. *Country Music Goes to War.* Edited by Charles K. Wolfe and James Edward Akenson. Lexington: University Press of Kentucky, 2005.

Fraser, Antonia. *A History of Toys.* London and New York: Spring Books, 1972.

Friedrich, Ernst. *War Against War!* Seattle: The Real Comet Press, 1987.

Fuchs, Wolfgang J., and R. Reitberger. *Comics: Anatomy of a Mass Medium.* Boston: Little, Brown & Co., 1972.

Georgakas, Dan. "The Hollywood Blacklist." In *Encyclopedia of the American Left,* edited by Mari Jo Buhle, Paul Buhle, and Dan Georgakas. Urbana and Chicago: University of Illinois Press, 1992.

Giddens, Anthony. *The Constitution of Society: Outline of the Theory of Structuration.* Berkeley and Los Angeles: University of California Press, 1984.

———. *Sociology.* Cambridge: Polity Press, 1993.

Giroux, Henry A. *Against the New Authoritarianism: Politics after Abu Ghraib.* Winnipeg, MB: Arbeiter Ring, 2005.

———. "The Emerging Authoritarianism in the United States: Political Culture under the Bush/Cheney Administration." *symploke* 14, nos. 1–2 (2006): 98–151.

Goldstein, Jeffrey. *Why We Watch: The Attractions of Violent Entertainment.* New York: Oxford University Press, 1998.

Gramsci, Antonio. *Selections from Cultural Writings.* London: Lawrence & Wishart, 1985.

Gravel, Mike. *The Pentagon Papers: The Defense Department History of United States Decisionmaking on Vietnam.* Senator Gravel Edition. 4 vols. Boston: Beacon Press, 1971.

Hall, Karen J. "A Soldier's Body: GI Joe, Hasbro's Great American Hero, and the Symptoms of Empire." *Journal of Popular Culture* 38, no. 1 (2004): 34–54.

Hall, Stuart. "Notes on Deconstructing 'The Popular.'" In *People's History and Socialist Theory,* edited by Raphael Samuel, 230–31. London: Routledge and Kegan Paul, 1981.

Hamm, Theodore. *The New Blue Media: How Michael Moore, MoveOn.org, Jon Stewart and Company Are Transforming Progressive Politics.* New York: New Press, 2008.

Hegarty, Marilyn E. *Victory Girls, Khaki-Wackies, and Patriotutes: The Regulation of Female Sexuality during World War.* New York: New York University Press, 2007.

Heller, Dana. "Introduction: Consuming 9/11." In *The Selling of 9/11: How a National Tragedy Became a Commodity,* edited by Dana Heller, 1–26. New York: Palgrave Macmillan, 2005.

Hemingway, Ernest. *A Farewell to Arms.* New York: Scribner, 1978.

Hendershot, Cyndy. *Anti-Communism and Popular Culture in Mid-century America.* Jefferson, NC: McFarland, 2003.

Herman, Edward S., and Noam Chomsky. *Manufacturing Consent: The Political Economy of the Mass Media.* Updated ed. New York: Pantheon Books, 2002.

Higonnet, Margaret. "War Toys: Breaking and Remaking in Great War Narratives." *The Lion and the Unicorn* 31, no. 2 (2007): 116–31.

Hitchens, Christopher. *No One Left to Lie To: The Triangulations of William Jefferson Clinton.* London and New York: Verso Books, 1999.

Hoare, Q., and G. Nowell Smith, eds. and trans. *Selections from the Prison Notebooks of Antonio Gramsci.* New York: International Publishers, 1971.

Hobson, John A. *Imperialism: A Study.* Ann Arbor: University of Michigan Press, 1905/1965.

Hoffmann, Stanley. "An American Social Science: International Relations." *Daedalus* 106, no. 3 (1977): 41–60.

Honey, Maureen. *Creating Rosie the Riverter: Class, Gender and Propaganda during World War Two.* Amherst: University of Massachusetts Press, 1984.

Hoyt, Carmen. *Daddy's in Iraq, but I Want Him Back.* Victoria, Australia: Trafford Publishing, 2005.

Jackson, Steven J., and David L. Andres. *Sport Culture and Advertising: Identities, Commodities, and the Politics of Repression.* New York: Routledge / Taylor and Francis, 2005.

Jaramillo, Deborah. "Ugly War, Pretty Package: How the Cable News Network and the Fox News Channel Made the 2003 Invasion of Iraq High Concept." Ph.D. diss., University of Texas at Austin, 2006.

Jarecki, Eugene, director. *Why We Fight.* DVD. Culver City, CA: Sony Pictures, 2006.

Jenkins, Henry. "Captain America Sheds His Mighty Tears: Comics and September 11." In *Terror, Culture, Politics: Rethinking 9/11*, edited by D. Sherman and T. Nardin, 69–12. Bloomington and Indianapolis: Indiana University Press, 2006.

Jensen, Robert. "Dan Rather and the Problem with Patriotism: Steps toward the Redemption of American Journalism and Democracy." *Global Media Journal* 2, no. 3 (2003). http://uts.cc.utexas.edu/~rjensen/freelance/attack41.htm (accessed August 3, 2009).

Johnson, Chalmers. *Sorrows of Empire: Militarism, Secrecy, and the End of the Republic.* New York: Metropolitan Books, 2004.

———. "American Militarism and Blowback." In *Masters of War: Militarism and Blowback in the Era of American Empire*, edited by Carl Boggs, 111–30. New York and London: Routledge, 2003.

———. *Blowback: The Costs and Consequences of American Empire.* New York: Henry Holt and Company, 2000.

Jowett, Garth S., and Victoria O'Donnell. *Readings in Propaganda and Persuasion: New and Classic Essays.* Thousand Oaks, CA: Sage, 2005.

Kelly, Andrew. *Cinema and the Great War.* New York: Routledge, 1997.

Kennedy, Paul M. *The Rise and Fall of the Great Powers: Economic Change and Military Conflict from 1500 to 2000.* New York: Random House, 1987.

King, Samantha. "Offensive Lines: Sport-State Synergy in an Era of Perpetual War." *Cultural Studies/Critical Methodologies* 8 (2008): 527–39.

Klein, Naomi. *The Shock Doctrine: The Rise of Disaster Capitalism.* Toronto, ON: Alfred A. Knopf Canada, 2007.

Kraska, Peter B. *Militarizing the American Criminal Justice System.* Boston: Northeastern University Press, 2001.

Li, Zhan. "The Potential of America's Army the Video Game as Civilian-Military Public Sphere." Master's thesis, Massachusetts Institute of Technology, 2003. www.gamasutra.com/education/theses/20040725/ZLITHESIS.pdf, 7 (accessed August 15, 2009).

Lockard, Joe. "Social Fear and the *Terrorism Survival Guide.*" In *The Selling of 9/11: How a National Tragedy Became a Commodity*, edited by Dana Heller, 221–32. New York: Palgrave Macmillan, 2005.

Loo, D., and P. Philips, eds. *Impeach the President: The Case against Bush and Cheney.* New York: Seven Stories Press, 2006.

Lorentzen, Lois Ann. "Feminists and Forward Command Posts." *The Scholar and Feminist Online* 2, no. 2 (Winter 2004). www.barnard.edu/sfonline/reverb/printllo .htm (accessed July 12, 2009).

Louw, Eric P. "The 'War against Terrorism': A Public Relations Challenge for the Pentagon." *Gazette* 65 (2003): 211–30.

Lutz, Catherine. "Making War at Home in the United States: Militarization and the Current Crisis." *American Anthropologist* 104 (September 2002): 723–35.

Lynch, Gordon. *Understanding Theology and Popular Culture.* Malden, MA: Blackwell, 2005.

MacDonald, J. Fred. "Soap Operas Go to War." In *Don't Touch That Dial! Radio Programming in American Life, 1920–1960.* 2009. http://jfredmacdonald.com/war.htm (accessed July 10, 2009).

Martin, Andrew. "Popular Culture and Narratives of Insecurity." In *Rethinking Global Security: Media, Popular Culture and the "War on Terror,"* edited by Andrew Martin and Patrice Petro, 104–16. New Brunswick, NJ, and London: Rutgers University Press, 2006.

Martini, Edwin A. *Invisible Enemies: The American War on Vietnam, 1975–2000.* Amherst: University of Massachusetts Press, 2007.

Mathieson, Eleanor. *Street Art and the War on Terror: How the World's Best Artists Said NO to the Iraq War.* London: Rebellion Books, 2007.

McKenna, George. *The Puritan Origins of American Patriotism.* New Haven, CT: Yale University Press, 2007.

Melman, Seymour. *Pentagon Capitalism: The Political Economy of War.* New York: McGraw-Hill, 1970.

Melnick, Jeffrey. *9/11 Culture: America Under Construction.* Malden, MA, and Oxford: Blackwell, 2009.

Miller, Laura. "War Is Sell." *PR Watch* 9, no. 4 (2002). www.prwatch.org/prwissues/ 2002Q4/war.html (accessed July 7, 2009).

Moon, Krystyn R. "'There's No Yellow in the Red, White and Blue': The Creation of Anti-Japanese Music during World War II." *Pacific Historical Review* 72, no. 3 (2003): 333–52.

Nohrstedt, Stig A. "Ruling by Pooling." In *Triumph of the Image: The Media's War in the Persian Gulf—a Global Perspective*, edited by Hamid Mowlana, George Gerbner, and Herbert Schiller, 118–27. Boulder, CO: Westview Press, 1992.

Olson, Scott Robert. "Hollywood Planet." In *The Television Studies Reader*, edited by R. C. Allen and A. Hill. London: Routledge, 2003.

Organski, A. F. K. *World Politics.* 2nd ed. New York: Alfred A. Knopf, 1968.

Oriard, Michael. *Brand NFL: Making and Selling America's Favorite Sport.* Chapel Hill: University of North Carolina Press, 2007.

O'Toole, Laura L., and Jessica R. Schiffman. *Gender Violence: Interdisciplinary Perspectives.* New York: New York University Press, 1997.

Ottosen, Rune. "The Military-Industrial Complex Revisited: Computer Games as War Propaganda." *Television New Media* 10, no. 1 (2009): 122–25.

Parenti, Michael. *Against Empire.* San Francisco: City Light Books, 1995.

Piven, Frances Fox. *The War at Home: The Domestic Costs of Bush's Militarism.* New York: The New Press, 2004.

Power, Dennis. "Personalized Dolls to Comfort Military Families." *The Maple Leaf* 11, no. 10 (March 2008). www.dnd.ca/site/Commun/ml-fe/article-eng.asp?id=4213 (accessed July 12, 2009).

Power, Marcus. "Digitized Virtuosity: Video War Games and Post-9/11 Cyber-Deterrence." *Security Dialogue* 38 (2007): 271–88.

Project for a New American Century. *Rebuilding America's Defenses: Strategy, Forces and Resources for a New Century.* Washington, DC: PNAC, September 2000. www.newamericancentury.org/RebuildingAmericasDefenses.pdf (accessed on June 3, 2009).

Raiti, Gerald C. "The Disappearance of Disney Animated Propaganda: A Globalization Perspective." *Animation: An Interdisciplinary Journal* 2, no. 2 (2007): 153–69.

Rich, Frank. *The Greatest Story Ever Sold: The Decline and Fall of Truth from 9/11 to Katrina.* New York: Penguin, 2006.

Robins, Kevin. *Into the Image: Culture and Politics in the Field of Vision.* New York: Routledge, 1997.

Runway Peace Project. *Fashion Resistance to Militarism.* DVD. Women of Color Resource Center, 2006.

Sampert, Shannon, and Treiberg, Natasja. "The Reification of the 'American Soldier': Popular Culture, American Foreign Policy and Country Music." Paper presented at the annual meeting of the International Studies Association, 48th Annual Convention, Hilton Chicago, IL, February 28, 2007. www.allacademic.com/meta/p179176_index.html (accessed July 13, 2009).

Sanders, Barry. *The Green Zone: The Environmental Costs of Militarism.* Oakland, CA, and Edinburgh: AK Press, 2009.

Scahill, Jeremy. *Blackwater: The Rise of the World's Most Powerful Mercenary Army.* Rev. ed. New York: Nation Books, 2008.

Scanlon, Jennifer. "'Your Flag Decal Won't Get You into Heaven Anymore': U.S. Consumers, Wal-Mart, and the Commodification of Patriotism." In *The Selling of 9/11: How a National Tragedy Became a Commodity,* edited by Dana Heller, 174–99. New York: Palgrave Macmillan, 2005.

Shaw, Tony. *Hollywood's Cold War.* Amherst: University of Massachusetts Press, 2007.

Sheppard, W. Anthony. "An Exotic Enemy: Anti-Japanese Musical Propaganda in World War II Hollywood." *Journal of the American Musicological Society* 54, no. 2 (2001): 303–57.

Silberstein, Sandra. *War of Words: Language, Politics, and 9/11.* New York: Routledge, 2002.

Stahl, Roger, director. *Militainment, Inc.* DVD. Media Education Foundation, 2007.
———. *Militainment, Inc: War, Media and Popular Culture.* New York: Routledge 2010.
Stauber, John, and Sheldon Rampton. *Toxic Sludge Is Good for You.* Monroe, ME: Common Courage Press, 2002.
Steinberg, Shirley R., and Joe L. Kincheloe. *Kinderculture: The Corporate Construction of Childhood.* Boulder, CO: Westview Press, 1997.
Steuter, Erin, and Deborah Wills. *At War with Metaphor: Media, Propaganda, and Racism in the War on Terror.* Lanham, MD: Lexington Books, 2008.
Stiglitz, Joseph E., and Linda J. Bilmes. *The Three Trillion Dollar War: The True Cost of the Iraq Conflict.* New York: W. W. Norton, 2008.
Storey, John. *Cultural Theory and Popular Culture: An Introduction.* 3rd ed. Athens: University of Georgia Press, 2001.
Strahan, Michael, and Jay Glazer. *Inside the Helmet: Life as a Sunday Afternoon Warrior.* New York: Penguin Group, 2007.
Sturken, Marita. *Tourists of History: Memory, Kitsch, and Consumerism from Oklahoma City to Ground Zero.* Durham, NC, and London: Duke University Press, 2007.
Suid, Lawrence H. "Hollywood and Vietnam." *Air University Review* 34, no. 2 (1983): 121–27.
———. Introduction to *Guts & Glory: The Making of the American Military Image.* 2nd ed. Lexington: University Press of Kentucky, 2002.
Taylor, Philip. "The Green Berets." *History Today* 45 (March 1995).
Tower, John. *The Tower Commission Report.* New York: Bantam Books / Times Books, 1987.
Troy, Gil. *Morning in America: How Ronald Reagan Invented the 1980s.* Princeton, NJ: Princeton University Press, 2005.
Turley, Jonathan. Foreword to *Operation Hollywood: How the Pentagon Shapes and Censors the Movies,* David L. Robb, 13–22. Amherst, NY: Prometheus Books, 2004.
Turse, Nick. *The Complex: How the Military Invades our Everyday Lives.* New York: Henry Holt and Company / Metropolitan Books, 2008.
Tuttle, William M. *Daddy's Gone to War: The Second World War in the Lives of America's Children.* Oxford: Oxford University Press, 1995.
Varney, Wendy. "Playing with 'War Fare.'" *Peace Review* 12, no. 3 (2000): 385–91.
Vescovi, Roberta. "Children into Soldiers: Sport and Fascist Italy." In *The European Sports History Review: Militarism, Sport, Europe—War Without Weapons,* vol. 5, edited by J. A. Mangan, 166–86. Portland, OR: Frank Cass, 2003.
Waltz, Kenneth. *Theory of International Politics.* Boston: McGraw-Hill, 1979.
Walzer, Michael. *Just and Unjust Wars: A Moral Argument with Historical Illustrations.* 4th ed. New York: Basic Books, 2006.
Wolf, Mark J. P. "A Brief Timeline of Video Game History." In *The Video Game Explosion: A History from Pong to Playstation and Beyond,* edited by Mark J. P. Wolf, xvii–xxi. Westport, CT: Greenwood Press, 2008.
Wolf, Naomi. *The End of America: Letter of Warning to a Young Patriot.* White River Junction, VT: Chelsea Green, 2007.

Wright, Micah Ian. *You Back the Attack! We'll Bomb Who We Want! Remixed War Propaganda.* New York: Seven Stories Press, 2003.

Yoe, Craig. *The Great Anti-War Cartoons.* Seattle: Fantagraphics Books, 2010.

Zinn, Howard. *On War.* New York: Seven Stories Press, 2000.

Zinn, Howard, and Mike Konopacki, Paul Buhle. *A People's History of American Empire.* New York: Metropolitan Books, 2008.

Zirin, David. *What's My Name, Fool? Sports and Resistance in the United States.* Chicago: Haymarket Books, 2005.

Index

About the Authors

Geoff Martin is assistant professor of continuous learning and political science at Mount Allison University.

Erin Steuter is professor of sociology at Mount Allison University.

Printed in Germany
by Amazon Distribution
GmbH, Leipzig